# HABERMAS AND AESTHETICS

*In memory of*
François van der Merwe
1961–1994


Is it possible that one day an emancipated human race could encounter itself within an expanded space of discursive formation of will and yet be robbed of the light in which it is capable of interpreting its life as something good?

Jürgen Habermas

# Habermas and Aesthetics

## The Limits of Communicative Reason

Pieter Duvenage

polity

First published in 2003 by Polity Press in association with Blackwell Publishing Ltd

*Editorial office*:
Polity Press
65 Bridge Street
Cambridge CB2 1UR, UK

*Marketing and production*:
Blackwell Publishing Ltd
108 Cowley Road
Oxford OX4 1JF, UK

Distributed in the USA by
Blackwell Publishing Inc.
350 Main Street
Malden, MA 02148, USA

ISBN: 0-7456 1597-X
ISBN: 0-7456 3120-7 (pb)

A catalogue record for this book is available from the British Library and has been applied for from the Library of Congress.

Typeset in 10.5 on 12 pt Berling
by SNP Best-set Typesetter Ltd., Hong Kong
Printed and bound in Great Britain by MPG Books Ltd, Bodmin, Cornwall

For further information on Polity, visit our website: www.polity.co.uk

193 HAB

# Contents

# Preface

I became aware of Critical Theory as an undergraduate student at the University of Stellenbosch (1982–4), but it was mainly Marinus Schoeman (who directed my Master's degree on hermeneutics at the University of Pretoria, 1986–8) and Johan Snyman who alerted me to the importance of this intellectual tradition for twentieth-century philosophy. Bert Olivier (who supervised my doctorate on Habermas at the University of Port Elizabeth, 1991–3) further facilitated an awareness of the tensions, but also the possibilities, for a critical *Auseinandersetzung* between Critical Theory, postmodernity and aesthetics.

As a student at Frankfurt University (summer semester 1989), I had the opportunity to attend the third of a series of three seminars on aesthetics in the twentieth century, presented by Jürgen Habermas and Axel Honneth. In retrospect, this seminar was in many ways the starting point of this study. I am grateful to Jürgen Habermas, who allowed me to attend his doctoral colloquium and gave me the opportunity to ask him, during that semester and on subsequent occasions, some uncomfortable questions regarding an area of his work that he himself acknowledges as being on the periphery. During my semester in Frankfurt I also benefited from seminars by Karl-Otto Apel, Richard Dreyfus, Axel Honneth and Hauke Brunkhorst. I am especially thankful to Axel Honneth, who by then was already involved in creating a space for new perspectives in Frankfurt amongst a younger generation of scholars. It was therefore a privilege for me to be his host (sponsored by the Human Sciences Research Council, now the National Research Foundation) in South Africa during October 1997.

The Social Philosophy Group that meets annually in Prague (since 1992) has been a further fruitful context for me to develop my ideas on Critical Theory and aesthetics. In this connection I would like to thank Alessandro Ferrara and David Rasmussen, more specifically, for their intellectual and moral support. Alessandro Ferrara was kind enough to read certain parts of the manuscript and provided me, on many occasions, with valuable suggestions. Through the years in Prague (1994, 1996, 1997, 1998 and 2000) I have benefited from discussions with Martin Jay, Peter Dews, Martin Matuštík, Maria Pia Lara, Rainer Forst, Jodi Dean, Lambert Zuidervaart, Aletta Norval, Maeve Cook and Jeffrey Alexander. During a few short visits to the USA (in 1995, 1997 and 2000) I also benefited from discussions with Christoph Menke, Joel Whitebook, David Ingram and Martin Matuštík. Nikolas Kompridis was kind enough to answer many questions by email and made encouraging comments on an earlier draft of this study. At a late stage of my research Eduardo Mendieta also provided me with valuable information.

In South Africa I am grateful to have a circle of colleagues and friends who have always provided me with a creative space in which to test and to refine my philosophical ideas. They are Bert Olivier, Andrea Hurst, Johan Snyman, Marinus Schoeman, Danie Goosen, Christoff Mans, Petrus de Kock, Gail Presbey, Dirk Louw, Johann Rossouw and Louise Mabile.

I should also like to thank Jean van Altena for her careful copy-editing and the many people at Polity Press – especially Elizabeth Molinari, Sarah Dancy, Ali Wyke, Sandra Byatt, Rachel Kerr, Carolyn Twigg, Gill Motley and Pam Thomas – who have helped, at one stage or another, to prepare this book for publication.

Finally I want to thank two people: Jörn Rüsen, historian and currently president of the *Kulturwissenschaftliches Institut* in Essen (Germany), who has been, since our first encounter in South Africa (1987), a warm and powerful interlocutor, and John Thompson, my skilled, patient and very professional editor at Polity, for entrusting me with a project that took a considerable time to finish.

Johannesburg

# Acknowledgements

The author and publisher wish to thank MIT Press for excerpts from J. Habermas, *The Philosophical Discourse of Modernity*, 1987.

Every effort has been made to trace all copyright holders, but if any have been inadvertently overlooked, the publisher will be pleased to make the necessary arrangements at the first opportunity.

# Introduction

From my earliest studies of Critical Theory I was struck by the paradox that although the first generation of Critical Theorists (Horkheimer, Adorno, Marcuse, Benjamin and Löwenthal) used aesthetically informed arguments in their respective socio-philosophical projects, this was much less the case with Habermas – the most prominent member of the second generation of Critical Theorists, who almost single-handedly steered this philosophical tradition in a new direction.[1] I addressed this paradox initially in my doctorate in South Africa, but it has continued to puzzle me.[2] It is well known that the first generation of Critical Theorists took the interaction between the rational and sensual aspects of humankind seriously. Adorno, for example, argues in his aesthetically informed philosophy for the possibility of a non-alienated relationship between humankind and nature, subject and object, reason and the senses. Quite similarly, Marcuse saw the student unrest of the sixties as a sign that the ethical issue of freedom and emancipation could not be separated from rational and aesthetic issues. The slogan of the Parisian students, 'all power to the imagination', signified for him an ideal of political emancipation leading to an aesthetic experience of reconciliation.

Aesthetic issues, however, do not feature prominently in the work of Jürgen Habermas. More than two decades ago Sherry Weber Nicholsen noted that Habermas's 'interest in the subjective or interactional components of domination has led to a more systematic return to the original problems of the nature of reason and its role in history, without, as yet, a similar reconsideration of the nature of the aesthetic and its relation to reason'.[3] Habermas has also been forthright about the "hidden" dimension of aesthetics in his socio-philosophical thinking.[4] In a rejoinder to Martin Jay, he refers to his scattered remarks on aesthetic modernity: 'In every case these remarks had a secondary character, to the extent that they arose only in the context of other themes and always in relation to the discussions among Adorno, Benjamin and Marcuse.'[5] Even though Habermas allows for the differentiation between the modern cultural spheres of cognitive-scientific, moral-judicial and *expressive-aesthetic* reason, in his recent work, the first two forms of rationality are emphasized, while the third plays a much more subdued role. One could describe this development as the fate of aesthetics in Habermas's work. It has also contributed to how little attention has been given to aesthetics in the vast secondary literature on Habermas. Apart from a few articles and shorter studies, no extensive effort has been made to interpret the role of aesthetics in his social philosophy.[6]

This study, then, is an attempt to interpret the fate of aesthetics in Habermas's work. First, it is in many ways an intellectual history of Habermas. It is well known that the event of the Second World War and the philosophical tradition of Critical Theory have played major roles in the development of Habermas's intellectual career. Consequently, the main outlines of his socio-philosophical career will be reconstructed in this study – from his first work on the literary public sphere to his later formulation of a theory of communicative reason. Against this background, Habermas's work on aesthetics divides into two phases. The first phase starts with the publication of his early study, *The Structural Transformation of the Public Sphere*, and ends with his essay on Benjamin's aesthetics in the early 1970s. The second phase starts in the early seventies and finds its culmination in *The Theory of Communicative Action*, *The Philosophical Discourse of Modernity*, and subsequent work in the eighties and nineties. Secondly, and related to the previous point, this study is also an exploration of the complex relationship between the first generation of Critical Theorists (Horkheimer, Adorno and Benjamin) and Habermas (the second generation). As indicated, the first generation used cultural and aesthetic arguments from their earliest studies, while this is much less the case with Habermas. Thirdly, the intellectual reconstruction of Habermas's career is also coupled with a critical systematic examination of his use of aesthetic concepts and categories. One such concept is instrumental reason – Adorno, for example, interprets instrumental reason as a totalizing kind of reason that can be addressed by certain autonomous artworks that serve as a model of non-coerced reconciliation, whereas Habermas interprets instrumental reason as a restricted kind of reason that entails an objective attitude to the empirical world.

I have referred to the first and second generations of scholars in Critical Theory. 'Generation' is used in this study as a sociological term that, following a cue from Matuštík, neither ascribes collective guilt nor exonerates individuals by depicting them as members of a 'generational cohort'. Against this background the first generation of Critical Theorists can be broadly interpreted as a group of scholars who grounded theoretical reflection in the ordinary self-understanding of participants in the social world – particularly in the domain of labour. As Anderson indicates, this core focus was complemented by related work in the aesthetics of experience and work in political economy and political theory. This generation came of age in the struggle to understand the consciousness of the majority of German workers, and then faced, as mature theorists, the discovery of National Socialism's crimes against humanity – a trauma that motivated Adorno, for example, to try and salvage, through aesthetic means, what was valuable out of the debris of national and personal destruction. The second generation (including Habermas), on the other hand, were too young to be aware of the Nazi regime, but old enough to be existentially affected by the events. This generation came of age in the face of revelations of Nazi atrocities, and experienced the transformations around 1968 as mature theorists. In this process Habermas's motivating concern (as a member of this generation after the devastating effects of an authoritarian tradition) was to restore, defend and radicalize the universalistic imperatives of liberal democracy, procedural rationality and modernist culture – an endeavour that made less use of aesthetic arguments than the first generation.[7]

In this study Habermas's work on aesthetics will be divided into two phases. The first phase is discussed in chapter 1 with reference to his early work *The Structural Transformation of the Public Sphere* (1962), which is a provocative formulation of the communicative role of art in society from a socio-historical perspective. Habermas argues that the Enlightenment opened a space for a rational public debate on political as well as *literary-aesthetic* issues (in the literary public sphere). In this process certain institutions (such as coffee houses and theatre spaces) served as new forums of debate contributing to the reception of literature and artworks by various audiences. This positive socio-communicative description of the literary-aesthetic sphere deviated from Horkheimer and Adorno's ideas of mass culture and aesthetics in their influential *Dialectic of Enlightenment*. Despite using some of their insights, in the second part of his study, Habermas did not relinquish the conceptual and normative potential of the enlightened public sphere at the end of this early study. The very motif of a rational public sphere also guided his work in the 1960s and early 1970s. In one of his studies the decline of the public sphere is sketched as a series of legitimation crises created by a winnowing away of the cultural and aesthetic life-world. Habermas's essay on Benjamin's 'redemptive aesthetics' is an interesting juncture at the end of the first phase of his aesthetics. It is argued that at this point Habermas favours a Benjaminian 'materialistic aesthetics of redemption' over Marcuse and Adorno's 'idealistic aesthetics of consciousness' – in this process Habermas provides the first outlines of a model of communicative reason through a critique of a philosophy of consciousness.

Before moving on to the second phase of Habermas's aesthetics, I explore further his complex relationship with the first generation of Critical Theorists, in the second chapter. The starting point here is Habermas's interpretation of the role played by aesthetics in the philosophical work of the first generation. Habermas here makes a distinction between an inner and an outer circle amongst the first generation of Critical Theorists (according to an influential essay by Honneth). The point is that the inner circle (represented by Horkheimer, Adorno and Marcuse) gradually became sceptical about the possibilities of a rational understanding of society. The infiltration of instrumental reason into the life-world, according to them, contributed to societal degeneration and the phenomenon of the culture industry. Eventually, according to Habermas, Horkheimer and Adorno came to describe all everyday conceptual and symbolical thinking as instrumental reason. Within such an interpretative framework only certain modern artworks represent, for Adorno, the last remains of 'reason' in a world of identity thinking, where 'aesthetic synthesis', opposed to conceptual thinking, does not violate the particular and non-identical, but exposes the irrational character of reality by a proposal of social reconciliation of another world.[8] The outer circle (which was constituted by figures such as Kirchheimer, Neumann, Fromm and Benjamin) did not share this pessimistic sense of instrumental rationality, according to Honneth's Habermasian reconstruction of Critical Theory. In Benjamin's aesthetics, for example, there is a less functionalist view of social communication and rationalization. Habermas holds that Benjamin does not limit the aesthetic healing of the fragmented modern rationality to the modern autonomous artwork itself (like Adorno), but gives art a positive public role to play.[9]

Habermas's favourable reading of the communicative aspect of art in Benjamin's thinking runs parallel with the linguistic turn that formed the core of his philosophical work during the 1970s and culminates in his *Theory of Communicative Action* (1981) and *The Philosophical Discourse of Modernity* (1985) – and inaugurates the second phase of his aesthetics. In chapter 3 this phase of Habermas's aesthetics is reconstructed in terms of a theory of argumentation, a theory of social rationalization and three case studies. With regard to a theory of argumentation, Habermas emphasizes the interaction between the validity claims of speaking and acting subjects and their relations with an objective, social and subjective world. In a similar way, the differentiation and communication between learning processes in the cultural spheres of science, law and art are sketched by Habermas in his theory of societal rationalization.[10] Here the different rationalities (of the three modern cultural spheres) stand in a communicative relation with one another without damaging the particular logic of each. In this context Habermas adds the dimension of the differentiation of modernity into life-world and system – where the separation of modern societies in the communicative life-world, on the one hand, and systems of means–end rationality, such as the market and bureaucracy, on the other, enables Habermas to refer to the infiltration of systematic imperatives into the fragile sphere of the communicative everyday praxis as a particularly modern pathology (the colonization of the life-world).[11] In the second part of chapter 3 the aesthetic implications of Habermas's theory of communicative reason are elaborated in terms of his theory of argumentation, his view of social rationalization and differentiation between life-world and system. Finally, these aesthetic implications are concretized with reference to Habermas's interpretation of the role of aesthetics in the work of Schiller, Hegel and Heine.

In chapter 4 the second phase of Habermas's aesthetics is further explored in terms of his reconstruction of the 'philosophical discourse of modernity'. Habermas holds that whereas Hegel's counter-discourse of modern differentiation (*Entzweiung*) never abandons the broad project of modernity, it is only with Nietzsche's anti-discourse that the certainties of modernity are radically challenged from an aesthetic perspective. Nietzsche thus becomes the 'turntable' between modernity and postmodernity, and also the forerunner and inspiration for an aesthetically informed and totalizing critique of modernity. Habermas argues that two groups of thinkers continue Nietzsche's aesthetic critique of rationality in the twentieth century. On the one hand, Heidegger, with his critique of Western metaphysics, and Derrida, with his levelling of the genre distinction between philosophy and literature, pursue an ontological or quasi-ontological reversal of modernity by aesthetic means. On the other, Bataille and Foucault attempt a more scientific, sceptical aesthetic approach. The location of the two groups of post-Nietzschean philosophers at different junctures in the philosophical discourse of modernity allows Habermas to propose his alternative of communicative reason – which forms, as indicated, the basis for the second phase of his aesthetics. At this point of the study, the merits of Habermas's alternative are critically engaged. This is done, at the end of chapter 4, by placing Habermas's position in a creative tension with those of a number of postmodern thinkers. Lyotard, for example, is very critical of Habermas's model of consensus and the presence of a hidden form of unity in his thinking, while Derrida, Nancy, Lacoue-Labarthe and De Man warn against a form of art becoming ideological.[12]

These critical remarks provide a good background for a critical investigation of the two phases of aesthetics in Habermas's work. In chapter 5 this is done by focusing, in the first place, on the status of the aesthetic sphere in Habermas's theory of communicative reason.[13] Important issues in this regard are the restriction of the validity of art to the subjective judgement of the author or creator and the distinction (made by Habermas) between 'normal' and 'abnormal' language use. The critique of the formal and abstract nature of Habermas's formal-pragmatic analysis of language action is, secondly, connected with the issue of nature. Foucault's notion of an *aesthetics of existence* and Whitebook's rehabilitation of inner and outer nature in psychoanalysis both emphasize that the restriction of the poetical dimensions of language could contribute to the problem that the creative and natural dimensions of human beings could disappear in a formalist theory of reason, language and action.[14] (The question seems to be: is the body an original unity of predispositions, habits and intentions that leads to intentional and expressive socializing, or is it a non-reflexive, mechanical and linguistic behavioural system?) Thirdly, Habermas's concept of social rationalization is critically examined by studying the restriction of the validity of art to the subjectivity of the author or the creator (a kind of subjective production aesthetics) versus reception aesthetics – which proposes a more communicative understanding of the nature of aesthetic experience. To this latter idea the concept of post-avant-garde art is also added – a move that opens a more appropriate mediation between art and life.[15] This perspective also suggests a reopening of the debate between Habermas and Adorno. In the final part of this chapter two possible answers are offered in this regard. Whereas Jay Bernstein aligns himself more strongly with Adorno, Wellmer initiates a cautious, but thorough, critique of Habermas by placing the issues of instrumental rationality, aesthetic reconciliation and truth in a communicative framework.[16]

By taking Wellmer's critique, amongst others, seriously, the fate of aesthetics in Habermas's work is explored in the final chapter through a consideration of the world-disclosing and discursive-rational reciprocity of language.[17] It starts with a discussion of Heidegger's original contribution on the creative linkage between world disclosure and reason – a position that is strongly influenced by his artwork essay. But the strong opposition that Heidegger draws between the processes of world disclosure and the practices of discursive reason giving is criticized. On the other hand, Habermas's theory of communicative reason, with its restriction of the transformative and subversive qualities of novel disclosures to the aesthetic edges of our self-understanding and social practices, is also criticized. The argument is that both Heidegger and Habermas (although on the opposite sides) retain too strong an opposition between world disclosure and reason giving. Given this *impasse* between Heidegger and Habermas, I argue that a pragmatic proposal of art as communicative experience could be a possible answer. This proposal (emphasizing the de-centring and centring effects of world disclosures – i.e. the complementarity and interdependence of world disclosure and rationality) also opens the way to some exploratory remarks on the moral and political implications of world disclosure for contemporary individuals, communities and societies.

# *1*
# Habermas and Aesthetics: The First Phase

The experience of the Second World War, and more specifically the occurrence of the Holocaust, made a lasting impact on the intellectual career of Jürgen Habermas.[1] As a young student, after these events, he had to find his way out of the physical and spiritual ruins of Germany. In an interview, he describes his reaction to the Nüremberg trials as one of shock: 'Our own history was suddenly cast in a light that made all its essential elements appear radically different. All at once we saw that we had been living in a political criminal system. I had never imagined that before.'[2] In this context of world disclosure Habermas had to answer some very painful questions: how was it possible that the intellectual accomplishments of a Kant or a Marx, in which the themes of critical rationality and practical realization of freedom are predominant, could have been such a fertile ground for the rise of Hitler and totalitarianism? Why did this development not encounter greater resistance from the Germans? How was it possible for Nazism to develop within the logic of modernity? Habermas's response to these questions came down to nothing less than a careful, comprehensive reconstruction of the trajectory of modern reason. In pursuing this issue, it was inevitable that his path would cross that of Critical Theory, in which figures such as Horkheimer, Adorno, Marcuse and Benjamin were prominent. The interesting aspect of these figures, in comparison to Habermas, is the important role that aesthetically informed arguments play in their attempt to come to a critical understanding of modern society.

In order to trace the fate of aesthetics in Habermas's reconstruction of modern reason, this chapter starts with a brief intellectual-historical sketch (section 1.1). Habermas started his career with a

Heideggerian study of Schelling before turning to Critical Theory and other intellectual traditions in the 1950s. His relationship with the Critical Theory of Horkheimer and Adorno (the focus of chapter 2) is filled with paradoxes and complexities, however. The complexity of the relationship is already present in his first major work, *The Structural Transformation of the Public Sphere*, in which his earliest reflections on the public sphere and aesthetics are formulated (sections 1.2 and 1.3). The differences between Habermas and Horkheimer/Adorno are especially discernible in the first part of the book, where a relatively optimistic picture is provided of the historical development of the public sphere. This must be seen against the pessimistic view of the public sphere found in the *Dialectic of Enlightenment*. Eventually these differences intensified in the 1960s and early 1970s (section 1.4). A work such as *Knowledge and Human Interests*, for example, is more a reflection on the methodology of the social sciences than a substantive questioning of cultural and aesthetic issues. Only with the publication of his interesting essay on Benjamin (1973) did Habermas return to the relationship between aesthetics, language and society (section 1.5). This essay, which stands at an interesting juncture in Habermas's intellectual development (and marks the end of the first phase of his aesthetics), did not lead to a further exploration of aesthetic issues, however, but rather to the development of a systematic and formal analysis of rational communication in contemporary society.

## 1.1  Initial influences and themes in Habermas's work

As a student in Göttingen, Zurich and Bonn, Habermas studied in a provincial intellectual atmosphere. After the war, most of the professors of philosophy, who were appointed before and during the Nazi era, remained.[3] Generally there was an apolitical and inward-looking mood in German academia. Intellectually, little was known or heard of analytical philosophy or Critical Theory, both having German origins. In these circumstances Habermas wrote a Heidegger-informed thesis in Bonn on Schelling's transcendental reconciliation between nature and spirit. This study, which has received little attention from commentators and critics, is in many ways fascinating.[4] It is an attempt not just to critique Cartesian dualism from the tradition of Jewish-Christian mysticism and Heideggerian ontology, but also to interpret the social and aesthetic implications of

Schelling's thinking. This study is in style and atmosphere quite different from Habermas's later studies on the rationality of modern culture and society. Habermas's break with the philosophical tradition in which he grew up came when Heidegger republished his *Introduction to Metaphysics* (first published in 1935) without any explanation in the 1950s.[5] It was unacceptable to the young doctoral student that an influential philosopher could treat the political implications of Nazism so uncritically. At the same time, Habermas's readings of Marx, Lukács and Löwith convinced him that the spiritual fragmentation and alienation of the modern era were of a social-rational rather than an ontological or metaphysical nature – a conviction that had profound implications for aesthetics.

During the 1950s Habermas became interested in the pathology of modernity as seen from the viewpoint of the distorted realization of reason in history.[6] This concern with the modern paradox – that is, the loss of freedom in the face of technical rational progress – brought him into contact with the Institute for Social Research, which relocated to Frankfurt in 1950. As Adorno's assistant (1956–9), he enthusiastically studied Marxist economy, Freudian psychology, and the sociology of Weber, Durkheim and Parsons. In addition, he was influenced by philosophical anthropology, hermeneutics (Gadamer), pragmatism (Pierce/Mead/Dewey) and analytical language theory (Wittgenstein).[7] Habermas writes:

> I saw myself as someone who, in the face of a very narrow, almost dog-matic selection of acceptable texts, carried on philosophical and academic traditions in a less strict manner . . . it became clear to me that the 1920s, in which I have lived theoretically during my student years, were, after all, the 1920s. That became a stimulus to become interested in American sociology for example. Analytical philosophy came afterward . . . In principle, I considered worthwhile anything that had a cognitive, structural, or hermeneutical element.[8]

At this time Habermas also discovered the seminal essays of the Institute for Social Research of the 1930s. This discovery persuaded him to revisit the critical and normative foundations of social rationality as defended by Horkheimer and associates in their interdisciplinary research programme of the 1930s.

Through his studies in the 1950s and 1960s, and the intellectual influences as indicated, Habermas became more and more critical of Horkheimer and Adorno's interpretation of post-1945 Western societies (including West Germany), and more specifically their concepts of history and instrumental reason.[9] One of the main issues at this stage, as will be argued in greater detail in the next chapter, was their reductive interpretation of history as well as their pronounced negative view concerning the democratic potentials of a rational public sphere.[10] Habermas's differences with Horkheimer and Adorno became more substantial after their deaths (that of Adorno in 1969 and Horkheimer in 1973). This is the historical moment when Habermas, as the most prominent member of the second generation of Critical Theorists, consolidated his reconstruction of Critical Theory – a project that found its most programmatic formulation in *The Theory of Communicative Action* (1981). In this process Habermas had to find an alternative to Adorno's critique of conceptual thinking via the idea of a mimetic and aesthetic rationality, as well as to Horkheimer's Schopenhauerian pessimism pointing in the direction of a negative theology of the other and Marcuse's sensual-aesthetic bid to save the lost revolution.[11] In contrast, Habermas (and his generation of intellectuals) responded differently to the challenges of twentieth-century society.

On the occasion of Habermas's seventieth birthday, Pierre Bourdieu, also a member of Habermas's generation, provided the following explanation for their intellectual response. Habermas and his generation had to confront Western Marxism, and especially the work of the young Hegelians (of *History and Class Consciousness*); they had to critically confront the life, work and influence of Martin Heidegger in post-1945 Europe; they had to come to terms with powerfully victorious American social sciences, which provided the theoretical and practical criteria for thinking about the social in the post-war years; they had to deal with the late discovery that university life in Europe moved quite arrogantly in closed circles; they discovered the Anglo-Saxon philosophy of Peirce, Mead, Dewey and the later Wittgenstein; and finally (and perhaps most important, according to Bourdieu) there was the influence of a theory of argumentation.[12] What is quite striking about this sketch is the absence of an aesthetic view of language and reason, and in its place a formal argumentative one. It is this view, and its aesthetic implications (the fate of aesthetics), that will be investigated in this study.

## 1.2   The public sphere and the role of art

Habermas made his début in the German intellectual life with the publication of *The Structural Transformation of the Public Sphere*, in which he explores the historical and normative evolution of the public sphere since the Enlightenment. The public sphere is, according to him, an institutional location for practical reason and for the valid, if often deceptive, claims of formal democracy. Holub writes: 'What attracted Habermas to the notion of a public sphere then and now is its potential as a foundation for a critique of society based on democratic principles.'[13] In this sense Habermas follows Kant as a theorist who offered the fullest articulation of the ideal of the bourgeois public sphere through his concept of procedural rationality and its influence on 'our views in the three areas of objective knowledge, moral-practical insight, and *aesthetic judgment*'.[14] In his study Habermas proposes to develop a critique of the public sphere, on the one hand, and to intimate its possible element of truth and emancipatory potential, on the other. This section starts with the latter aspect – reconstructing the important transition from the representative public sphere (feudal era) to the bourgeois public sphere (modern era). An important issue here is the role that art and culture play in the communicative relationships between participants in the public sphere. In the next section Habermas's sketch of the decline of the socio-cultural and political functions of the bourgeois public sphere will be examined. Although this shift is indebted to some extent to Adorno and Horkheimer, it is executed in a less pessimistic fashion.

Habermas describes feudal society as a historical phase wherein art and culture are 'represented' in public.[15] It is a sphere in which the public and private spheres are not separated, making representation in a democratic sense impossible.

> Representation in the sense in which the members of a national assembly represent a nation or a lawyer represents his clients had nothing to do with this publicity of representation inseparable from the lord's concrete existence, that, as an 'aura,' surrounded and endowed his authority . . . As long as the prince and the estates of his realm 'were' the country and not just its representatives, he could represent it in a specific sense. They represented their lordship not for but 'before' the people.[16]

In other words, through art and culture the higher classes established their right and higher authority to represent themselves in the public sphere on behalf of the people. Habermas continues that the transformation of the feudal public sphere into the modern bourgeois public sphere is the outcome of a change in power relations between the monarch and his or her subjects and also of early capitalist commercial economy. This leads to a situation wherein the society (public sphere) is separated from the ruler (state) and the private sphere.[17] Through this enormous influential change, the public sphere is characterized by a conflict between those of the bourgeois civil society, on the one hand, and those of the state, on the other. The free citizens of the 'bourgeois society' in the public sphere soon debated this conflict over the rules of exchange of social goods and ideas.[18]

In the next step of his argument Habermas indicates that the members of the bourgeois public sphere did not just defend their interests against the state; they also institutionalized a range of rational-critical practices whereby reasonable (*räsonierende*) citizens could critically challenge the political norms of the state and its monopoly on interpretation and institutions. This is the historical moment when validity claims become more important than power claims in the public sphere. It is also the moment when public discussion becomes the cornerstone and medium of debate through the press, political parties and parliament. Only in a power-free discussion, according to this line of thought, can the strongest argument triumph in the struggle of private and public opinions – and can *voluntas* proceed to ratio.[19] Two processes helped, according to Habermas, to institutionalize this concept of the public sphere: the reconstitution of the family as an intimate sphere represented by the patriarchal head in public and the emergence of the world of letters, or literary public sphere, which paved the way for the political public sphere. In both cases an essential humanness is involved, one that no economic or other kind of interest could remove.[20] Novels like those of Richardson, Rousseau and Goethe reinforced this. Habermas writes: 'The relation between author, work, and public changed. They became intimate mutual relations between privatised individuals who were psychologically interested in what was "human", in self-knowledge, and in empathy.'[21]

Habermas continues that the value of the literary public sphere was advanced not only through the construction of modern subjectivity, as the result of a distinctly modern idea of an autonomous art and culture, but also through the development of certain institutions in the political public sphere. He provides the following concrete examples of places where literary and other matters were publicly debated: English coffee houses, French salons, and German table societies (*Tischgesellschaften*).[22] According to Habermas, all of these institutions operated with a similar rationale: they constitute a public sphere that disregards status (*Takt der Ebenbürtigkeit*). By suspending the laws of the state and the market (for the duration of the debate), they render official prestige, power and economic status absent, in principle at least. Secondly, rational argument is the sole arbiter of any issue. Everything is open to criticism in the literary public sphere. Thus philosophical and literary works are no longer 'represented' by the Church, court or authorities. Private citizens, to whom cultural products become accessible, are able to interpret aesthetic and philosophical issues independently. Thirdly, the literary public sphere is conceived as a universal auditorium. Anyone with access to cultural products – books, plays and journals – has at least a potential claim on the attention of the culture-debating public. In this way the public sphere is not simply the forum of an insulated power clique, but is rather part of a more inclusive public (read: educated private citizens) comprising all those who are qualified to participate in an independent, critical discussion.[23]

These institutions of the literary public sphere also contributed, according to Habermas, to the practice of literary and art criticism. He describes the relationship between the public and the art critic (*Kunstrichter*) as one of communicative reciprocity.[24] The critic both influences and depends on the public. Persuasion here succeeds on the basis of the better argument. Although the critic exposes dogmas and fashionable opinions in public, his or her expertise holds only as far as it is not contradicted. Habermas writes: 'The *Kunstrichter* retained something of the amateur; his expertise only held good until countermanded; lay judgment was organized in it without becoming, by way of specialization, anything else than the judgment of one private person among all others who ultimately were not to be obligated by any judgment except their own.'[25] The first part of *The Structural Transformation of the Public Sphere* thus portrays a positive picture of the role of art in opening up critical discursive practices in early modern society. The *Empfindsamkeit* (empathic identification) with the characters in the bourgeois novel and drama, the importance of a rational-aesthetical debate in salons, journals and newspapers, and the educational role of the art critic all contribute, in Habermas's view, to the institutionalization of the literary public sphere as a kind of *Vorform* of the political public sphere. All of these aspects thus institutionalized a form of rational-critical discourse about objects of common concern, which flowed over into political discussions.

According to Habermas, this evolution of the world of letters into the world of politics used the vehicle of public opinion to 'put the state in touch with the needs of society'.[26] But this evolution could only happen on the basis of a new economic order. This order was capitalism, and its crucial contribution to the public sphere was the institutionalization of a new, stronger sense of privacy and free control of productive property. In Europe it was reflected in the codification of civil law, in which basic private freedoms were guaranteed. A fundamental parity among persons was thus established, corresponding to owners of commodities in the market and educated individuals in the public sphere. Although not all people were full legal subjects at this stage, all subjects were joined in a more or less undifferentiated category of persons. The extension of these notions into the doctrines of *laissez-faire* and even free trade among nations brought the development of 'civil society as the private sphere emancipated from public authority' to its fullest extent. Habermas argues, though, that this moment lasted for only 'one blissful moment in the long history of capitalist development.'[27] In the second part of his book he changes his argument, almost like Horkheimer and Adorno, by arguing that the aesthetic-communicative and political model of the bourgeois public sphere was undermined by historical and economic developments in the latter part of the nineteenth century.

## 1.3   The decline of the public sphere

Habermas interprets the decline of the public sphere, in the second part of *The Structural Transformation of the Public Sphere*, as a shift from rational discourse (*Räsonnement*) to consumption. This shift took place, according to him, in the last quarter of the nineteenth century, when liberal competing capitalism was transformed into the monopolistic capitalism of cartels and protectionism. The classical function of public opinion – namely, the free debate of matters of general interest – was from then on undermined by the state's and other interest groups' intervention in the social life-world and the public sphere. Even institutions such as parliaments could not prevent this erosion of a free public sphere.[28] 'Discussions, now a "business" becomes formalized; the presentation of positions and counter positions is bound to certain prearranged rules of the game, consensus about the subject matter is made largely superfluous by that concerning form.'[29] Against this background, the relationship between the private and public spheres and their relation with the state changed. State and society, once distinct, became interlocked, leading to the refeudalization of the public sphere.[30] The public (literary) sphere thus changed from a forum for critical and rational debate to an instrument for the manipulation of public discourse, in which bureaucratic and economic actors use advertising, marketing and 'public relations' to create a perfect 'social engineering' of voter behaviour and cultural consumption.[31]

At this historical moment, according to Habermas, the literary Enlightenment and the cultural emancipation of the masses failed. In this process the public (literary) sphere changes from a forum for critical and rational debate to an instrument in the manipulation of discourse by powerful bureaucratic and economic interests. Following Horkheimer and Adorno, Habermas describes the decline of the literary public sphere into a minority of art connoisseurs (high art), on the one hand, and a large mass of art consumers (cultural industry), on the other. Art gradually distances itself from involvement, while the cultural industry manipulates the critical discussion for political purposes.[32] The arrival of new technologies, leading to lower book prices, did not enhance cultural life either. Mass media such as the press (and later radio and television) became the commercialized instruments of powerful advertising interests. Habermas's argument is that these new forms of media, which have become so powerful since the latter part of the nineteenth century, speak directly to the consumer and ignore the idea of a rational discourse between participants in a critical public sphere.[33]

> With the arrival of the new media the form of communication as such has changed; they have had an impact, therefore, more penetrating ... than was even possible for the press ... They draw the eyes and ears of their public under their spell but at the same time, by taking away its distance, place it under 'tutelage', which is to say they deprive it of the opportunity to say something and to disagree. The critical discussion of a reading public tends to give way to 'exchanges about tastes and preferences' between consumers.[34]

Where works of literature had previously been appropriated through individual reading, group discussion and the critical discourse of literary publications, modern mass media and the modern style of appropriation made this impossible. Thus, the world of the mass media is a public sphere in appearance only. With the expansion of access, the form of participation is significantly altered. 'Serious involvement with culture produces facility, while the consumption of mass culture leaves no lasting trace; it affords a kind of experience which is not cumulative but regressive.'[35] Habermas refers here to both the depoliticization of the public sphere and its impoverishment by the removal of critical discourse. Nothing remains of the cultural circumstances in which Richardson's *Pamela* was once read by the entire public – that is, by 'everyone' who could read at all. This structural change involves not only segmentation of audiences but also the transformation of the once intimate relationship between cultural producers and consumers. It is precisely at this point that intellectuals begin to form a distinct stratum of those who produce culture and those who critique it.[36] Habermas also cites the social and psychological effects of consumption on the members of the bourgeois family. This comes to the fore in a loss of individuality and moral autonomy in this important socializing institution. 'To a greater extent individual family members are now socialized by extra familial authorities, by society directly.'[37]

These arguments on the structural change of culture and individualization have clearly been influenced by Horkheimer and Adorno's interpretation of contemporary society in the *Dialectic of Enlightenment*.[38] This is reflected in Habermas's use of concepts like 'mass culture', 'objectification' and 'manipulated culture'. But Habermas does not fully endorse their defence of autonomy against a fully instrumentalized public sphere. Rather, he sketches a more complex picture of the relationship between emancipation and consumption. His disagreement with Horkheimer and Adorno is revealed in the following words:

> Conflict and consensus (like domination itself and like the coercive power whose degree of stability they indicate analytically) are not categories that remain untouched by the historical development of society. In the case of the structural transformation of the bourgeois public sphere, we can study the extent to which . . . the latter's ability to assume its proper function determines whether the exercise of domination and power persists in a negative constant . . . of history – or whether as a historical category itself, it is open to substantive change.[39]

In contrast with the first generation of Critical Theorists, Habermas's reading of the 'dialectics of Enlightenment' focuses on the contradictions in liberal capitalism, rather than on the instrumental nature of historical development. *The Structural Transformation of the Public Sphere* thus challenges the argument of an instrumental public sphere in the *Dialectic of Enlightenment*.

Habermas's work on the transformation of the public sphere has been read critically from various perspectives.[40] His liberal critics are sceptical about the historical comparison between the ideal-typical liberal public sphere and its decline in late capitalism, while Luhmann (from a system-theoretical position) judges the communicative social function of public opinion as unsuited to contemporary societies characterized by specialized systems.[41] From a Marxist perspective, Habermas's sketch of the decline of the bourgeois public sphere is accepted, while the idealistic and communicative-rational suppositions of his normative model of the public sphere find less favour.[42] More recently, Habermas's treatment of the public sphere has become important for debates on the politics of identity. For some commentators, the very emphasis on rational-critical debate implies an inability to deal adequately with 'identity politics' and concerns of difference. This criticism is also implicit in the whole rethinking of the boundary between public and private broached by feminist discourse. The argument runs that although Habermas's initial discussion of the literary public sphere shows how fiction serves to facilitate a discussion about selfhood and subjectivity and to reinforce a vesting of primary identity in a newly constructed intimate sphere, his position eventually imposes a neutralizing logic on differential identity by establishing a qualification for publicness entailing abstraction from private identity.[43]

The remarkable aspect of Habermas's *The Structural Transformation of the Public Sphere*, though, remains its (early) discussion of the role of the literary public sphere. This discussion points to a stage in early bourgeois capitalism when a democratic exchange of aesthetic-political values was important and possible prior and adjacent to the wider debate of political issues in public. The fascinating aspect here is the importance granted to artworks and institutions in contributing to the rational exchange of ideas in the public sphere. Unfortunately, Habermas's sketch of the decline of the public sphere took his ensuing work in another direction. The point is that whereas his early work on structural transformation located the basis of practical reason in the historically specific social institutions of the public sphere, his subsequent work shifts to the trans-historical, intersubjective and communicative capacities of reason. In this process Habermas's account of the decline of the public sphere (in the second half of his book) serves as the basis from which to recover the normative ideal of formal democracy from early bourgeois political theory and practice.[44] The details of this argument (and its implications for aesthetics) will be explored in chapter 3.

## 1.4   Towards a normative and rational public sphere

In this section I will argue that the aesthetic potential of Habermas's first study receded into the background of his work in the

1960s and early 1970s (thereby contributing to the fate of aesthetics in the first phase of his career). In this period Habermas started with an ambitious project to ground the formal-rational requirements for the public sphere, thereby taking leave of the more socio-historically informed strategy that played such an important role in *The Structural Transformation of the Public Sphere*. Habermas now sought a more formal-normative (transcendental) and less historically informed basis for democracy. This shift to a more formal understanding of public reason is perceptible, for example, in his study of Weber's account of the rationality of political decision making and the influence of elites on public opinion.[45] Even though Habermas sided with Adorno in the so-called positivism debate of the early 1960s, he was already well on the way to developing an alternative to Horkheimer and Adorno's concept of instrumental reason.[46] His strategy in this regard was to defend practical reason against the close link between modern social philosophy and the natural sciences.[47] The point is that science's illusion of pure knowledge hides its interests, thereby contributing to a one-sided form of knowledge, 'objective science' (scientism), which inhibits understanding of the social dimension of knowledge.[48] At this early stage Habermas argued that the complex, sophisticated, technical nature of science should not affect the fine balance between scientific knowledge and social interest (common sense). This critique of positivism's exclusive understanding of knowledge led to a differentiated model of reason in *Knowledge and Human Interests* (1968), in which empirical-analytical, historical-hermeneutical and critical-social science each has a role to play.[49]

Following broadly in the footsteps of Kant's three Critiques, Habermas's study sketches a differentiated model of knowledge and reason in which empirical-analytical, historical-hermeneutical and critical-social science each has a role to play in a self-reflective style. The first outline of this epistemological model is already included in Habermas's inaugural lecture at the University of Frankfurt (1965), where he states that while the first mode of knowledge (empirical-analytical) is geared toward 'expanding our power of technical control', and the second (historical-hermeneutical) seeks to facilitate 'action-orientation in the context of shared traditions', the last mode of knowledge (critical-social) pursues the goal of releasing 'the subject from dependence on hypostatized powers'.[50] Habermas continues that when clarity is gained regarding the changeable nature of social standards or traditions, their hold can be broken, leading to practical emancipation.[51] Finally, the three modes of knowledge originate, according to Habermas, 'in the interest structures of a species which is tied essentially to distinct means of socialization: work, language and power' (where work and power appear as non- or extra-linguistic categories).[52] In other words, whereas natural or empirical science has a technical interest in the causal and controlled explanation of (unconscious) natural processes, and the human sciences have a practical interest in understanding cultural or symbolic meanings (a process important for aesthetics), critical-social science has an emancipatory interest in analysing structural and social deformations in the hope of promoting more equitable arrangements through self-realization.[53]

It is with this latter point in mind – the emancipatory interest of the social sciences – that Habermas introduces psychoanalysis, a model that could recover the impaired ego and superego structures through the interaction and therapeutic exchanges between analyst and patient.[54] Once a patient finds an explanatory proposal that is applicable to his or her case, according to Habermas's proposal, it is assumed that the deformed inner nature is healed in favour of self-understanding and a restored ego identity. In contrast to Adorno, Habermas seems to see therapy as capable of resoloing the conflict between the instinctual-libidinal and societal norms (including linguistic norms) and thus being able to sublate inner nature in reflective rationality. Building on this construal, Habermas's subsequent writings further mitigated libidinal factors and the impact of psychoanalysis in general by subordinating the latter progressively to formal-pragmatic and 'reconstructive' modes of analyses. As a corollary of this shift, Habermas explicitly limited the role of psychoanalysis to individual experience and private 'self-reflection', while integrating critical social inquiry more closely than before with general societal and linguistic structures and with the basic 'rationality claims' embedded in such structures – a point that will be critically discussed in the context of Whitebook's interventions in chapter 5.

In the early 1970s Habermas expanded his reflections on the rational nature of the public sphere. In *Legitimation Crisis*, a work that builds on *The Structural Transformation of the Public Sphere*, he provides a critical discussion of extensive state intervention in the public sphere through new educational curricula, urban planning, medical insurance, the scientization of professional practices and the administrative regulation of social interaction. For Habermas, all of these interventions lead to the legitimation, motivational and rational crises of late capitalism.[55] The point is that state intervention disrupts those critical traditions that are needed for broad democratic legitimization and leads to the promotion of a kind of means–end rationality in the communicative and cultural spheres of society. Legitimation crises stem, for Habermas, 'from the fact that the fulfilment of governmental planning tasks places in question the structure of the depoliticized public realm and, thereby, the formally democratic securing of the private autonomous disposition of the means of production'.[56] Motivational crises, on the other hand, stem from a weakening of the cultural tradition and an exhaustion of the central aspects of bourgeois ideology. In an argument that is very similar to that of *The Structural Transformation of the Public Sphere*, Habermas argues that interaction between the political system (state) and the sociol-cultural system, which relies on the mass loyalty of the bourgeois in market liberal capitalism, breaks down in modern monopoly capitalism. When the interaction becomes frozen as a result of a shortage of motivation, the legitimacy of the political system falls away, thereby endangering a critical and rational public sphere.

This is the point in Habermas's intellectual career when he seriously started to search for a way to meet these public crises. In *Legitimation Crisis*, Habermas finds a way through the discursive standards embedded in science, universal morality and (interestingly enough) post-auratic art. With regard to these cultural spheres Habermas comments that: although science creates the appearance of objectivity (by means of depoliticization), it also contains critical elements that can be used against technocracy. The normative standards of a universal morality can also be used, in a similar way, against the demands of the political and economic sub-systems of late capitalism.[57] Finally – and this is important for the first phase of Habermas's aesthetics – he emphasizes a role for post-auratic art in contributing towards a rational-critical public discussion. 'Bourgeois art, unlike privatised religion, scientistic philosophy, and strategic-utilitarian morality, did not take on tasks in the economic and political systems. Instead it collected residual needs that could find no satisfaction within the "system of needs". Thus along with moral universalism, art and aesthetics (from Schiller to Marcuse) are explosive ingredients built into bourgeois ideology.'[58] This reference to the role of post-auratic art in a rational-democratic public sphere, should be qualified, though. Habermas did not elaborate on the 'explosive ingredient' of aesthetics, but rather cautioned against a surrealist integration of art into everyday life, where art destroys 'the shell of the no-longer-beautiful illusion in order to pass desublimated over into life'.[59] Habermas is thus ambiguous at this point about the possible contribution that modern art can make in addressing the crises of late capitalism in a rational-democratic public sphere.

Habermas's ambiguity about the possible public role of art must be seen in the context of the development of his philosophical reflections from *The Structural Transformation of the Public Sphere* up to the early 1970s. Although he provides a role for post-auratic art, together with science and moral universalism in *Legitimation Crisis*, he did not elaborate on the possible role of art and culture in contemporary society. Despite a brief discussion of Benjamin's aesthetics (see next section), his intellectual interests shifted during the rest of the 1970s in the direction of a formal-discursive account of communicative reason that allowed even less of a role for aesthetics in public reason.

## 1.5   An aesthetics of redemption: Habermas's Benjamin essay

Habermas's remarkable essay on Benjamin (1973), 'Consciousness-raising or rescuing critique', in which he still regards aesthetics as offering a possible way to deal with the dilemmas of modern reason, also contains the outlines of his concept of communicative reason. It is this concept of communicative reason, and its normative-critical role in the public sphere, that eventually direct aesthetics to a more marginal position in his work, thereby contributing to its fate. Habermas's Benjamin essay, which remains one of his most focused writings on aesthetics, can also be interpreted as the end of the first phase of his aesthetics (where aesthetics still has a critical role) and the beginning of the second phase (where there is a less critical role for aesthetics). In discussing the potential public role of art in this essay, Habermas makes an important distinction between the 'consciousness-raising critiques' of Marcuse and Adorno, on the one hand, and the 'rescuing critique' of Benjamin, on the other. Against this background, the difference between the critique of Marcuse and Adorno (which he criticizes) and that of Benjamin (which he appreciates) is addressed with reference to four areas: (i) criticism, (ii) symbolism, (iii) the avant-garde and (iv) technical reproduction.[60] In the final part of the essay Habermas discusses the relevance of Benjamin's aesthetic understanding of experience and language for his own emerging model of communicative reason.

(i) Habermas describes Marcuse's position on art (and Adorno's by implication) as a 'consciousness-raising critique' – a critique whereby the subject uses self-reflection to arrive at some 'aesthetic truth' about reality.[61] In this process autonomous artworks (like Kafka's novels and Beckett's dramas for Adorno) provide the concrete material for consciousness raising and the political transformation of society by opposing ideal to reality. Autonomous art thus unmasks material relationships of life and initiates a self-reflective overcoming of everyday culture. Habermas describes Benjamin's rescuing critique, by contrast, as a procedure that transposes what is worth knowing from the medium of the beautiful (its truth) into the world and thereby rescuing it.[62] Here modern artworks lose their autonomy through new technology (such as the gramophone, film and radio) that operates through accessibility and shock.[63] Benjamin's theory of aesthetic experience thus rescues its objects – whether baroque tragedy, Goethe's dramas, Baudelaire's poetry, or Soviet films – for present-day purposes.[64] Such a rescuing critique is further explained in terms of Benjamin's philosophy of history, where the emphasis falls not on the continuity of time, but on its interruptions. It is the moment in which art forces 'progress' to a standstill and exposes the utopian experience of the 'new-in-the-always-same'. Habermas holds that Benjamin's criticism aims, in contrast with that of Marcuse (and Adorno), to rescue a past charged with *Jetztzeit* – to redeem the past in the 'now'. Benjamin's concept of the de-ritualization of art is, in Habermas's language, part of a world-historical process of rationalization caused by a revolutionary change in the mode of production.[65]

(ii–iii) Habermas relates Marcuse's emphasis on happiness, freedom and reconciliation to the classical symbolic work, such as the novel and the bourgeois drama, in the tradition of Idealist aesthetics. Benjamin's aesthetics, on the other hand, is linked with the non-affirming, non-totalizing, allegorical nature of artworks. In Benjamin's investigation of the baroque tragic drama (*Trauerspiel*) the allegory is contrasted with the individual totality of the transfigurative work of art. It is thus a contrast between the unreconciled and the reconciled – a contrast that has been questioned. It is, for example, an open question whether Marcuse, but definitely Adorno, is in favour of a reconciled artwork.[66] Habermas sketches the third difference between Marcuse and Benjamin in terms of their positions on autonomous art and the avant-garde. He writes: 'Marcuse spares the transformation of bourgeois art by the avant-garde from the direct grasp of ideology critique, whereas Benjamin shows the process of elimination of autonomous art within the history of modernity.'[67] Habermas seems to suggest at this point that the elimination of autonomous art in Benjamin's materialistic aesthetics leads inevitably to an appreciation of the avant-garde wherein the urban masses play an important, critical role in renewing and transforming the traditional concept of bourgeois art.

(iv) On the issue of the technical reproduction of art, Habermas also sides with Benjamin. In this context he faults Adorno's argument that mass art and the new techniques of aesthetic reproduction lead to cultural consumption and degeneration in twentieth-century capitalism.[68] Habermas interprets Adorno's specific historical interpretation as one in which the dissolution of traditional images of the world is countered by an attempt to establish a mimetic relation with inner and outer nature – the need for solidarity removed from the imperatives of public deliberation.[69] Consequently, Adorno defends a position in which the hermetic dimensions of modern art (the novels of Kafka and the music of Schönberg), and not the secular enlightenment of mass art, allow an aura-encapsulated experience to become public. Habermas finds Adorno's position to be 'a defensive strategy of hibernation', such that formal-modern artworks exist only as individual reading practices (literature) and contemplative listening experiences (music) – both being examples of bourgeois individualization. Habermas's problem here is that there is no place in Adorno's aesthetics for collective art forms such as architecture, drama and popular literature.[70] It is also precisely amongst such collective artworks, where repeatability replaces uniqueness, that Benjamin feels himself at home and where post-auratic aesthetic objects move closer to the masses.[71] This is the case in the cinema, where the experiences of film audiences are influenced by the constantly changing images – a situation that Habermas, as opposed to Adorno, and in concert with Benjamin, judges favourably.

Habermas's appreciative reading of Benjamin's hope for secular illumination allows him the opportunity to place Benjamin's emphatic notion of *experience* in the openness of the public sphere. Such a form of experience (which needs to be critically conserved and appropriated if the 'messianic promise of happiness' is ever to be redeemed) must overcome the esoteric and cultic access to the autonomous artwork. The collapse of the aura, on Habermas's reading of Benjamin, opens up the chance of universalizing and stabilizing the experience of happiness. In this context a field of surprising correspondences between animate and inanimate nature appears where things appear to us in the form of vulnerable inter-subjectivity. Benjamin's position, according to Habermas, is thus 'a condition in which the esoteric experiences of happiness have become public and universal, for only in a context of communication into which nature is integrated in a brotherly fashion, as if it were set upright once again, can human subjects open their eyes to look in return'. This is also the point at which Benjamin turns against the esotericism of private fulfilment, happiness and solitary ecstasy.[72] Benjamin's theory of aesthetic experience is thus, unlike that of Marcuse and Adorno, not an example of ideology critique and linked to subjective reflection. In Benjamin's concept of secular illumination, the experience of aura has burst the productive auratic shell and become exoteric. In the next part of his essay Habermas links this reading of Benjamin's concept of experience to language.

The original source of meaning for Benjamin is, according to Habermas, a mixture of mimetic and expressive language wherein words are not related to reality accidentally.[73] There is an intimate link between words and names in Benjamin's theory of meaning. Naming is a kind of translation of the nameless into words, a translation from the incomplete language of nature into the language of humans. Habermas continues that it is not the specifically human properties of language that interest Benjamin, but its links it with animal languages, thereby meaning that the oldest semantic stratum is the expression. Benjamin, on this reading, is attracted to the combination of expression and mimesis, because it precedes the break between subject and object, as in the Schillerian motive of reconciliation. The interesting question here, though, is how Habermas responds to Benjamin's theory of language and meaning. On the one hand, he agrees that if the dependence on nature should be liquidated, leading to a blocking of the powers of mimesis and the streams of semantic energies, it would be a loss to the poetic capacity to interpret the world in the light of human needs.[74] The conservation of these mimetic linguistic experiences, according to Habermas, constitutes for Benjamin the centre of the *promesse de bonheur* of art – humans need these semantic potentials if they want to interpret the world in terms of their needs. It is only in such a context that the appeal for a happy and good life can succeed.[75] On the other hand, Habermas has problems with a theory of experience based on a mimetic theory of language. He expresses his reservations by confronting Benjamin's messianic conception of history and his mimetic view of language with historical materialism and the idea of politicized art.

It is an open question for Habermas whether the theologian in Benjamin succeeds in putting the messianic theory of experience and his mimetic theory of language at the service of historical materialism.[76] Habermas continues that although Benjamin found the politicizing of art ready at hand, he also admitted that an immanent relation to praxis could not be gained from his theory of experience: the experience of shock is not an action, and secular illumination is not a revolutionary deed. Consequently, the intention to 'enlist the services' of historical materialism for a theory of experience ends in an identification of ecstasy and politics that Benjamin, according to Habermas, could not have wanted. The liberation from the cultural tradition of semantic potentials that is sacrificed to the messianic condition is not the same as the liberation of political domination from structural violence. Benjamin's relevance for Habermas is thus not his theology of revolution, but the applicability of his theory of experience for historical materialism.[77] On this note Habermas returns with appreciation to Benjamin's reminder that emancipation without happiness and fulfilment is senseless. In other words, the claim to happiness can be made good only if the sources of the semantic potentials we need for interpreting the world, in the light of our needs, are not exhausted.[78] In this context Habermas asks the following remarkable question at the end of his essay: 'Is it possible that one day an emancipated human race could encounter itself within an expanded space of discursive formation of will and yet be robbed of the light in which it is capable of interpreting its life as something good?'[79] The danger of such a 'discursive formation of will' is that right at the moment of overcoming age-old repressions, it harbours no violence but also no content.

In the final twist of his Benjamin essay, Habermas states that a theory of linguistic communication that wants to bring Benjamin's insights back into a materialist theory of social evolution should consider the following two theses – the possibility of a proper sphere of mutual linguistic understanding, on the one hand, and the non-linguistic and dangerous trust in technology, on the other – at the same time. This is the interesting way in which Habermas ends his essay on Benjamin. One of the most fascinating aspects of the essay is the way in which he attempts to construct a model in which there is a kind of role for aesthetics in communicative reason, yet without deepening this insight. At the same time, though, Habermas was starting to steer his intellectual work towards a theory of communicative action and rationality – a theme that will be further explored when we come to the second phase of Habermas's aesthetics (see chapter 3).[80]

## 1.6   Habermas's early reflections on aesthetics

If one studies Habermas's career in the 1960s and early 1970s (the first phase of his aesthetics), a distinctive shift becomes clear. It is one where aesthetics moves from the foreground to the background. In Habermas's first work, *The Structural Transformation of the Public Sphere*, aesthetics (in the form of a historical and institutional construction of a literary-public sphere) still has an important role to play in the process of democratic will formation. The fascinating aspect of the first part of this work is the importance given to artworks and cultural institutions in contributing to the rational exchange of ideas in the public sphere. Even the more pessimistic analysis of the public sphere, in the second part of the work, still allows space for critical aesthetic interventions in an era of consumption. The process of modernization and rationalization is thus, in opposition to Horkheimer and Adorno's *Dialectic of Enlightenment*, not interpreted exclusively in terms of reification, alienation and instrumental rationality.[81] Although some aspects of the first generation's vision of the culture industry are acknowledged here, Habermas disagrees with Horkheimer and Adorno's interpretation of the public sphere in the contemporary era. Although Habermas agrees in this work that it is impossible to return to a liberal public sphere, as it once existed, he is also unwilling to sacrifice the conceptual and normative aspects of public rationality. Such a move, for Habermas, would threaten public emancipation. Already at this early stage of Habermas's intellectual career, it is clear that the dark side of the Enlightenment does not cancel out the hope for a non-foundational modern ideal of freedom, justice and happiness.

It has also been argued in this chapter that Habermas's concern to develop a rational and normative concept of the public sphere (in the 1960s and early 1970s) contributed to a weakening of aesthetic interests in his work. In this process the inherent potential of a concept such as the literary public sphere fell by the wayside. Clear examples of Habermas's shift on aesthetics are detectable in his works of the late 1960s and early 1970s. In *Knowledge and Human Interests*, for example, he links the idea of emancipation with psychoanalysis as a critical social science leading to critical self-reflection. Although one might expect Habermas to explore themes such as the libido and inner nature here (themes that have rich aesthetic potential), instead he interprets psychoanalysis as the communicative interaction between analyst and patient recovering the unimpaired ego and superego structures. In this process critical social inquiry is closely linked with general societal and linguistic structures. In *Legitimation Crisis* Habermas deepened his study of a rational public sphere by focusing on the manner in which extensive state intervention in the economy leads to legitimation, motivational and rational crises in late capitalism. Habermas's alternative to these crises was interesting at this stage, because a certain kind of scientism, universal morality and post-auratic art were mentioned as examples of cultural resources that could counter the encroachment of planned systems in the cultural life-world. Unfortunately, Habermas did not elaborate on the possible role of art in the public sphere.[82]

Habermas's Benjamin essay, which brings the first phase of his aesthetics to a close, is in many ways remarkable. First, it is Habermas's most substantive essay on aesthetics to date. Secondly, it provides a clear outline of the differences between his position and the aesthetic legacy of Critical Theory (an issue that will be explored in greater detail in the next chapter). Thirdly, Habermas defends Benjamin's rescuing critique against the consciousness-raising critique of Marcuse and Adorno. The point is that criticism is not the result of artworks that raise consciousness, but a form of activity that rescues various aesthetic experiences for public debate. The interest in Benjamin's aesthetics also stems from Habermas's view that theoretical and normative dimensions can be expanded by developments in popular culture such as photography and film. Fourthly, Habermas's defence of Benjamin is further explored in terms of the Benjaminian concepts of experience and language. I have already indicated that Habermas seems to agree with Benjamin that without the influx of semantic energy, with which Benjamin's rescuing criticism is concerned, practical discourse is weakened. At another juncture in the essay, however, Habermas is cautious about a theory of experience grounded in a mimetic theory of language. In this context he questions Benjaminian concepts such as mimesis, ecstasy and shock in the public sphere. This qualified critique of Benjamin allows Habermas, in the fifth place, to defend a view of the public sphere that includes material and communicative aspects. At the end of the essay, though, Habermas acknowledges that a model of linguistic communication seeking to bring Benjamin's insights into a materialist theory of social evolution must deal with the complex ambiguity of communication and technology.

The discernible shift in the first phase of Habermas's aesthetics (from the 1960s to the early 1970s) has been mentioned. It is a shift from the institutional construction of a public sphere as the basis for democratic will formation in *The Structural Transformation of the Public Sphere* (via a model of self-reflection in psychoanalysis) to the validity claims that are universally implicit in all speech. This shift can also be described as a turn away from a historically specific grounding of democracy (in his early work) towards reliance on the trans-historical and intersubjective evolving communicative capacities of reason.[83] This shift, which inaugurates the second phase of his aesthetics, is a further refinement of the final paragraph of his essay on Benjamin's aesthetics, where Habermas states that the challenge is to deal with the problem of universal human communication in light of the danger of a non-linguistic technology. Already at this juncture of his career it is clear that aesthetics finds only a reduced and specified position within communicative reason. This motive is also one of the driving forces behind Habermas's main philosophical accomplishment – *The Theory of Communicative Action*. Before discussing the aesthetic implication of Habermas's theory of communicative action (which forms the heart of the second phase of his aesthetics), in chapter 3, we will focus on the relationship between Habermas and the first generation of Critical Theorists, in the next chapter. We have seen that aesthetic arguments fulfil an important role in the works of Horkheimer, Adorno, Marcuse and Benjamin. In the development of his own project of Critical Theory in the direction of a more formal understanding of reason, and before he could launch the second phase of his aesthetics, Habermas had to deal with this aesthetic legacy.

# 2

# Habermas and the Legacy of Aesthetics in Critical Theory

Habermas's relationship to the first generation of Critical Theorists is an important leitmotiv of this study. The question is: how did Habermas come to terms with the aesthetic legacy of Critical Theory in the unfolding of his own philosophical project since the 1970s? One way to address this question is to reconstruct Habermas's interpretation of the first generation of Critical Theorists. It is clear, from many interventions, that Habermas had a special affinity with the initial research programme of Critical Theory in the 1930s as it emerged under the guidance of Horkheimer. This programme was closely attached to left-wing Hegelianism and historical materialism (section 2.1). Horkheimer and his associates' reading of historical materialism had a distinctive angle based on an epistemological critique of positivism and the development of an interdisciplinary research model. In this model historical materialism, as philosophy of history, was articulated in economic, psychological and cultural terms. It is via the last of these that aesthetics found its interdisciplinary place. In the next step of his argument Habermas claims that this ambitious formulation of societal reason in the 1930s was shipwrecked during the Second World War on the rocky coast of Horkheimer and Adorno's pessimistic view of reason, as articulated in the *Dialectic of Enlightenment*. As members of the inner circle (a term stemming from Axel Honneth), Horkheimer and Adorno became haunted by the image of the functional systematization of twentieth-century society through instrumental rationality (section 2.2).[1]

It is in this context that Adorno became the main articulator of Critical Theory in the 1950s and 1960s, a period in which he defended a socio-philosophical position that was strongly influenced by aesthetic themes. Part of Adorno's answer to a functionalist society was that modern art could provide a kind of escape from instrumental reason (section 2.3). Although Habermas was closely associated with Adorno in the 1950s and 1960s, it should be clear (on the basis of the previous chapter) that art and cultural themes played a less significant role in the first phase of his aesthetics. I also indicated that Habermas, in an early essay, preferred Benjamin's model of aesthetic redemption to Adorno's (and Marcuse's) model of consciousness raising. The issues that are at stake here will be further explored in section 2.4. It is important at this stage to note that in the period leading up to the publication of *The Theory of Communicative Action* in 1981, which finally inaugurated the second phase of Habermas's aesthetics, he did not interpret the differences between Adorno and Benjamin in purely aesthetic terms, as was the case in his Benjamin essay; rather, he positioned them within the unfolding of his theory of communicative reason. It is in this context that a less-known group of the first generation of Critical Theorists, the so-called outer circle (Neumann, Kirchheimer, Fromm and Benjamin), became important for Habermas's project.

## 2.1   The initial research programme of Critical Theory

Critical Theory has its roots in the Frankfurt of the early twentieth century. This city – with its enlightened citizenry, a liberal university and press, an experimental radio station and the Jewish Academy (*Freien Jüdischen Lehrhaus*) at that time – was the site of an unusual concentration of intellectual energy and provided a fertile milieu for socio-philosophical work. It is in these surroundings that an *Institut für Sozialforschung* (Institute for Social Research) was founded at the University of Frankfurt in 1924, with the brief to provide a sound academic basis for research on socialism. The first director, Carl Grünberg, who had an Austro-Marxist background, kept the research programme close to orthodox Marxism.[2] The work directed by Grünberg tended to be empirical, historical and oriented toward problems of the European working-class movement, although theoretical works by Karl Korsch and Georg Lukács were also considered. When Max Horkheimer took over as director of the Institute in 1930, a more independent material theory of society emerged. The contours of this approach were presented in Horkheimer's inaugural lecture and were further developed in the Institute's journal (1932–41).[3]

In his inaugural lecture Horkheimer defined social philosophy as an attempt to elucidate 'human fate . . . the fate of humans not as mere individuals, however, but as members of a community. It is thus above all concerned with phenomena that can only be understood in the context of human social life: with the state, law, economy, religion . . . in short, with the entire material and intellectual culture of humanity.'[4] Horkheimer began his argument by pointing to the limitations of both the classical social theories of Kant and Hegel, on the one hand, and of metaphysical and positivist philosophies of his day, on the other. Kant is criticized for grounding social philosophy in the experience and faculties of the particular individual. Hegel's attempt to situate philosophy within society and history is presented as an improvement over Kant, yet Hegel's idealism and tendency to justify the existing order is rejected. Hegel's legacy is then, sketched by Horkheimer as a last attempt to unite an empirical analysis of social reality with a philosophico-historical concept of reason.[5] But post-Hegelian social philosophy split into two directions: modern metaphysics and positivism. Horkheimer then criticizes the forms of idealism in neo-Kantian, neo-Hegelian, phenomenological and existential philosophies (of Scheler, Hartmann and Heidegger) for their questionable speculative metaphysics and for their tendencies to celebrate a higher, transcendental sphere of being (*Sein*) and meaning (*Sinn*) over concrete existence. But he also criticizes the positivist schools which root their theories in isolated facts for their unsupportable metaphysical presuppositions and their methodological limitations such that empirical knowledge is deprived of all philosophical reflection and reduced to mere 'factual research'. The task of a social philosophy, according to Horkheimer, is to confront the disintegration of the classical Hegelian synthesis.[6]

Horkheimer, ably assisted by a group of talented associates, reacted to the disintegration of the Hegelian legacy in two way. First, they provided an epistemological critique of positivism from the perspective of the young Marx.[7] The point is that the empirical sciences are steered by social labour. The problem is that the empirical approach becomes alienated from a practical and social consciousness. For Horkheimer this was also the problem of modern theory *überhaupt* – the tradition of positivist consciousness since Descartes. Horkheimer termed this tradition of scientism, so indicative of modernity, *traditional theory*. Against it he placed *critical theory*, as a kind of reflection that is aware of its social roots as well as its practical context of application.[8] This insight was worked out within the framework of a materialistic epistemology.[9] In the 1930s Horkheimer and his associates added to this epistemological model a type of Marxist philosophy of history. Accordingly, social progress was regarded as the development of production forces that, with each technological step, imposed a new level of development in the relationships of social production. This reading, which was connected with the idea of emancipation, referred to the potential for a non-exploitative, democratic and rational society – which was not merely a utopian ideal, but part of the unfolding of history. Marx, for example, described his position as one that could resolve the antagonism between man and nature and man and man.

This epistemological critique of positivism was not really a significant redirection of Marxism. Only with a second step, in developing a programme of interdisciplinary research, did Horkheimer and his associates effect a new methodological interpretation of historical materialism.[10] Here the argument runs that the conflict between production forces can be interpreted only from the comprehensive perspective of different social-scientific disciplines, in which a philosophy of history is combined with interdisciplinary (empirical) research in a dialectical research programme. Philosophy, as the general theoretical discipline, is placed here in a position to direct the specialized sciences, but it is also seen as being amenable to the results of empirical studies. The optimistic contention was that the various scientific disciplines could mediate the fragmentary nature of human existence and knowledge. It is a research programme wherein neither philosophy nor any of the individual sciences could discern 'reality' on its own.[11] According to Horkheimer, such a research project would bring

> philosophers, sociologists, economists, historians, and psychologists . . . together in permanent collaboration to undertake in common that which can be carried out individually in the laboratory in other fields. In short, the task is to do what all true researchers have always done: namely, to pursue their larger philosophical questions on the basis of the most precise scientific methods, to revise and refine their questions in the course of their substantive work, and to develop new methods without losing sight of the larger context.[12]

This is Horkheimer's socio-philosophical answer to the fate of theory after Hegel.

It should be noted that this exposition of interdisciplinary research harbours a certain concept of reason in order to deal with the relationship between the particular and the universal in the research process. This concept of reason, which the first generation of Critical Theorists (under the guidance of Horkheimer) used in their interdisciplinary research programme of the 1930s, reflected their Hegelian-Marxist roots; but, in contrast to Hegel, the particular is not sacrificed here to the universal. This means that universal ideas such as truth, justice and freedom were confronted with particular, contingent and concrete demands for happiness and an end to suffering. This position presupposes a situation in which the difference between the *volonté générale* and the individual will, as well as the contrast between the rational abilities and the sensual nature of humankind, is bridged. In developing this concept of reason, the first generation of the Frankfurt School arrived at two conclusions: that rationality could be a living reality in modern, industrialized and technologized societies if individuals would grasp this specific idea of reconciliation, truth and happiness – between the universal and the particular. On the other hand, there was already an acknowledgement by some Critical Theorists that the 'rationalization process of modern society' (Max Weber) could lead to the formation of a closed system of instrumental rationality, reification, instrumentality and oppression.[13] In terms of Habermas's reconstruction of Critical Theory (as will be discussed in the next section), Horkheimer and Adorno eventually used this latter part of the conclusion to develop a comprehensive, pessimistic view of twentieth-century society.

With regard to the interdisciplinary research programme, Horkheimer argued that it allowed the questioning of 'the connection between the economic life of society, the psychical development of individuals, and the changes in the realm of culture in the narrower sense (to which belong not only the so-called intellectual elements, such as science, art, and religion, but also law, custom, fashion, public opinion, sport, leisure activities, lifestyle, etc).'[14] This interdisciplinary programme (with its emphasis on disciplines such as political economy, psychology and cultural studies) was somewhat unorthodox at that time for Marxian social theory, which tended to neglect the dimension of individual and social psychology and downplay the study of culture and leisure. Attention to these topics was thus another distinctive contribution of the first generation of Critical Theorists.[15] Political economy, the central discipline (of the three terrains), was judged to mediate between the philosophy of history and the specialized sciences. The process of capitalist production was thus interpreted as a historico-philosophical as well as an empirical process. This interpretation was linked to a study of the radical changes in capitalism since the end of the eighteenth century.

Friedrich Pollock, who was responsible for this part of the research at the institute, described the development of capitalist 'planned economies' as state capitalism – a characteristic that he found in Fascism as well as Soviet Communism. Pollock's argument regarding planned economies was intimately linked to Lukács's interpretation of reification (a concept that stems from Weber). Pollock argued that state capitalism frustrated the possibility of a progressive twentieth-century social culture – in the place of the free market came bureau-cratic planning strategies. Accordingly, the co-operation between capitalist conglomerates and political power elites changed social integration in a centralized and administrative manner. This analysis, which was originally known only within the inner circle of the Institute, later became an influential theory of post-liberal capitalism. More importantly, it provided the foundation for a functionalist and instrumental understanding of reason that influenced the Institute's work on psychology and cultural studies.

With regard to psychology, the Institute's research contains one of the first attempts to develop a synthesis of Marx and Freud and to incorporate psychoanalytic perspectives into an interdisciplinary research programme. Eric Fromm was assigned the task of develop-ing a model of the integration of historical materialism and the psyche.[16] The underlying question was: why do individuals submit themselves with such ease to the authority (the centrally adminis-tered power) of planned economies, and what psychological conditions produce authoritarian personalities who will submit to Fascism? Like Bernfeld, Reich and other left-wing Freudians, Fromm's point of departure was the individual's integration into capitalism via the social formation of psycho-sexual characteristics. According to this position, human drives are determined not only biologically, in accord with classical Freudian theory, but also by socio-economic circumstances. A good example here is the structural change in the bourgeois nuclear family under conditions of com-modity capitalism, such that the father figure lost the authority that he possessed under liberal capitalist conditions. The structural change of the family in the form of the disappearance of the 'authority system' resulted in the weakening of the adolescent's ego develop-ment and the emergence of an easily manipulated personality type. Critical Theorists thus analysed changes in socialization processes, which produced weak individual egos. Horkheimer took Fromm and his associates' different and often speculative reflections and integrated them with the results that were coming from Pollock and his associates' study of political economy.[17] This move by

Horkheimer opened the way to study twentieth-century culture and art together with political economy and psychology in the research programme.

Figures such as Löwenthal, Adorno and Benjamin (who worked in the third area of Horkheimer's interdisciplinary research programme) presented the view that socialized subjects do not merely react passively to culture, but use it actively in a complex process of social integration. Habermas writes that for them the arts 'were the preferred object of an ideology critique aimed at separating the transcendent contents of authentic art – whether utopian or critical – from the affirmative, ideologically worn-out components of bourgeois ideals'. He continues: 'Ironically, however, the critiques of ideology carried out by Horkheimer, Marcuse and Adorno confirmed them in the belief that culture was losing its autonomy in postliberal societies and was being incorporated into the machinery of the economic-administrative system.'[18] This change in the position of Critical Theory contributed, according to Habermas, to a situation in which the model of an open interdisciplinary research programme was left behind in favour of a closed model of instrumental reason. In this context, Horkheimer, who was strongly influenced by Adorno's work, returned cultural and aesthetic analysis, together with political economy and psychology, to a functional framework, in which the concept of instrumental rationality played a central role. From then on, the immanent logic of the capitalist modernization and commodification process pointed for Horkheimer and Adorno to the emergence not of a classless, emancipated society, but of an instrumental one. Habermas writes: 'Critical Theory had already lost too much ground and surrendered to a dialectics of the enlightenment that eroded reason and faith in reason. Resignation had already set in by 1941.'[19] It is within this context that Adorno, with his forceful articulation of aesthetically informed arguments, became the major figure in Critical Theory till his death in 1969.[20]

## 2.2  Society as the result of instrumental reason

The abandonment of an interdisciplinary theory of society by Horkheimer and his associates coincided with the exile of the Frankfurt School from Fascist Germany in the run-up to the Second World War. Horkheimer's articles in the last volume of the Institute's journal (1941) are drenched with a pronounced historico-philosophical pessimism.[21] In Habermas's view, '[t]he dark writers of the bourgeoisie, such as Machiavelli, Hobbes, and Mandeville, always had an appeal for Max Horkheimer, who was influenced by Schopenhauer early in his career.'[22] This new phase in the development of Critical Theory benefited Adorno, whose interests in aesthetic issues made him sceptical from the start about the historical-materialist notion of progress which was the basis of the initial interdisciplinary research programme. The three pillars of the research programme (political economy, psychology and cultural studies) thus received a new incarnation as economic steering mechanisms, psychological methods of oppression, and cultural manipulation strategies. Only those social processes that had a function in the reproduction and manipulation of social labour found a home in the project. Honneth argues that from the 1940s a functionalist framework directed the research programme of Critical Theory, wherein the idea of instrumental reason and a specific philosophy of history were combined. In this process the following two premises are dominant: that human reason stands in an instrumental relation to natural objects; and that history is a process that progressively enables humankind to control natural objects.[23]

In the *Dialectic of Enlightenment*, which Adorno and Horkheimer completed in 1944 and Habermas describes as 'their blackest book', the mistrust in progress and enlightenment is articulated from an epistemological, ethical-anthropological and aesthetic point of view.[24] The formulation of 'Dialectic of Enlightenment' plays on the paradoxical (dialectical) nature of the Enlightenment project. On the one hand, it refers to the social optimism inherent in the Enlightenment – the belief in human reason as the basis of freedom and the cultural source of light.[25] As Kant indicated, 'enlightenment' means that a person should free him or herself from immaturity by means of independent critical thinking. In place of a mythical interpretation of nature comes a rational explanation and 'disenchantment'.[26] In the process the following themes play an important role: the desacralization of nature, a rejection of myth, the coming of age of the subject, individual rights, the autonomous use of reason, separation between subject and object, the ascendence of science, and mechanization of labour and industrial production.[27] Going against Kant, Horkheimer and Adorno developed a crisis philosophy. The belief in progress and the dialectical development towards freedom are thus interpreted as a dialectical regression. In this process the points of reference for them are Schopenhauer (Horkheimer) and Nietzsche (Adorno) – both figures who used aesthetic arguments prominently. To this critique Horkheimer and Adorno added Weber's thesis of means–end rationality and Lukács's view of reification.[28] Weber's point is that belief in scientific progress and rationality lead not to progress, but to means–end rationality (*Zweckrationalität*). This type of rationality infiltrates economic, judicial, administrative and cultural systems. In place of the concrete realization of universal freedom, comes the 'iron cage' of bureaucratic control.[29]

The fact that Weber had a more differentiated model of rationalization (incorporating both instrumental and other forms of reason – a point that Habermas supported) was not important for Horkheimer and Adorno. Their doubts as to whether instrumental reason could be transformed into *Vernunft* (emancipated reason) were reinforced by the following catastrophes in the twentieth century: the failure of the proletarian revolution, the ascendence of Fascism, the capitalist resistance to radical transformation, and the degeneration of Marxism in the Soviet Union. Armed with such enlightenment pessimism, any kind of social action was viewed in the instrumental relation between subject and object. In this process the liberation of individuals became an illusion – in the place of freedom came the control of nature and the scientific laws of modern reason which mastered both humans and nature in a regressive dialectic of the Enlightenment. Thus the modern predicament is, not the result of the action of a dictator or an oppressive class; it is humans themselves, who are both oppressors and the oppressed – creators of the social system which eventually deforms them.[30] In this context, social labour is not a form of emancipatory activity, but contains the seed of objectifying and instrumental rationality.[31] The faint rumbling of the factory hall, the drone of disciplined labour, and the restless rhythm of diligence and clock time culminate in the conditioned loneliness of the many nameless, exchangeable workers in the production system.[32] This sombre picture of one-dimensional rationality, scientific objectification, and capitalist consumption made a liberating reason inconceivable. The imperialistic drive of the Western individual to understand physical and human nature is thus described by Horkheimer and Adorno as the 'Prinzip der blinde Herrschaft' (principle of blind domination), thereby anticipating Foucault's concept of a 'disciplined society'.[33]

In a provocative manner Horkheimer and Adorno describe the principle of blind domination as the transformation of enlightenment into myth.[34] For them, the mythical nature of seasonal cycles finds its equivalent in the rhythm of scientific laws – modern reason as the heir of *mythos* – and in the repetitive nature of identity thinking and exchange value (the central categories of *Dialectic of Enlightenment*).[35]

In this process, enlightened reason (*Aufklärung*), which claims man's independence from nature, eventually becomes its master. In the place of the 'abolition of the myth' comes a new, unyielding master – the totalitarian-scientific regularity of enlightened reason.[36] By conforming to this myth, humankind's concept of freedom is destroyed.[37] In the most radical paragraphs of *Dialectic of Enlightenment*, all forms of reason and action are portrayed as instrumental reason and identity thinking – even formal logic and the law of non-contradiction are equated with the process of means–end rationalization. Eventually this process runs the danger, according to Horkheimer and Adorno, of liquidating the autonomous subject in an oppressive rational system in which any form of emancipatory reason disappears. The only alternative is to turn against the reifying inclinations of conceptual thinking itself. Hence, despite this very sombre picture of enlightened reason – one in which weary labour practices, the spiritual poverty of the culture industry, and the concentration camp are all linked (and one in which the whole civilization process of humankind is determined from the start by a progressive reification which founds its logical conclusion in Fascism and the mega-bomb) – they still kept alive, on the other hand, the memory of some kind of reconciliation in philosophical thinking.[38] Adorno found this memory in modern art, whereas Horkheimer defended the mystical-religious experience of the other.

From Habermas's perspective, Horkheimer and Adorno's pessimistic philosophy in *Dialectic of Enlightenment* led to a position such that the possibility of reason fulfilling itself in the world became more and more remote. This is a position opposite to that of the interdisciplinary research programme of the 1930s (which was inspired by the Hegelian-Marxist tradition). Habermas asks: 'But then a question arises as to the motives that could have led Horkheimer and Adorno to commence their critique of the enlightenment at such a depth that the project of the enlightenment itself is endangered?'[39] Against this background of a shift from an interdisciplinary research programme to a philosophy of reified consciousness, Habermas offers two points of criticism. First, he is critical about the broad thrust of Horkheimer and Adorno's reductive and functional philosophy of history. Such a move runs the danger of excluding any form of intersubjective communication in the public sphere. The negation of a broadening of legal freedoms and individual action leads to a serious hiatus in *Dialectic of Enlightenment*.[40] The dimension of everyday communication, which allows socialized subjects to creatively develop common action orientations, is thereby lost.[41] Secondly, Horkheimer and

Adorno's philosophy of history is generalized to such an extent that all forms of social-scientific study get caught up in the process of reification. In this way the fruitful possibilities of the interdisciplinary social theory of the 1930s are abandoned.[42]

The details of Habermas's intersubjective and communicative alternative to Horkheimer and Adorno (with its implications for the second phase of his aesthetics) will be discussed in detail in the following chapter; but here it is necessary to revisit Adorno's aesthetic alternative to instrumental reason. This is necessary, because Adorno established himself in his philosophical-aesthetic contributions as the major representative of Critical Theory in the 1950s and 1960s – at the time when Habermas became his assistant and (later) colleague. Adorno who, alluded (together with Horkheimer) to a new relationship between reason and aesthetics in *Dialectic of Enlightenment*, proceeded to an alternative ethics in *Minima Moralia*, an alternative epistemology in *Negative Dialectics*. And finally, in *Aesthetic Theory*, he brought all these questions together in an ambitious aesthetic project. It is Adorno's aesthetic project that Habermas reacts to in the second phase of his aesthetics.

## 2.3   Adorno: instrumental reason and aesthetics

Adorno's position on instrumental reason (in *Dialectic of Enlighten- ment*) is intimately linked to culture and aesthetics. Instrumental reason is seen as something that infiltrates more and more life spheres by manipulating cultural and aesthetic objects. The point is that the production and consumption of cultural goods (the so-called culture industry) are the result of the imperatives of economic and political sub-systems – which constitute a monolithic power block that manipulates the cultural life-world. Under the monopoly of capitalism and the monotony of cultural consumption, everything becomes identical and stereotypical.[43] By excluding any deviation, the culture industry becomes completely integrated into capitalist society. More concretely, the mass media (constituted by radio, film, popular music, etc.) serve in the twentieth century as 'social cement' for the capitalist system of instrumental rationality, rather than for self- emancipation.[44] The commodification of commercial music, for example, contributes to a deterioration of the listening capacity. Under such circumstances the impressionistic colour effects of popular music genres easily overwhelm listeners – they are satisfied with a standardized repertoire and enjoy certain parts that are taken out of context. Contemporary listening thus becomes trapped in an infantile phase, where the audience is subjected to the meagre diet of the popular tune.[45] In his critical stance towards the culture industry, an essay of Marcuse, which holds that classical bourgeois art displays affirmative features and serves the existing power relations, influenced Adorno.[46] In becoming affirmative, art's revolutionary longing and utopian potential are rendered impotent. Even though certain art forms may lead to a temporary sensation of liberation, this does not really alter the *status quo*. The inner ambivalence of modern bourgeois art is that at the very moment in which social ills are articulated, they are aesthetically neutralized. In late bourgeois culture, especially in Fascism, the ambivalence between affirmative and negative moments of art is abolished in favour of the affirmative.

In broad agreement with Marcuse's position, Adorno presents his alternative – modern autonomous art.[47] Adorno finds examples of such art in aspects of idealistic aesthetics, and more specifically in the music of Schönberg and the writings of Valéry, Proust, Kafka and Beckett. In all these cases art transcends the system and ideology of mass culture in order to contribute to societal emancipation.[48] In this process art has a distinctive negative role: in the place of reconciliation, harmony and the whole (all elements of the traditional organic, closed artwork) comes disruption, dissonance and the fragmentary nature of the open artwork.[49] Adorno also defends the modern autonomous artwork as being free from any religious, political or social influence.[50] This becomes clear when he deals with the antinomy between autonomous and committed (engaged) art. Adorno holds that the latter constantly fails in its attempts to change fundamental political conceptions. Autonomous art, on the other hand, which does not specifically aim to change political attitudes, often succeeds in doing so. Adorno writes: 'This is not the time for political works of art; rather, politics has migrated into the autonomous work of art, and it has penetrated most deeply into works that present themselves as political dead.'[51] Autonomous works of art thus achieve without political considerations a political effect above that of committed art. Adorno proceeds: 'Kafka's prose and Beckett's plays ... have an effect in comparison to which official works of art look like children's games – they arouse the anxiety that existentialism only talks about ... Their implacability compels the change in attitude that committed works only demand.'[52] In his debate with Benjamin and Brecht (on theatre and related issues) and Lukács (on twentieth-century literature), Adorno deepened his position on autonomous modern art.

In addressing the tension between artistic autonomy and political commitment, through Brecht's concept of theatre, Benjamin takes the revolution in literary techniques and the transformation of the production system as significant and worth studying. Brecht's epic theatre is in this context an important example of such a transformation (*Umfunktionierung*).[53] Brecht uses, for example, the interruption of the story's plot via the montage effect of film and radio against the illusionary nature of the bourgeois drama. Through such a *Verfremdungseffekt* (alienation effect) the spectator recognizes the situation on stage as real, not with satisfaction, but with surprise and insight. The Brechtian theatre is thus, for Benjamin, both technically and politically progressive – a model for committed and humane social art. Adorno, on the other hand, is sceptical about whether such a concept of theatre can change the power relations of late capitalist societies. The uncompromising work of Beckett, with its autonomous resistance to consumption, is rather more open to the hidden contradictions of advanced capitalism and instrumental rationality than politically committed works. Adorno writes: 'Art works are less and more than praxis.'[54] Art is more than praxis, because by turning away from it, art denounces the narrow-mindedness and untruth of practical life. It is in this sense that Beckett's aesthetics points to a truth quality (*Wahrheitsgehalt*) beyond politics.

Although Adorno and Lukács share certain assumptions about twentieth-century society – the total commodification, reification and alienation of late capitalist culture; scepticism about worker emancipation; and an appreciation of autonomous art as a possible medium and source of resistance for uncovering global structures of alienation and reification – they differ on twentieth-century art movements.[55] Adorno, for example, defends the modern autonomous artworks of Picasso, Schönberg, Kafka and Beckett against politicized and mass-mediated art, while Lukács judges that these works reinforce man's ahistorical anxieties in advanced capitalism and lack of the perspective of a possible socialist future.[56] Only critical realism (Mann) and social realism (Gorki), despite their bourgeois elements, contain for Lukács a sober openness to socialism and historical optimism in the twentieth century. Adorno, on his part, judges the historical and technical elements of social realism regressive – especially the way in which they mask the oppressive social production forces of the East bloc countries of the 1950s. Critical realist works are also more modern than Lukács admits.[57] Against the background of these arguments, Adorno is thus able to judge aesthetic modernism positively as a 'negative knowledge of truth' of the socio-historical reality

– a dialectical truth of social alienation.[58] Aesthetic modernism, accordingly, has the experimental and technical depth at its disposal to resist the commodification of late capitalism. For Adorno, the critical technique of modern literature – for example, Beckett's *Endgame* – stands above suspicion in its polemic against a meaningless world.[59]

In his debates with Benjamin and Lukács, Adorno defends modern autonomous art that can transcend the social system of twentieth-century society and crack the cement of the culture industry. It is this principle of autonomy that also provides the pre-conditions for art's emancipatory role and its *Wahrheitsgehalt* (truth quality). One of the radical implications of the socio-aesthetic truth of reality (or the truth character of art) is that the 'rational idea' is no longer the exclusive property of discursive thinking. This awareness is forcefully articulated by the high-modern (autonomous) artwork that reminds us of the complex nature of reason in the world. Such artworks represent a 'logic' and a 'synthesis' that differ from the oppressive operation of identity thinking. Aesthetic synthesis also differs from conceptual thinking by considering the particular or the non-identical in a non-violent manner. Against this background the artwork serves for Adorno as the model of non-objectified thinking and a paradigm for a non-oppressive integration or reconciliation of elements. In other words, two social functions of art are emphasized: the artwork reveals through its structures the irrational, false and instrumental character of the existing world, and by way of aesthetic synthesis it anticipates a possible reconciled order. This is what Adorno means by aesthetic rationality – a transfiguration of the elements of empirical reality so that reality can emerge in the light of a reconciliation that is not of this world. Art thus makes a knowledge claim in its universal and particular moments as well as through its appearance (*Schein*). In this way the differentiation of reason into the isolated spheres of truth, normative correctness and expression is bridged.[60] In short, from Adorno's perspective the practice of art is a model for an alternative form of reason (especially instrumental reason) and an alternative form of praxis.[61]

Adorno expands his view of aesthetic rationality by considering the issue of conceptuality. He writes:

> To argue that concepts are interspersed with art is not the same as claiming the conceptuality of art in general. Art is no more a concept than it is vision (*Anschauung*). By its very existence, art protests against that dichotomy. Moreover the visual aspect of art differs from empirical perception because it always points beyond empirical perception

to spirit. Art is a vision of the non-visual; it is similar to the concept without actually being one. It is in reference to concepts, however, that art releases its mimetic, non-conceptual potential.[62]

In this quotation, Adorno links the non-conceptuality (and non-discursiveness) of truth to the dialectic interaction of art and philosophy. Art expresses the ineffable in an intuitive, sensual, particular and non-conceptual manner. There is, though, the danger that the non-discursive nature of art becomes a particular experience. On the other hand, philosophy needs the non-conceptual. It is at this point that Kant is paraphrased: art is blind without philosophy, and philosophy empty without art. In other words, art and philosophy 'overlap in the idea of truth content. The progressively unfolding truth of a work of art is none other than the truth of the philosophical concept.'[63] Adorno explains this reciprocity between art and philosophy through the example of the criticism of painting – without criticism we can't see the painting, but seeing the painting is not reducible to its criticism. Art thus points to an emphatic truth concept, which philosophy cannot give in a similar way. Adorno writes: 'Art works are true in the medium of determinate negation only. This constitutes the challenge of aesthetics today.' And, 'Actually, only what does not fit into this world is true.'[64] Ultimately, the inner authenticity, truth and validity of artworks supply evidence, for Adorno, against the universality of instrumental reason and point to an alternative concept of truth.[65] By suggesting that what appears outside meaning is meaningful, art risks the whole concept of meaning itself.

Adorno's aesthetically informed philosophy, with its view of truth and conceptuality, has various implications. His criticism of instrumental reason leads to a position where reason must also incorporate aesthetic rationality and aesthetic truth. This articulation, which indicates Adorno's Kantian inclinations when it comes to aesthetics, also reverses the modest position allocated to art in Hegel's and Marx's systems. Adorno is a Kantian in so far as he stresses the importance of aesthetic reason and the truth of art. In this sense aesthetic reason is not judged to be inferior to communicative reason. Adorno seems to suggest that truth is the result not *just* of a public or communicatively shared understanding or consensus (as Habermas would like to convince us), but also of a *world-disclosing*, non-discursive approach. He is thus clearly uneasy with the interdisciplinary research model of Critical Theory in the 1930s. Adorno finds himself at home, rather, in a tradition that includes a certain reading of Kant and of Schiller's aesthetics, one that moves from Schopenhauer and Nietzsche into the twentieth century. Although Adorno never openly aligned himself with Heidegger, there is an interesting similarity in their respective positions on the truth of art (an issue that will be further explored in chapter 6). Against this background, aesthetic synthesis or reconciliation serves as a kind of utopian model of the uncoerced relationship between individuals in a liberated society. Due to the oppressive nature of identity thinking, aesthetic rationality becomes for Adorno an alternative to instrumental rationality. The artwork could thus be interpreted as a model for a 'rational' and emancipated society, anticipating a non-oppressive social reconciliation.[66] It is obvious that Habermas's view of the normativity of language-anchored reason giving (as will be explored in the next chapter) is very critical regarding such an interpretation of societal reason.


## 2.4   The outer circle and the Benjaminian alternative

Habermas's discomfort with the first generation of Critical Theorists, and more specifically with how Adorno's aesthetically informed philosophy departs from the initial framework of the interdisciplinary research programme of the 1930s, necessitated a reconstruction of the history of Critical Theory. Axel Honneth, the most prominent member of the third generation of Critical Theorists, provided such a reconstruction by distinguishing between an inner circle (Horkheimer, Adorno and Marcuse) and an outer circle (Neumann, Kirchheimer, Fromm and Benjamin). The argument runs that although the inner circle's contributions differed thematically from one another, these individuals were united by their reductive philosophy of history (portrayed as a degenerative dialectic of enlightenment) and their functionalistic frame of reference when it comes to society. The outer circle, by contrast, differs from the inner circle on both these counts. In this section (and building on the insights of Honneth's reconstruction of the history of Critical Theory) we will discuss (i) Neumann and Kirchheimer's understanding of society, law, and economy, before addressing (ii) Fromm's ideas on psychology. This discussion will form the background to the actual aim of this section: to provide further evidence of the aesthetic differences between Benjamin and Adorno (iii).[67] By not sharing Adorno's very direct link between instrumental reason and aesthetics, Benjamin suggests a kind of aesthetics that seems to be nearer Habermas's model of communicative reason.

(i) For Neumann and Kirchheimer, who studied the steering mechanism of justice in civil society, constitutional law serves as a political compromise between interest groups in capitalism.[68] Changes in constitutional law reflect changes in the economic structure. As an alternative to Horkheimer and Pollock's thesis of state capitalism (see section 2.1), they introduced the concept of totalitarian monopolistic economy.[69] In his study, *Behemoth*, Neumann, for example, interpreted the phenomenon of National Socialism as a social compromise in which the party, private economic interests, and an administrative elite agreed about political measures with a view to increasing monopolistic gains.[70] Returning to the issue of the reconstruction of the outer circle in Critical Theory, the point is that the empirical results of their research led to another perspective on society than that of the inner circle – one that emphasized the phenomenon of political legitimacy in the constitutional state. From this it followed that the constitutional set-up of a society is always the expression of a general consensus between political role-players and powers.[71] Neumann and Kirchheimer thus contested the inner circle's thesis of the totalitarian state as a homogeneous centre of power (power centralism). For them as legal-political thinkers, the process of social integration is not the product of functional imperatives, but one of political communication between interest and power groups.

(ii) Although Fromm initially worked closely with Horkheimer and Adorno, his encounter with the works of Karen Horney and Harry Stack Sullivan during his exile led to an interactionistic review of basic psychoanalytic presuppositions.[72] This encounter influenced his work *Escape from Freedom* (1941), where the formation of the civilian personality is placed in a new socio-psychological framework – one in which Freud's idea of an unchanging libidinal drive structure is supplemented by a more flexible framework of drives. Apart from the biological, room is made here for socio-historical influences on human drives. These two basic kinds of drives constitute, for Fromm, the motivation potential for individuation and socialization.[73] Special importance is given here to the role of social interaction in the socialization process. It should be noted, though, that Fromm qualified this view of character development (as interaction between individual motivation and the imperatives of the socio-cultural milieu) by stating that social influences do not completely sweep away the individual character structure. But this qualification did not satisfy Adorno and Marcuse.[74] They interpreted the interactionist model as constituting a neo-analytical revisionism, wherein psychoanalysis is replaced by conformist therapy. Against Fromm,

Adorno and Marcuse remained faithful to the validity of instinctual theory as a helpful model for describing the instrumental relations of modern society – an issue that has a lot of implications for aesthetics, as the recent interventions of Joel Whitebook indicate (see chapter 6).

(iii) According to Honneth's Habermasian reconstruction of Critical Theory, Benjamin also interpreted the conflict between social classes in an anti-instrumental manner as a lively and communicative experience of society.[75] An eclectic mix of theological, literary-aesthetic and material-political interests influenced Benjamin. Hannah Arendt formulated this eclecticism as an interest in the strange correlation 'between a street scene, a speculation on the stock exchange, a poem, a thought, with the hidden line which holds them together and enables the historian or philologist to recognize that they must all be placed in the same period'.[76] The influence of Lukács and Brecht's materialist aesthetics made it very difficult for Benjamin to share Horkheimer and Adorno's fear that bourgeois culture would be totally destroyed by Fascism. In his famous essay 'The work of art in the age of mechanical reproduction' (1936), he deals with this issue by addressing the loss of the quality of uniqueness (*aura*) in modern autonomous art – a quality it once possessed under ritual conditions. Like Adorno, he acknowledges the empirical fact that the thousandfold potential for reproduction in modern life shatters the authenticity and uniqueness of art.[77] In the 1930s this was especially pertinent to new developments with regard to film, photography, radio and the gramophone.[78] But Benjamin differs from Adorno in arguing that the masses are not merely passive objects of an objective cultural apparatus (the culture industry), but are actively involved in the transformation of an esoteric culture into an exoteric one. Where distance, the core of idealistic aesthetics, disappears, the artwork becomes publicly accessible. This avant-garde idea became important in Benjamin's discussion of the changed nature of reflection in films.[79]

Benjamin argues that in the case of films collective reception is no longer disinterested reflection (the reflective stance towards a specific image, as in the case of Idealistic aesthetics), but rather is constituted by active surprise, multiple fragmentation and physical shock effects (the result of a fast spread of a number of images). Shocks cause experiences totally different from those of reflection and concentration – a state of affairs leading to a new appreciation of art. The reception of a film as a focused but playful public sphere replaces the disinterested, private reflection of the privileged art-viewer.[80]

Benjamin writes: 'Mechanical reproduction of art changes the reaction of the masses toward art. The reactionary attitude toward a Picasso painting changes into the progressive reaction toward a Chaplin movie. The progressive reaction is characterized by the direct, intimate fusion of visual and emotional enjoyment with the orientation of the expert. Such fusion is of great social significance.'[81] In place of the ritual and religious function of traditional artworks comes the political function of photography and film. On this basis the film theatre is seen as an instrument of mass emancipation and progress.[82] Although Benjamin was aware of the possible abuses of art (especially films) as reproduction, he still defended the critical ability of new production forces to challenge the existing production relationships.

As regards the disappearance of the aura and Benjamin's defence of art in the era of its reproduction, it is worth stating Adorno's opposing view again. Although he acknowledges that modern technology moves art beyond a sphere of magical aura, Adorno remains critical of Benjamin's optimistic defence of publicly accessible art (which bids farewell to the essential characteristics of Kantian aesthetics – autonomy and distance). From such a perspective, Benjamin's position is an oversimplified sketch and insufficiently dialectical, one that does not deal adequately with the reduction of the art-observer to a passive, non-reflective consumer through the new reproduction techniques of mass art. For Adorno, the culture industry remains a means of control, and popular art embodies rational regression. When these ideas are linked with the notion of the systematic steering process of society, it becomes impossible for individuals and groups to unlock the world creatively via technological forms of art.[83] Against Benjamin's positive view of the destruction of the aura (and the fact that the technical progress of modern art justifies its continued relevance amidst the loss of ritual function), Adorno criticizes Benjamin for ignoring the progressive side of autonomous art and the regressive side of mass-mediated art. The problem is that Benjamin identifies himself so strongly with the technological demolition of the magical aura and of the individual subject in favour of the unmediated realities of mass culture (through film), that he cannot see modern art as both a reflection of, and a protest against, those processes. In his alternative, Adorno claims that modernist art is itself anti-auratic *and* aesthetic – it has a dialectical relationship with the moment of magical aura that it has lost. It is also a position that could provide, compared to that of Benjamin, a more dialectical interpretation of art in its era of reproduction.[84]

In Honneth's Habermasian reconstruction of Critical Theory, Benjamin's aesthetics (like the politico-theoretical perspective of Neumann and Kirchheimer and Fromm's socio-psychological perspective) moves beyond the instrumental framework of the inner circle of Critical Theory. For Benjamin, according to Honneth, society is not an instrumental association of individual attitudes and orientations, but rather the result of group-specific experiences and fragments that develop independently and imaginatively in the process of communicative association. In Honneth's language, the cultural struggle of social classes determines the integration of society. It is thus necessary for the oppressed to have access to creative perception, which will hopefully contribute to collective fantasies and the politicization of the aesthetic. Honneth then compliments Benjamin (and other members of the outer circle) for providing a more differentiated evaluation of forms of capitalist integration and for giving the first tentative insights, in the tradition of Critical Theory, on the communicative infrastructure of societies. None of them, according to Honneth, utilized these insights as a basis for an independent social theory – this had to wait for the work of Habermas. Returning to the debate between Benjamin and Adorno, the following concluding remarks can be made: the debate reveals very different positions on the nature of aesthetics and its role in society. Benjamin differs from the exclusive perspective of instrumental reason – a position that enabled him to study the role of mass and reproductive art in a positive manner. For Benjamin, according to Honneth, truth is to be found in the aesthetic-communicative struggles among individuals and groups attempting to make sense of the world. For Adorno, on the other hand, truth is found mainly in the autonomous modern artwork that shields itself from the retrogressive elements of the modern public sphere.[85]

## 2.5   Summary

I have argued that Habermas's critique of the aesthetically informed philosophy of the first generation of Critical Theorists takes the form of a reconstruction of the intellectual history of Critical Theory itself. The main feature of this reconstruction (as Honneth indicates) is a differentiation between an inner and an outer circle among the first generation. On this reading, the aesthetic perspectives of the inner circle changed from positioning of cultural studies in the interdisciplinary research programme (of the 1930s) to the pessimistic, aesthetically informed concept of instrumental reason in *Dialectic of Enlightenment* in the 1940s. It is Adorno, on this reading, who provides the aesthetic backbone to the argument. On the basis of his linkage between instrumental reason and cultural commodification (culture industry), Adorno's alternative takes the form of modern autonomous artworks that provide a critique and determined negation of society. In Adornian terms, art, as opposed to instrumental reason, becomes a model for non-identical thinking and an uncoerced reconciliation that contributes to a certain aesthetic truth of reality. Adorno is quite negative about the possibilities of a critical public sphere and the possibility of a collectively accessible, public, mass art. Only art's uncoerced reconciliation provides a hopeful ray for an emancipated public sphere. Habermas (and Honneth) argue, though, that this view is not shared by a lesser-known group of the first generation (the outer circle).

In Honneth's Habermasian reconstruction of the intellectual history of Critical Theory, the outer circle does not reduce all forms of rationality to instrumental reason. In Benjamin's model of aesthetics, unlike Adorno's, room is made for mass art, new production techniques, and the political and committed nature of art. As I indicated in the previous chapter, Habermas supports Benjamin's argument that the fragmented nature of modern rationality needs more attention than the mere exclusive engagement with the autonomous work of art through individual aesthetic experience. Mass art forms – for example, film, with its collective emancipation potential – have an important role to play in the public sphere. Benjamin's aesthetic perspectives (as Honneth indicates) lead not only to a differentiated appreciation of capitalist forms of integration, but also to the first preliminary insights into the communicative infrastructure of society. It is Habermas, according to Honneth, who transforms these insights (stemming from the anti-functionalist perspectives of the outer circle's societal studies) into an explicit critique of a functionalist view of society.[86] In this process, Habermas's reconstruction of Critical Theory (as sketched in this chapter) can be linked with the outlines of the first phase of his aesthetics (as sketched in the previous chapter). The guiding line here is Habermas's movement away from an aesthetically informed philosophy towards the (emerging) model of communicative reason. From this juncture onwards (which also opens the beginning of the second phase of Habermas's aesthetics), he uses all his intellectual energies to defend communicative reason – a focus that gives aesthetics a reduced role to play.

# 3

# Habermas and Aesthetics: The Second Phase

The aim here is not to provide an in-depth discussion of Habermas's theory of communicative reason. The brief discussion of the theory of communicative reason (sections 3.1 and 3.2) serves here only as a point of reference for reconstructing the second phase of Habermas's aesthetics. Habermas describes communicative rationality as the replacement of a philosophy of consciousness (the objective paradigm) by the mutual understanding between subjects who are competent in language and action (the communicative paradigm).[1] This move, also known as Habermas's 'linguistic turn', is already present in his inaugural lecture in Frankfurt (1965), where he states that '[w]hat raises us out of nature is the only thing whose nature we can know: language. Through its structure, autonomy and responsibility are posited for us.'[2] This leitmotiv, which is initially substantiated as a programme of universal pragmatics (in the 1970s), finds its consolidation in *The Theory of Communicative Action* (1981).[3] In this work Habermas connects communicative rationality with a theory of argumentation (or rational discursiveness) that includes validity claims and a model of world perspectives (section 3.1). To this more systematic side of his theory, Habermas adds a theory of societal rationalization, consisting of a model of evolutionary learning processes, the concepts of system and life-world, and a defence of modernity (section 3.2). After discussing the main aspects of the theory of communicative reason, its aesthetic implications will be reconstructed (section 3.3). This reconstruction will then be contextualized in terms of Habermas's case studies of Schiller, Hegel and Heine (section 3.4) and of Nietzsche and his followers (next chapter).

## 3.1   The theory of communicative action
## and rationality

I have already indicated that Habermas is critical of the monological image of the subject-centred, self-referential mind that plays such a central role in the modern tradition of the philosophy of consciousness since Descartes. Such a solipsistic relationship with the world corresponds, according to Habermas, with a teleological model of action orientated to success (strategic action). The dilemma here is that participants instrumentalize other subjects (as if they were objects) in their quest to achieve their respective goals. This concept of action (which Habermas links with a philosophy of consciousness) is also determined by a one-world ontology, where the agent is one-dimensionally dependent on the objective world.[4] In such a context the subject–object polarity provides the frame of reference into which all problems (inner versus outer nature, reason versus senses, mind versus body, culture versus nature, autonomy versus heteronomy, liberation versus alienation) are translated. Such a model of action is further complicated, according to Habermas, by using truth and effectiveness as the only criteria for the rationality of action – in other words, it reflects a cognitive-instrumental view of rationality.[5] In his alternative to such a narrow concept of strategic and instrumental rationality – one that Habermas also links with the intellectual framework of Horkheimer and Adorno in *Dialectic of Enlightenment* – he develops the concept of communicative action and rationality.

In place of the subject–object model of objectification and strategic action, Habermas proposes a model of the intersubjective use of language.[6] Consequently, he distinguishes between strategic-oriented action stemming from instrumental reason (as discussed in the previous paragraph) and the understanding-oriented action of communicative reason. This language-oriented view of understanding (*Verständigung*) is based on the presupposition that participants interact with one another in a decentred manner. Habermas holds (following Piaget's developmental psychology) that the decentred consciousness of communicative participants in the modern world allows them to take on different positions vis-à-vis the world – an objective relationship to the objective world, a normative relationship to the social world, and an expressive relationship to the subjective world.[7] Communicative action is thus based on a three-world ontology. It is the last of these worlds (the subjective world in which Habermas locates expressive and *aesthetic* experience) that is of par-

ticular importance for this study. The important question here (one
that will be discussed in greater detail later) is the status of the subjective world in the broader context of Habermas's theory of communicative action. For the moment, though, it is important to note
that although Habermas acknowledges that participants in everyday
communication can adopt different attitudes toward one and the
same world (for example, an expressive attitude in the objective
world), he nevertheless cautions that this must be viewed with a
healthy sense of scepticism. He continues that if we fail to differentiate between the various worlds, the following dangers surface:
objectivism (an objectifying attitude to the world), moralism (a
norm-conformative attitude towards the world) and *aestheticism* (an
expressive attitude towards the world).[8]

In the next step of his argument Habermas links his three-world
ontology with validity dimensions. Communicative action is an
explicit and concentrated attempt to obtain agreement between
validity claims that are made by participants in the three worlds.[9]
Communicative competence is thus not only the ability of a speaker
or participant to distinguish between these worlds, but also the ability
to know which attitude and validity claim are applicable.[10] The point
is that a modern decentred consciousness allows communicating participants to develop an ability to distinguish between a variety of
validity dimensions. In other words, the ability to recognize that the
validation of an empirical truth claim ('It is raining outside') requires
different procedures of validation from a normative validity claim
('Abortion is wrong') or the validity claim associated with subjective
truthfulness ('This painting is beautiful'). In the framework of communicative reason, Habermas refers to three validity claims that cor-
respond to the three worlds mentioned above: the claim for truth,
rightness and truthfulness (he also adds a fourth one – comprehen-
sibility). While truth claims are concerned with the denotative or
referential aspects of speech (statements referring to 'objective'
and 'external nature'), and claims regarding rightness are applicable
to intersubjective relations (the normative-regulated social domain,
or 'society'), Habermas, interestingly enough, describes claims to
truthfulness (which point to the speaker's inner nature and are related to aesthetics) as not discursively redeemable. In short, although
Habermas's model of the differentiation of validity claims in communicative reason contributes to a network of relationships (which
link language and society with one another), he has a problem
dealing with the relationship between inner and outer nature – an
issue that will be fully investigated in chapter 5.[11]

In a further step of his argument Habermas links the different validity claims (as discussed) with speech-acts. The point of speech-acts is the achievement of understanding (*Verständigung*) and consensus (*Einverständnis*) between participants.[12] In following the later Wittgenstein, Austin and Searle, Habermas holds that speakers both speak and act in language. Both the propositional (locutionary) content and the performative (illocutionary) power of a speech-act are bona fide categories of meaning. These two dimensions of language mirror the double structure of intentionality in all speech-acts. Habermas continues that the different kinds of speech-act make different claims on effectivity, truth, correctness and truthfulness (or expressiveness).[13] In this context communicative interaction succeeds only if the hearer responds to the validity claim raised by the speech-act of the speaker.[14] A speech-act is a discursive offer that can be accepted or rejected in accordance with the stand taken by the participants toward the validity claims offered. Through the validity claim of every speech-act the speaker enters into an interpersonal relationship of mutual obligation with the hearer. Interestingly enough (especially with reference to the aesthetic implications of Habermas's theory of communicative reason), this obligation is a *cognitive-rational one* (and not moral or expressive-aesthetic).[15] As performances, the utterances or actions of a subject involve knowledge claims that can be criticized or defended by other speakers and agents: in this sense, rationality means openness to argumentation (critique and justification).[16]

Finally, Habermas's position in his theory of communicative reason, which comes down to a theory of argumentation, can be summarized as follows. (a) Speakers (participants) have an objectifying attitude toward the external (objective) world and lay claim to propositional truth. In such a context cognitive instrumental rationality is expressed through strategic action.[17] The appropriate form of valid argumentation here is a theoretical discourse (of intersubjectively shared propositional knowledge). (b) Speakers in the social world, on the other hand, have a normative attitude towards the world and lay claim on correctness or rightness (i.e. judging the correctness of social rules). In this context moral practical rationality is the result of the possible consensus flowing from different moral judgements. The appropriate form of argumentation for the justification of moral claims is practical discourse. (c) Towards the inner world speakers assume a *subjectifying* attitude and lay claim on *sincerity* or *truthfulness* (i.e. on an honest revelation of their needs and desires). Here Habermas states that *aesthetic-expressive* rationality is the correct way to interpret one's own and other's needs and desires. The appropriate argumentative form for revealing subjectivity is aesthetic criticism. In short, Habermas's presentation of the dimensions of validity, justification and argumentation comes down to nothing else but a differentiated concept of rationality.[18] In this process rational-discursive co-operation is stressed. 'This concept of communicative rationality carries with it connotations based ultimately on the central experience of the unconstrained, unifying, consensus-bringing force of argumentative speech, in which different participants overcome their merely subjective views and, owing to the mutuality of rationally motivated convictions, assure themselves of both the unity of the objective world and the intersubjectivity of their lifeworld.'[19]

## 3.2   The theory of societal rationalization

As well as his theory of rational argumentation (as discussed above), Habermas added a theory of social rationalization, which will be discussed in this section in terms of (i) the dialectic of social rationalization; (ii) the concepts of system and life-world; (iii) a critical diagnosis of modernity/postmodernity.[20]

(i) Habermas connects his theory of argumentation with a socio-historical model of evolution that distinguishes between mythical and modern understanding. The problem with mythical stories and experiences is, according to Habermas, the absence of a distinction between fact and fantasy, word and description, emotions and natural events. The modern processes of differentiation and disenchantment (*Entzauberung*), for their part, correct the power of mythical and religious interpretations of natural and social events. Habermas, like Weber, describes this process of differentiation and learning processes as contributing to the rationality of the modern cultural spheres of science, morality and art – each with its respective validity claims as sketched in the previous section.[21] This evolutionary argument is also used as a perspective whereby the rationalization of world images is connected with internally reconstructed learning processes (an idea stemming from Piaget).[22] Hence the transition from mythical-poetical, cosmological, religious and metaphysical world-views to modern forms of understanding coincides with moral and cognitive decentring.[23] In the mythical world, as in the childhood world, there is a correspondence between objective and subjective realities.

Habermas describes the distinction between archaic and developed civilizations with interesting implications for aesthetics: narrative accounts of reality are replaced by the formal principles of discursive reasoning and learning processes.[24] In this way the historical institutionalization of learning processes and the systematic dimension of communicative rationality constitute complementary possibilities of modern rationalization.

Thus, emancipated human relations, no longer require exclusive liberation from nature (Adorno), but can be developed according to their own communicative logic. In a similar manner, universal morality and law do not function as mere ideological mirrorings of the capitalistic production process (Marx), but are rather the result of collective learning processes that can be corrected. The problem with thinkers like Adorno and Marx, in Habermas's view, is that they identify social rationalization exclusively with a philosophy of consciousness. Both the technological optimism of the critique of political economy (Marx) and the anti-technical pessimism of the critique of instrumental reason (Adorno) are caught in the constraints of a philosophy of consciousness, where emancipation depends either on the control of, or reconciliation with, nature. Habermas, on the other hand, reformulates the relationship man/nature in terms of a theory of differentiated rationality and communicative ethics.[25] With this argument he deals with the opposition between emancipation from, and control of, nature – rationality versus technical progress.

(ii) Habermas uses the argument of social rationalization – in which modernity is not linked exclusively to the objectifying rationality of social production (labour), but also to the communicative rationality of internal learning processes – to explain the historical differentiation between the *life-world* and the *system*.[26] Habermas interprets the phenomenological idea of the life-world (which is influenced by Mead,[27] Husserl and Schütz) as the *Verweisungszusammenhang* (unproblematic background) for linguistic and symbolic interaction. Rationalization occurs here as the differentiated transformation of taken-for-granted structures in the life-world. This process of differentiation in the life-world offers a clearer distinction between form and content, and when the distinctions (or ways of differentiation) are thwarted, then crises appear.[28] Habermas describes these crises as the dangers of subjectivism, culturalism and idealized fictions like the autonomy of agents, art and culture, and the transparency of communicative interaction in the life-world. In such a crisis atmosphere, social reproduction is merely symbolic reproduction, and the life-world runs the risk of degenerating into a *hermeneutic idealism* of participants who are blind to the causes, connections and consequences of systematic distortion. It is at this point that Habermas adds a second perspective of social reproduction – the material reproduction of social systems.[29]

Habermas's concept of system is influenced by Marx's explanation of the pathological forms of symbolic reproduction, Durkheim's study of the distribution of labour, Parsons's work on the rationalization of the life-world, and the work of Luhmann.[30] System-theoretical (functional) analysis is thus added to the hermeneutical theoretical (structural) analysis of the life-world.[31] Systems play an important role in the modern world, where functions of material reproduction shift from the life-world to formally organized sub-systems such as the market and the law.[32] Here, though, the co-ordination of specialized tasks requires a delegation of authority to experts or institutions. Hence there is a danger that such systematic mechanisms may become detached from the life-world and steered by strategic action – for example, the exchange principle of the market economy and the institutionalization of political power and bureaucracy in the modern state.[33] It is at this point that the danger of *Entsprachlichung* appears: where communicative co-ordination of action shifts to non-linguistic media. The implication is that media such as money and power disconnect action from validity claims and neutralize the requirements for communication and consensus in the life-world.[34] This leads to the paradox of societal rationalization: 'formally organized domains of action emerge that – in the final analysis – are no longer integrated through the mechanism of mutual understanding, that sheer off from lifeworld contexts and congeal into a kind of norm-free society'.[35]

As an alternative to the crises of the infiltration of more and more systems into the communicative structures of the life-world, Habermas sets his hopes on new social movements – such as the ecological, anti-nuclear, feminist and liberation movements.[36] The argument is that these movements can hopefully address the paradox that systems also need communication. Interestingly enough, Habermas gives a certain priority to the life-world in so far as it corresponds to the basic structures of a communicatively mediated reality. On the other hand, he uses the tension between life-world and the system to sketch a paradoxical picture of modernity in terms of the positive aspect of progressive rationalization in the life-world and its negative, systematic and institutionalized aspect.[37] Habermas describes the latter as the colonization of the life-world – the imperialistic invasion of monetary and bureaucratic systems in areas that are intrinsically related to symbolic interaction (a phenomenon that can also be described in terms of pathologies or social crises in the life-world).[38] Habermas's analysis of the positive and negative sides of modernity enables him to argue, in contrast to the first generation of Critical Theorists (Horkheimer and Adorno), that the problem of modernity is not instrumental rationality *per se*, but its generalization. A critique of modernity should, therefore, not be directed exclusively against the instrumental use of reason, but against the failure to develop and institutionalize the different dimensions of reason (with its objective, normative and expressive moments) in a balanced way. In short, he opts for a differentiated reason, where the life-world is communicatively open.[39]

(iii) By situating the malaise of modernity in modernity itself, Habermas performs an immanent critique of Western reason. The challenge for a communicative rational life-world is to develop institutions in which practical questions of general interest are discussed in the public sphere and decisions can be made on the basis of rational discursivity. In this process, the Enlightenment's promise of a reasonable life remains a practical hypothesis for a critical social theory of science.[40] McCarthy puts Habermas's position very succinctly as 'an enlightened suspicion of enlightenment, a reasoned critique of Western rationalism, a careful reckoning of the profits and losses entailed by "progress" . . . reason can be defended only by way of a critique of reason'.[41] With regard to modernity, Habermas argues that learning processes are not forgotten in social evolution, except when they are consciously or subconsciously suppressed. The achievement of modernity, then, is that problems can be solved in the different cultural spheres of science, morality and art without 'alien' intervention. Habermas offers this view as an alternative to postmodern trends that advocate, in his view, a new organic unity, wherein differentiations are revoked to reconcile man and nature (an argument that will be more fully examined in the next chapter).[42]

### 3.3   The aesthetic implications
### of communicative reason

The aesthetic implications of Habermas's theory of communicative reason will be discussed in terms of the same four motives that are, Habermas says, the driving forces behind his *Theory of Communica-*

*tive Action* (and which were discussed in the previous two sections): (i) a theory of argumentation; (ii) a theory of social rationalization; (iii) the difference between life-world and system; and (iv) a defence of modernity. This discussion (together with the case studies in section 3.4 and the next chapter) also provides the framework for addressing the second phase of Habermas's aesthetics.

(i) It has been mentioned that Habermas situates the aesthetic valid-ity claim of truthfulness in the subjective sphere of speaker's inner nature.[43] The rational status of aesthetic judgements is thereby an open question. On this issue Habermas provides two possible answers. First, he holds that aesthetic validity claims cannot be tested *directly* through rational argumentation. Such validity claims are settled, rather, through sustained debate in which speakers express their sincere or insincere subjective intentions. He continues that, philosophically speaking, it is difficult to distinguish between 'real' and 'false' self-expressions and emotions. One can only decide among sincere or insincere emotions by studying the behaviour and evidence of a person's expressions, including the possibility of self-deception. Substantive criteria like truth and correctness are difficult to apply in circumstances in which the subjective authority of the actor is involved. Secondly, though, Habermas proposes a procedural crite-rion whereby to evaluate claims of sincerity. He writes: 'We call a person rational who interprets the nature of his desires and feelings (*Bedürfnisnatur*) in the light of culturally established standards of value, but especially if he can adopt a reflective attitude to the very value standards through which desires and feelings are interpreted.'[44] Of these two answers of Habermas regarding the rational status of aesthetic validity claims, the more plausible one seems to be the first, where aesthetic validity claims are restricted or even reduced to the subjective sphere of emotions, self-expressions and intentions – with the implication that their possible rational-discursive potential is inhibited. This point is made by Habermas in a complex table in *The Theory of Communicative Action* which sketches the various relation-ships between cognitive-instrumental, moral-practical and *aesthetic-expressive* forms of rationality.[45]

In this table the validity claims of propositional truth and norma-tive rightness are linked to the idea of universal agreement.[46] These two validity claims are, according to Habermas, supported by theo-retical discourses (with their propositional truth claims) and practi-cal discourses (with their moral validity claims). On the other hand, Habermas restricts aesthetic or evaluative validity claims to particular and local contexts, by stating that such speech-acts (aesthetic speech-acts) 'raise no clear-cut validity claim'.[47] The implication of this position is that the subjective nature of aesthetic experience has a disclosing potential for truth only in the complexity of life experience. Artworks thus claim validity through a process of disclosure that is not linked to the rational discursiveness of theoretical or practical discourses. Habermas goes on to say that although aesthetic 'truth' claims affect the cognitive and moral dimensions of life, they are justified only with reference to the subjective experience of those affected, and not with reference to facts or theories. This aesthetically restricted conception of communicative reason, in which aesthetic validity claims do not contribute to rational discursiveness, but only to a kind of world disclosure (thereby contributing to the fate of aesthetics in Habermas's work), will be critically revisited in chapter 5.

(ii) Despite Habermas's restriction of the status of aesthetic validity in his theory of argumentation, he nevertheless acknowledges in his theory of social rationalization that art (as a differentiated cultural sphere of modernity) has its own learning process. He says that the differentiation between art and the other cultural spheres (objective science and universal morality) allows each one to liberate its respective cognitive potential from more esoteric forms.[48] On the other hand, despite this differentiation (where each of the cultural spheres deals in a distinct, rational way with issues in the world), they remain communicatively open to one another.[49] At this point Habermas restates his position on objectivism, moralism and aestheticism (see section 3.1) in the following way: it is possible to apply non-objectivist modes of inquiry (such as moral and aesthetic points of view) in science, but this should not violate science's primary orientation toward truth. Similarly, post-avant-garde art has been influenced by cognitive elements (realism) and moral-practical elements (committed art), but not at the expense of the internal validity of truth, normativity and aesthetic expressiveness.[50] In other words, while the different cultural spheres (each with its own validity claims) communicate with one another, they also remain autonomous.[51] Here Habermas focuses on two issues: first, the specific rational content (or learning process) that art accomplishes in the process of differentiating among modern cultural spheres, and, second, the historical aspect of the differentiation that runs from the Renaissance to the contemporary world and is closely linked to the debate about autonomous and mass art (see (iii) below).

In line with the logic of social evolution, Habermas describes the internal learning process of autonomous art (which is closely linked to Romanticism and the nineteenth-century position of *l'art pour l'art* – 'art for art's sake') as a progressive constitution and expansion of a particular domain of experience that is purified from cognitive and moral contents.[52] Art as a laboratory and the medium of a learning process is thus for Habermas a concentrically expanding, continuous exploration of a sphere of possibilities that is structurally opened by the differentiation of the cultural value spheres. In this process, he continues, talented artists give authentic expression to their experiences, divorced from the limitations of everyday action, in a decentred manner. These experiences are described as the opening up of suppressed elements of the subconscious, the fantastic, the wild and physical; in short, everything which is connected to the *non-linguistic contact with reality*, 'which is fleeting, so contingent, so immediate, so individualized, simultaneously so far and so near that it escapes our usual categorical grasp'.[53] In its disconnectedness from social and traditional limitations, aesthetic experience is, according to this line of thought, more reflexively open to the structure of human needs (*Bedürfnisnatur*). Art is thus described as a medium through which individual experience can be communicated and transformed. The artist, on his or her part, opens a space for free play and experimentation via a reflexive handling of materials, methods and techniques – and thereby opens a space in which formal decision-making processes are opened up for aesthetic experience.[54] This implies that the specific rational content of autonomous artworks and art judgements (*sensus communis*) can be interpreted, evaluated and put in language (*Versprachlichung*). It is interesting to note here that although Habermas acknowledges the 'truth' (the unity, harmony, *Stimmigkeit*, authenticity and expressive success) of art as a modern learning process, and although he concedes that pragmatic argumentative logic provides the most appropriate medium for expressive rationality, he still insist that art as learning must conform, in the final analysis, to rational discursiveness.[55]

(iii) In the next step of his argument, Habermas provides a sociohistorical perspective on the differentiation and institutionalization of art as a modern culture sphere – a move that has implications for his view of autonomous versus popular art and their respective relationships to system and life-world and his case studies (which will be discussed in the next section and the following chapter). The Renaissance, according to Habermas, is the moment when a movement towards greater autonomy started in the practice and definition of art. In its wake, and especially since the eighteenth century, fine arts, literature and music became institutionalized independently of both Church and State. In this process concepts like the 'beautiful' and the 'sublime' were separated from the merely useful and the desirable. Aesthetics, like science and law, acquired its own claim to validity – with its own inner logic, learning process and *Eigensinn* (meaning), leading to a different functional action system (as described above). Habermas nevertheless criticizes certain Enlightenment philosophers (such as Condorcet) who had the (inflated) expectation that autonomous art could fully control natural forces, interpret the world and the self, enhance moral progress, expand fair institutions, and increase human happiness – who, in other words, succumbed to aestheticism.[56] In an argument similar to that of *The Structural Transformation of the Public Sphere*, Habermas cites a historical moment when the optimism in autonomous aesthetics became suspect. This was when commodity capitalism and technological developments began to undermine the idea of modern, classical aesthetics. Despite Baudelaire's attempts in the mid-nineteenth century, according to Habermas, the crisis of autonomous art intensified towards the last quarter of that century – hence colour, line, narrative and movement stopped being the sole attributes of artistic representation.

Habermas continues that the new media of expression (the systems of technical art production) eventually problematized art as a whole, 'its inner life, its relation to society, even its right to exist'.[57] It is against this background that movements such as Surrealism and the avant-garde react against the autonomous inclinations of art for art's sake in the twentieth century. The loss of the aura, the importance of the allegory, and the destruction of the total meaning of the organic artwork all reflect a revolutionary change of life. As in his arguments in *The Structural Transformation of the Public Sphere* and his Benjamin essay, Habermas interprets the collective reception of aesthetic fields, such as architecture, popular art and music, in a favourable light – a point that Wellmer expands: 'Under the impact of technology, art becomes a vaccine against those collective psychoses in which the enormous tensions that technological innovations generate in mass populations would otherwise vent themselves . . . it appears to me that Benjamin's analysis at least points towards a positive potential in modern mass culture – from film to rock music – which Adorno was unable to see because of his traditionalism and his theoretical preconceptions.'[58] For Wellmer, the disinterested contemplation of autonomous art disappears in the contemporary experience of a rock concert. In the change of sound and image, rock creates a basic attitude of sensual delight. This is similar to the Benjaminian analysis of modern mass culture, which anticipates an explosive mixture of aesthetic and political imagination. But Habermas also cautions against the Surrealist attempt to negate the difference between art and life – fiction and praxis, appearance and reality – so that everything is art and everyone an artist (a caution that is a restatement of an earlier argument, see section 1.4).

Habermas offers two reasons why the Surrealist rebellion failed. First, when the sides of the autonomously developed cultural sphere are simply broken, the content is lost, and nothing emancipatory remains of the desublimated meaning of a destroyed form. Secondly,

> [E]veryday communication, cognitive meanings, moral expectations, subjective expressions and evaluations must relate to one another. Communication processes need a cultural tradition covering all spheres – cognitive, moral-practical and expressive. A rationalized everyday life, therefore, could hardly be saved from cultural impoverishment by breaking open a single cultural sphere – art – and so providing access to just one of the specialized knowledge complexes. The surrealist revolt would have replaced only one abstraction.[59]

To this caution Habermas adds his interpretation of Benjamin's distinction between the politicization of aesthetics and the aestheticization of politics. In the case of the latter (as in Hitler's Germany), politics is ruined when the masses are reduced to mere extras in an orchestrated, totalized, Fascist aesthetic spectacle. Benjamin's concept of the politicization of aesthetics is far more acceptable in Habermas's view, because it amounts to an appropriation of politics wherein the masses have a role to play.[60] It thus seems that Habermas's reconstruction of modern aesthetics keeps two ideas operative. On the one hand, he acknowledges that mass production and consumption have transformed the traditional concept of the autonomous artwork as a product of individual creativity; mass production leads to an aesthetic situation in which the 'artist' of a film (record or television programme) is no longer obvious. On the other hand, Habermas also defends the validity claims of traditional autonomous aesthetics against those of popular art.

Habermas's defence of the complex normativity of autonomous art against the 'total onslaught' of Surrealism, the avant-garde and post-avant-garde (and their attempts to aestheticize the life-world) has been articulated by Wellmer, who argues that a transformed art institution does not bring an end to the 'culture of experts'.[61] He writes:

> [I]t is not clear why a change in the function of art that is related to a democratic opening-up of society should exclude the idea of the great work of art. The opposite seems to me to be the case: without the paradigmatic productions of 'great' art, in which the imagination, the accumulated knowledge and the skill of obsessively specialized artists is objectivized, a democratically generalized aesthetic production would presumably decline into an amateur arts-and-craftism.[62]

Zuidervaart has also added his voice to this point by stating that Habermas's positive evaluation of mass art doesn't exclude normative categories of art such as structures, standards and criteria.[63] *Structures* refer, according to him, to the relatively stable patterns of a social institutional differentiation in modern society, on the one hand, and the interwovenness of the different cultural spheres, on the other. *Standards* refer to prevailing norms within a social institution such as an art community. Practising artists among the public, for example, need some kind of technical expertise. *Criteria* refer to public standards and normative propositions as formulated by practising artists. Criteria are not only the result of discourses in art institutions themselves, but also the product of a 'normal discourse' between critics, educationists, students and the public. In such a discourse it is legitimate to ask: why are certain works regarded as more valid than others? Is there an anti-democratic moment when popularity is equated with success?[64] Zuidervaart continues that in the complex network binding experts and popular culture a democratic praxis can productively draw from the innovating and communicative potential of art. Against this background his proposal can be read as a mediation between elements of Adorno's normative and autonomous aesthetics, on the one hand, and the radical integration of art and life as advocated by the avant-garde and Surrealism, on the other.

(iv) In studying Habermas's position on autonomous and mass art, it becomes clear that he polemicizes against both a false *Aufhebung* of art (mass art) and an aestheticization of the life-world (autonomous art), because both options exclude the possibility of a discursive mediation between art and the life-world.[65] In a Hegelian manner, Habermas holds that any attempt to assign reconciliation to a 'philosophy of nature' (or the technical *Aufhebung* of art) pays the price of a de-differentiation of categories and forms of knowledge, behind which we cannot escape anymore. He writes: 'All this is not really an argument, but more an expression of skepticism in the face of so many failed attempts to have one's cake and eat it too: to retain both Kant's insights and, at the same time, to return to the "home" (*Behausung*) from which these same insights have driven us.'[66] In contrast to the false totalities and the aestheticization of the life-world, Habermas offers his alternative. According to him, a mediated aesthetic truth reaches 'into our cognitive interpretations and normative expectations and transforms the totality in which these moments are related to each other. In this respect modern art harbours a utopia that becomes a reality to the degree that the mimetic powers sublimated in the work of art find resonance in the mimetic relations of a balanced and undistorted intersubjectivity of everyday life.'[67] By placing the concept of 'mediated aesthetic truth' in the (intersubjective) life-world, Habermas goes beyond a strict distinction between high and low art. Even the most autonomous artwork fulfils, for him, a function in the social system (e.g. as economic object, legal possession and object of social interaction). The problem with an autonomous, individual, aesthetic life-world expression is the danger of aestheticism and the exclusion of the role of social systems. The problem with social systems, on the other hand, is that art can easily disappear in technological reproduction.

In summarizing the aesthetic implications of Habermas's theory of communicative reason, the following remarks can be made. In the first place, Habermas assigns a restricted place to aesthetic rationality in his theory of argumentation. This implies that aesthetics must be translated into language and must conform to rational discursivity. On the other hand, Habermas acknowledges that art is a distinctive learning process in the rational differentiation of modernity, contributing to autonomous art. In addition, he acknowledges the changes in production processes and new technological developments – the reality of mass art. He posits a way beyond a blunt choice between autonomous art and mass art, through an alternative that preserves the tension between differentiation and integration. It is thus misleading, according to Habermas, to reduce the modern aesthetic discourse to the autonomous beautiful, on the one hand, or the de-differentiated sublime, on the other hand. A communicative aesthetic experience must enable us to live in a world of social as well as cultural differentiation that is not dissolved in a discredited subject-centred rationality or an ecstatic community of subjectless heterogeneity and endless *différance*.[68] Habermas concludes that the relationship between art and the life-world can be successfully mediated only when the internal learning processes of cognitive, moral and aesthetic spheres of specialized knowledge are made accessible to one another in a rational discourse of intersubjectivity.

## 3.4   Three case studies: Schiller, Hegel and Heine

Habermas uses various case studies to concretize the second phase of his aesthetics. These case studies relate to the aesthetic positions of (i) Schiller; (ii) Hegel; and (iii) Heine.

(i) In his communicative model Habermas interprets Kantian aesthetics as a mediation of the imaginative act of the senses and the disinterested contemplation of the reason, coming together in the shared taste (*sensus communis*) of cultivated persons. Taste is thus not an a priori category, but is cultivated through education and the critical discussion of values in the public sphere. In this process, common sense is consolidated by discursive, pre-discursive and mimetic communication. Habermas interprets Schiller's aesthetics in terms of a natural mimetic drive (*Stofftrieb*) and a rational reflexive drive (*Formtrieb*) being communicatively mediated in a play drive of public art (*Spieltrieb*). On this reading, Schiller avoids both a total differentiation of rational structures, as in modern society, and an aestheticization of life such as the avant-garde and postmodernism propose.[69] Thus, aesthetic experience does not emerge in the monological terms of organic unity. Intersubjective judgements of artworks, rather, constitute a medium through which human impulses, wishes and fears enter the public sphere of rational debate and communication.

(ii) In his *Philosophical Discourse of Modernity* Habermas claims that in Kantian terms modernity meant basically the refinement of consciousness and subjectivity, specifically in the differentiation of reason into the respective domains of science, ethical freedom and *aesthetic judgement*.[70] Whereas Kant did not problematize the costs of this differentiation, it was Hegel, according to Habermas, who addressed this problematic in his discourse of rational synthesis. By countering the negative aspect of modern differentiation – namely, its *Entzweiungen* (divisions and cleavages) – Hegel sought to reconcile the dichotomies of theoretical and practical reason, knowledge and faith, judgement and imagination, without abandoning the modern project. Hegel arrived at this point, according to Habermas, only after going through different phases in his career. First, in his *Early Theological Writings* (influenced by Schelling and Hölderlin's mythical-poetic version of reconciliation), he confronted the abstract nature of the Enlightenment with the positive nature of established religion. At this stage Hegel defended a 'national religion' (as did Rousseau), which mediated the expressive-emotional and the rational.[71] Hegel used this concept of national religion, according to Habermas, to describe public celebrations, cult activities and myths (heart and fantasy) – an emotional and religious intelligence that permeates society. Hegel thus hoped to reconcile pre-modern life forms, such as the Greek *polis*, and aspects of modern German culture. Secondly, in his Frankfurt phase, according to Habermas, Hegel defended art and artistic imagination as the way to reconcile a divided modernity. Here the monotheism of the mind (and the religion of the heart) is reconciled with the polytheism of the imagination. It is a programme that resembles Schiller's aesthetic letters, Schelling's transcendental idealism, and Hölderlin's poetic thinking.

Thirdly, Habermas argues that Hegel left all of these initial, aesthetically influenced positions to interpret modernity as a dialectical process – that is, a reflexive process through which the mind distinguishes itself practically (objectively) from nature so that it can be understood theoretically (subjectively). In this process, art, religion and philosophy represent various levels of how truth and the objective/subjective unity of reason can be known. Hegel thus bases modernity on a critical self-reflection, where only philosophy or thinking can bring about reconciliation and avoid the trap of solipsistic and dominating subjectivism. Rationality is thus a positive power of self-objectification, whereby particular motives and natural feelings make their way under universal moral laws. In this way the philosophy of subjectivity is used to overcome a subject-centred rationality.[72] In this process, art plays a less important role. Habermas continues that Hegel (like Schiller) preferred Romantic art to Classical art. For Romantic art necessitates the transcendence of the sensual art medium in the direction of philosophical reconciliation, whereas Classical art stresses the unparalleled beauty and aesthetic harmony of art with the world. For Hegel, this same process of sublimation also occurs in the case of religion. Both aesthetic experiences and religious representations thus depend on subjective forms of modern speculative reason. Habermas indicates that Hegel's social and political philosophy has a similar logic. In modern society a distinction is made between the particular interests of civil society

(*Sittlichkeit*) and the universal (moral) interests of the state – a sphere of social antagonism. In this context Hegel develops a model wherein the interests of the class of property owners must be mediated with the legislative power of a strong, neutral bureaucracy in a monarchy.[73] As in the case of art and religion, reconciliation between the opposing groups can be achieved only at the level of philosophical reflection and public reason, where the advantages of such a social arrangement can be pointed out to everyone.

Habermas appreciates Hegel's important orientating role in the philosophical discourse of modernity, but he also argues that Hegel's concept of (absolute) reason is based on a self-objectifying subjectivity rather than a communicative intersubjectivity.[74] Hegel therefore remains trapped in a subjectivist model of thinking (philosophy of consciousness) that impedes a mediated position on modernity. Such a unilateral reconciliation by an absolute consciousness actually robs it of participating in actual world processes. In its absoluteness the Hegelian concept of reason (*Vernunft*) achieves at most a partial reconciliation in the sphere of theory (philosophy), but at the cost of the public sphere of intersubjectivity that was, interestingly enough, present in Hegel's earlier writings, where a public mediation between the aesthetic-sensual and rational is mentioned. Habermas finds the absence of a critical public sphere particularly acute in Hegel's *Philosophy of Right*. Here, existing reality is no longer criticized but merely subjectively understood. This move amounts to an underestimation of the relationship between philosophical reflection and reality. Such a subjectivist understanding of political modernity also fails to interpret the complexities of social modernity, thereby leading to a situation where philosophical reflection takes precedence over public (democratic) demands. Against this background, Habermas's critique of Hegel allows him to propose his model of communicative rationality as a way of reconciling the universal and the particular. Instead of entrusting the freedom of the individual to the 'higher subjectivity of the state', his model is based on the intersubjectivity of unrestrained will formation and communication within society – 'In the universality of an uncoerced consensus arrived at among free and equal persons, individuals retain a court of appeal that can be called upon even against particular forms of institutional concretization of the common will.'[75]

Habermas thus offers his theory of communicative reason as an alternative to the dilemmas inherent in the Hegelian model – an alternative that has, as indicated in this chapter, implications for the second phase of Habermas's aesthetics. Like Hegel, Habermas places art under the watchful eye of reason – in his case, not absolute subjectivist reason, but the communicative reason of rational discursivity. Taking his inspiration from Hegel, Habermas argues that the unity of reason cannot be re-established in terms of a substantive world-view, as various romantic models of aestheticism have attempted to do (and postmodern thinkers attempt to do today). Rather, Habermas defends the 'unity of reason' in a non-objectified, everyday, communicative practice. Such unity of reason is then the appropriate way to mediate between morality and ethical life (theory and practice, art and life-world) in a process of undistorted intersubjectivity. Humans, according to Habermas, have an intuitive knowledge of a unifying reason in communicative action. A philosophy that wants to bring this intuition to a conceptual level must consequently reconstruct the diffused tracks of reason in communicative practice without getting trapped in a discredited theoretical image of the world as a whole.[76] Habermas adds that such a communicative proposal is materialistic enough not to lose inner nature and aesthetic experience in a formalistic model.[77] Habermas then points to a historical event in Berlin (1937) that he sees as an example of a mediated concept of communicative art. This example, borrowed from Peter Weiss, describes the attempt by a group of politicized workers to make the cultural heritage of Europe, which was systematically distorted by the Nazis, accessible for their own life-world. Habermas writes approvingly of their visits to the museum of art:

> These were young people, who, through an evening high school education, acquired the intellectual means to fathom the general and the social history of European art. Out of the resilient edifice of the objective mind, embodied in works of art which they saw again and again in the museums in Berlin, they started removing their own chips of stone, which they gathered together and reassembled in the context of their own milieu. This milieu was far removed from that of traditional education as well as from the then existing regime. These young workers went back and forth between the edifice of European art and their own milieu until they were able to illuminate both.[78]

(iii) In a fine essay on Heinrich Heine's legacy, Habermas found a further opportunity to explain the second phase of his aesthetics in the concrete terms of the role of the artist-intellectual in the public sphere. He starts by arguing that Heine stands as a solitary example of a committed artist-intellectual in the public sphere of nineteenth-century Germany up until the Weimar Republic.[79] Habermas then lists a host of thinkers who, unlike Heine, had an image of the artist-intellectual as an abstract thinker with no roots, patriotism or loyalty. In such an atmosphere, where intellectuals or artists were seen as decadent and unstable personalities who lent their ears to the destructive critique of the enemy ('foreigner' and Jew), there was no scope for Heine's social-democratic and humanistic stance to develop in Germany as an intellectual and poetic role model till well into the twentieth century. This view of the artist-intellectual as the enemy, or 'other', is, according to Habermas, discernible in five important intellectual movements of the Weimar Republic.[80] Apolitical authors and mandarins (such as Hesse, early Thomas Mann, Curtius and Jaspers) made such a strict division between the sphere of the spirit and that of power that a 'politicized spirit' was regarded as treason with respect to the call of the creative, cultured person. Second, *realpolitik* thinkers (such as Weber and Heuss) regarded politicized authors and philosophers as constituting an unstable element invading the sphere of specialized rationality of professional politics.[81] The politician and the artist must each remain loyal to their own domain of categories. Third, activists (such as Hiller) and Expressionists (such as Schickele, Carl Einstein and Bloch) invaded the political arena rhetorically by emphasizing political commitment. Their mistake, according to Habermas, was to confuse public aesthetic involvement with political power – dreaming of an international intellectual *Areopagus*. With their emphasis on 'spirit and action', leftist party political intellectuals (such as Lukács and Becher) also neglected the role of autonomous intellectuals. Fourth, Habermas mentions cultural workers who were critical of the hesitation, disloyalty and ideological power of the 'petit-bourgeois intelligentsia'.[82] Finally, rightist intellectuals (such as Stapel) contested the slogans of artistic and intellectual freedom by pointing to the ruined thinkers of the 'Literatencafés' blowing on Heine's freedom trumpet. The alternative for such intellectuals was selfless service to the people (*Volk*). As Benn said, 'Don't waste your time on arguments and words, be lacking in reconciliation, shut the gates, build the state.'[83]

Against the background of these 'intellectuals who did not want to be intellectuals', Habermas finds Heine's intellectual and aesthetic legacy an enlightening example of reflection on themes such as nationalism, political commitment and artistic autonomy.[84] He notes the following influences on Heine: the French Revolution, young Hegelianism, and Feuerbach's critique of religion. These forms of a radicalized bourgeois revolution accordingly charge Heine's prose and poetry. It is this intellectual heritage that also made Heine, as a Jewish intellectual, painfully aware of the ambiguous nature of nationalism as a republican and cosmopolitical idea. The problem is that while nationalism is associated with patriotism and certain liberties, on the one hand, it also runs the danger of succumbing to xenophobia precisely at the point where national unity overshadows the emancipatory content of bourgeois individual liberties. As an alternative, Heine distinguishes, according to Habermas, between the mobilization of the masses under the principles of the 'French liberty doctrine' of 'cosmopolitanism and the rationality of the youth', on the one hand, and the mobilization of the uninformed masses with the credo 'German fatherland – the belief of our fathers', on the other. It is not Heine's radical Enlightenment views that were a thorn in the flesh of the German mandarins, according to Habermas, but his reinterpretation of the radical origin of Romanticism liberated from a fatal nationalistic idealization and false historicizing. Heine's critical-aesthetic work was thus a potent reminder to rightist intellectuals about the danger of subjecting the role of the artist-intellectual to a political and nationalist movement.[85]

On the issue of political commitment and aesthetic autonomy, Habermas reads Heine, according to his model of communicative aesthetics, as a figure of mediation. Heine was fascinated, on the one hand, with the July revolution in Paris, and on the other, with the idea that the poet should fight with his or her own weapons on the side of the revolutionary masses – a position that raises the issue of the relation between art and politics and mind and power. Heine is, on this reading, sensitive to the way in which literary products exert an influence in the public sphere and media. 'Condensed journalistic forms of communication', for example, change the nature of art and writing. Heine's modern aesthetics was especially receptive to these changes. In this process the reading public was confronted with the sociological perspective of cultural dissemination and media analysis. Habermas argues that Heine regarded the July revolution as the axis of the public sphere – the point where the political public sphere emerged from the literary public sphere. This structural transformation influenced and changed the classical autonomous conception of aesthetic forms and the relationship between the poet and the public. From that moment on, the words of intellectuals became public, potential acts. Heine, for example, writes about the writers of 'Young Germany' who do not distinguish 'between life and writing, who never separate politics from science, art, and religion, and who are simultaneously artists, tribunes, and apostles'.[86]

In an argument that should be familiar by now, Habermas points to Heine's defence of some kind of autonomy of art, on the other hand, without making it a fetish. Heine criticized the excessive autonomy claims of both the Goethe epigones and the iconoclasts who destroyed the marble statues of his 'beloved art world' with their 'red fists' and their politicized opinions. Heine thus opposed the false alternative between the fetishization of the spirit and an aestheti-cized politics. Habermas puts Heine's response to the iconoclast Börne as follows: 'For Heine, the autonomy of art and scholarship, remains a necessary condition if the locked granaries (*Kornkammern*) that the intellectual wants to open for the people are not to be empty.'[87] The young Hegelian pathos of the philosophy of the deed or the 'workers of the spirit' (*Kopfarbeitern*), as propagated by Herzog and Hoernle, is thus not convincing. The Hegelian-Marxist concep-tion of theory and practice end in either inflated Idealism or inflated Leninism – the relationship between power and spirit becomes either elitist or instrumental. In the unfolding of his argument, Habermas seems in agreement with Heine's detachment from left-wing and right-wing politicians, his ambivalent relationship with Marx, and the 'godless self-gods'. Eventually Heine's position amounts, for Haber-mas, to the negation of a simple instrumental association between word and deed. In this process both the tribunalization of art and the doctrinalization of writing are questioned. In short, Heine serves for Habermas as a concrete example of an artist-intellectual who goes beyond the aestheticization and politicization of the life-world towards a model of communicative intersubjectivity.

## 3.5   Recapitulation: Habermas and the fate of aesthetics

It is necessary at this point to provide a brief summary of the different aspects of the two phases of Habermas's aesthetics that have been discussed so far. In the first phase of Habermas's aesthetics (as sketched in chapter 1) the importance of the concept of the public sphere, and more specifically the literary public sphere, was empha-sized. Habermas focuses in *The Structural Transformation of the Public Sphere* on socio-historical as well as normative developments of the public sphere since the seventeenth century. In a significant move (in the first part of *The Structural Transformation of the Public Sphere*), the importance of artworks and cultural institutions are highlighted as contributing to the rational exchange of ideas in the public sphere.

Despite the more sombre picture of the culture industry and consumption that is sketched in the second part of the study (thereby acknowledging some aspects of the first generation of Critical Theorists' vision of instrumental reason, bureaucratization and cultural manipulation), Habermas retains the idea of a rational public sphere at the end of his early study. During the 1960s and early 1970s Habermas further deepened his ideas of a public sphere in the direction of a theory of rationality. In *Knowledge and Human Interests*, rationality is explained in terms of self-reflection, but in his work of the early 1970s it becomes increasingly clear that Habermas links rationality to a concept of public communication. It is in this context that Habermas wrote his Benjamin essay, in which he opted for a Benjamin-informed aesthetics (against Marcuse and Adorno) that stands communicatively open to public reason giving. This essay, as argued in chapter 1, and supplemented by Habermas's interpretation of the aesthetic legacy of the first generation of Critical Theorists, as discussed in chapter 2, also marks the end of the first phase of Habermas's aesthetics.

The second phase of Habermas's aesthetics, as sketched in this chapter, is closely linked to his linguistic turn, which culminated (via a theory of universal pragmatics) in *The Theory of Communicative Action*. Here Habermas links a theory of argumentation (based on a differentiation of worlds and forms of rationalities) with a theory of societal rationalization. In the theory of argumentation it is clear that Habermas gives a restricted position to aesthetic rationality – an issue that will be critically challenged in chapter 5. On the other hand, he acknowledges art as a differentiated sphere of modern culture with its own learning process in his theory of social rationalization. Art's learning process has, according to Habermas, crystallized around two important aesthetic positions: autonomous art (which seeks a reconciliation with nature and runs the danger of aestheticizing life) and mass art (which through new reproduction techniques also wants to integrate art and society). Against these two attempts at aesthetic reconciliation Habermas offers his alternative that art belongs to the life-world and systems, but that reconciliation can be accomplished only if art as a learning process is brought into communication with the other aspects of a modern differentiated reason. Ultimately, rational discursiveness is for Habermas the criterion that art, as a modern learning process, must conform to. In this sense a modern cultural ethos is linked to the reflexive experiences of unrestrained subjectivity and the general experimental approach to phenomena and experiences that are made possible by a decentred consciousness.

A radicalized aesthetic consciousness (like experimental-scientific thinking and post-conventional ethical consciousness) is thus available only to the modern socialized subject. This is also an important point for Habermas in his debate with postmodern thinkers (whom he accuses of using aesthetic experience to launch a totalizing critique of modern rationality) – a debate that concludes the second phase of his aesthetics.

# 4

# The Second Phase
# Continues:
# The Postmodern Challenge

In the process of grounding a model of communicative reason, Habermas developed the second phase of his aesthetics (as indicated by the discussion in the previous chapter). This phase of Habermas's aesthetics is further consolidated in his debate with the major representatives of postmodern thinking. The contours of postmodernity first became discernible in aesthetic debates, in which it was contrasted with classical modernism. In architecture, for example, the glass and steel functionalism of the International style, of Le Corbusier and Lloyd Wright, was challenged by a new style of historical references, local traditions, eclectic pastiche, and a return to ornamentation and decoration.[1] In the late 1970s the (post)modern debates in aesthetics shifted to the (post)modern discourses in socio-philosophical debates. Against this background they entered the philosophical circles of Europe in Paris, Frankfurt and elsewhere. In particular, the works of Lyotard (and other French figures such as Foucault, Derrida and Kristeva) and the reaction of Habermas (and other German figures such as Gadamer, Frank, Wellmer and Honneth) played a major role in heightening the philosophical and broader intellectual importance of this debate. Habermas's position, which is the focus of this chapter, is closely connected with his *Philosophical Discourse of Modernity*.[2] In this work he holds that the discourse of modernity, which was initiated by thinkers such as Descartes and Voltaire, came to full fruition in the rational theories of Kant, Fichte and Hegel. Whereas Kant did not problematize the costs of modern rational differentiation (in the respective domains of science, ethical freedom and aesthetic judgement), it was left to Hegel to provide a 'counter-discourse' of rational synthesis. By countering the negative side of differentiation, namely the divisions and cleavages (*Entzweiungen*) resulting from modernity, so the argument runs, Hegel sought to reconcile the dichotomies of theoretical and practical reason, knowledge and faith, judgement and imagination, without abandoning the modern project. The Hegelian legacy was, Habermas continues, modified and extended in the nineteenth century by the opposing camps of young Hegelians (interpreting reason on the basis of praxis and productivity) and right Hegelians (interpreting the objective rational structures of the state, economy and/or technology).[3]

In his reconstruction of the modern/postmodern debate Habermas situates Nietzsche as the figure who provides a more radical anti-discourse (*Sonderdiskurs*) – one seeking not so much to modify Hegel's position on modernity as to cancel the whole modern project. In this context Nietzsche's *heroic-aesthetic* anti-discourse is geared towards erasing the rational aspects of modernity with aesthetic means (section 4.1). Nietzsche becomes, for Habermas, the turntable (*Drehscheibe*) between modernity and postmodernity and also the instigator for an aesthetically-informed (and totalizing) critique of modernity. Habermas's next step, which forms the heart of his *Philosophical Discourse of Modernity*, holds that this legacy has been continued by two different (but also interdependent) aesthetic-philosophical positions in the twentieth century. On the one hand, Heidegger's critique of Western metaphysics (section 4.2) and Derrida's levelling of the genre distinctions between philosophy and literature (section 4.3) pursue an ontological or quasi-ontological reversal of modernity, while Bataille and Foucault (section 4.4) attempt a more sceptical and empirical approach, on the other hand. In short, Habermas places his version of cultural modernity against the radical critique of reason inaugurated by Nietzsche and continued by postmodern thinkers. Whether Habermas's position is convincing will be briefly investigated in the section 4.5, where his views are juxtaposed with those of some other contemporary postmodern thinkers. Here Lyotard's critique of Habermas's 'modernism', amongst others, also serves as a starting point for the various critical perspectives on Habermas's aesthetics that will be continued, in a more focused manner, in the next chapter.

## 4.1   Nietzsche's aesthetic anti-discourse of modernity

Habermas situates Nietzsche's work in the shadow of that of Romantic thinkers – for example, Schiller's educational model of aesthetic mediation and Schelling's system of transcendental idealism.[4] In Schelling's system it is not Hegel's model of reason, but public poetry, that replaces the unifying power of religion. Nietzsche, though, shows the greatest affinity, according to Habermas, with Friedrich Schlegel. Both thinkers leave the possibility of a philosophical system behind to shelter in Homer's temple of new poetry. Habermas interprets this move of a philosophically informed mythopoetics, coupled with a messianic hope, as the anti-Enlightenment core of Romanticism. The mythopoetic quality of art functions in the Romantic context as a return to archaic sources of social integration that constitute the original state of human nature. Habermas writes:

> Schlegel no longer understands the new mythology as rendering sensuous of reason, the becoming aesthetic of ideas that are supposed to be joined in this way with the interest of the people. Instead, only poetry that has become autonomous, that has been cleansed of associations with theoretical and practical reason, opens wide the door to the world of primordial forces of myth. Modern art alone can communicate with the archaic sources of social integration that have been sealed off within modernity. On this reading the new mythology demands of a dirempted modernity that it relate to the 'primordial chaos' as the other of reason.[5]

Habermas singles out Dionysus, the Greek god of intoxication and endless forms, as the key theme in early Romantic literature. Hölderlin, for example, interprets Dionysus as a strange mythical figure whose absence implies the hope of a transformed return, like the Christian Second Coming. Nietzsche, according to Habermas, did not share the attempt to regenerate modern society by a messianic promise of Christianity.[6] Rather, he used the figure of Dionysus to contribute to a heightened aesthetic subjectivity that transcends the objective boundaries of reason, social convention and action. Only when the subject loses itself, when it shrugs off pragmatic experience in space and time, when the norms of everyday life are destroyed and the illusion of normality collapses – only then is an unforeseen world disclosed: 'the realm of aesthetic illusion, which neither hides nor reveals.'[7] Habermas's problem with Nietzsche's interpretation is that Dionysian aesthetic phenomena are purified of all theoretical, practical and moral action, thereby thwarting the possibility of social emancipation. In his reaction to instrumental reason, Nietzsche places the 'other of reason' in an archaic sphere beyond all cognitive and moral claims. Under such circumstances the only meaning-giving force, for Nietzsche, is the authentic core of the 'will to power'. From the ruins of rationality rises the *Übermensch* (overman), who glorifies the continuous return of the 'will to power', without any hope of future redemption or termination of suffering. Reconciliation is achieved by means of the pure ecstasy of 'evaluation for the sake of evaluation'.

Habermas disagrees with two further points of Nietzsche's radical aesthetic critique of modernity. In the first place, he argues that Nietzsche's decentring of subjectivity leads to a position where all normal conventions of perception and action are suspended. The retreat into subjectivism is, according to Habermas, expressed in a number of ways. On one level it is a crucial aspect of Nietzsche's break with Enlightenment traditions, thereby removing the subject from all limiting rules of cognition and instrumental activity and all imperatives of utility and ethics. On another level the retreat surfaces in the notion of the 'will to power', in a form in which subjective power claims are disguised behind validity claims. In the second place, and linked to his charge of subjectivism, Habermas criticizes the Nietzschean abandonment of rational standards and the tendency to strip aesthetic experience of all cognitive and moral substance. Dionysian experience and subjective-aesthetic preferences use aesthetics against the spheres of theoretical cognition, moral action and the everyday life-world and drift in the direction of a metaphysically sublimated irrationalism. Such a lack of rational standards contributes, according to Habermas, to a theoretical inability to legitimize its own position, which ends up without a reasonable philosophical foundation. The problem is that Nietzsche places his power-focused, critical concept of modernity beyond the frontiers of reason. In short, without a modern aesthetics of reason, Nietzsche cannot justify the standards of aesthetic judgement. Aesthetic experience is carried back to an archaic past, and the critical ability to appreciate art is severed from rational argumentation or a procedural rationality.[8]

Given Habermas's communicative understanding of aesthetics, as sketched in the previous chapter, and his case studies of Schiller, Hegel (as the pivotal modernist) and Heine, his interpretation of Nietzsche comes as no surprise. One of the central issues for Habermas (in the second phase of his aesthetics) is that the differentiated nature of modernity does not imply that the autonomous sphere of aesthetics is communicatively closed to other cultural spheres. Compared to Hegel, who reconciles aesthetics with speculative reason, Nietzsche intensifies aesthetics to such an extent that it explodes any trace of cognitive or moral reason. Habermas finds such a strong aestheticization of life, as in the twentieth-century case of Surrealism (as discussed in sections 1.4 and 3.3), improbable. Nietzsche earns his problematic status for Habermas by radicalizing Hegel in the wrong direction, with the result that he becomes the *Drehschiebe* ('turn-table') between the defenders of modern reason and the champions of postmodernism.[9] This move allows Habermas to make the following historical reconstruction. First, he situates Heidegger (section 4.2) and Derrida (section 4.3) as figures who continue the project of a radical critique of Western metaphysics. Secondly, he sees Bataille's and Foucault's work as attempts to unmask the perverse 'will to power' by means of anthropological, psychological and historical methods (section 4.4). These thinkers are all of interest to Habermas because they continue to develop the relationship between reason and modernity in Nietzsche's radical-aesthetic manner. They are therefore, like Nietzsche, criticized for neglecting a more balanced and differentiated interpretation of modernity.

## 4.2   Art and ontology: Heidegger

Heidegger's originality consists, for Habermas, in portraying the modern dominance of the subject in terms of the history of metaphysics. Habermas makes the following distinction between Heidegger and Nietzsche: 'Nietzsche had spanned the arch of the Dionysian event between Greek tragedy and a new mythology. Heidegger's later philosophy can be understood as an attempt to displace this event from the area of an aesthetically revitalized mythology to that of philosophy.'[10] Habermas argues that whereas Nietzsche used aesthetic experience to move beyond modernity, Heidegger, with his radical rehabilitation of the project of Western metaphysics, remains within the framework of the Enlightenment. In place of a subjectively elevated, radically differentiated concept of art that acts as the protector of a new mythology, Heidegger links aesthetics with the ontological phenomenon. Beauty and truth are thereby dependent on Being.[11] The sacred voice of the poet is accessible to the thinker. Poetry and thinking (*Dichten und Denken*), or the work of the *Dichter*, all depend upon each other, even though poetry originates before thinking.[12] In such an ontological conceptualization of art, philosophy receives the task that was assigned to religion and art in Romanticism – to heal the *Entzweiung* (division or differentiation) of modernity. Whereas Nietzsche attributes the victory over nihilism to an aesthetic regeneration of the Dionysian myth, Heidegger projects it onto the screen of a metaphysical critique of world-historical import.

Habermas deals with Heidegger's argument as follows. First, he argues that Heidegger attempts to reinstate philosophy to the position it had before being expelled by young Hegelian criticism. Heidegger's view, according to Habermas, is that the historical destiny of a society is determined by a collective ontological pre-understanding and metaphysics, rather than by freely chosen projects and actions of its members. In this sense the history of Western metaphysics bears the stamp of ontological fatalism (*Seinsgeschick*). In modern times – and this is the second step – metaphysics has progressively taken the form of defending technology. Based on the philosophy of subjectivity inaugurated by Descartes, modernity has increasingly given rise to calculated rationality, the instrumental control of nature, and finally to an all-out struggle for the control of the earth. In this process of global domination and nihilism, being is reduced and even disregarded in a quantifiable manner. This forgetfulness of being (*Seinsvergessenheit*) and the technological objectification of human beings indicate for Heidegger, in the third step of Habermas's argument, the end of metaphysics and the crisis in our time. Heidegger's alternative, which is almost similar to Nietzsche's Dionysian hope, is to argue for a kind of recollective thinking that waits for an 'exiled god' to announce the apocalyptic arrival of a new era, wherein being appears only to those who prepare themselves for its fateful arrival. This brings Heidegger, according to Habermas, to the conclusion that only a recollective or anamnestic way of thinking can transgress the bounds of calculated reason. But this concept of 'ontological differentiation' places thinking ('a thinking more rigorous than the conceptual') beyond the sphere of traditional self-reflection and discursive reasoning.[13] In place of reflexive autonomy, Habermas continues, comes a new heteronomy, wherein a self-denying subjectivity has to learn to persevere modestly. In the Heideggerian constellation, reason is merely an imperfect activity of forgetfulness and displacement.

Against this background, Habermas's criticism of Heidegger is to be expected. His main problem with a critique of metaphysics that explodes the framework of discursive reason is that the subject–object scheme of conceptual and performative language is put on a par with the objectified 'will to power'. The experience of truth as disclosure also provides no clue for solving the problem of performative language – it also underestimates the communicative praxis of the life-world. Secondly, Heidegger remains squarely within the parameters of the philosophy of consciousness, in which the onto-logical experience of unconcealed truth is preferred to intersubjec-tivity. Although Heidegger places the problem of self-identity within the intersubjective horizon of social interaction, he does not see it as an original sphere of communicative reciprocity.[14] Thirdly, Habermas raises some objections regarding the issue of modern discourse and the autonomy of human thinking and action. The surrender of the subject to Being creates, according to Habermas, a new form of heteronomy such that Being becomes unspecified in a poetic tran-scendence of propositional truth, conceptual thinking and discursive reason. Against this background, Heidegger's critique of modern reason culminates in a radical but substantively empty attitude. With the glorification of heteronomy and the subjection of the subjective self-confirmation of *Dasein* to the power of the non-verifiable meaning of Being, the existential-ontological concept of freedom dis-appears in Habermas's view.

McCarthy describes Habermas's critique of Heidegger very aptly as follows:

> The 'palpable distortions' of a one-sidedly rationalized world get enci-phered into an 'impalpable *Seinsgeschick* administered by philoso-phers'. This cuts off the possibility of deciphering the pathologies of modern life in social-theoretical terms and frees their critique from the rigors of concrete historical analysis. 'Essential thinking' consigns questions that can be decided by empirical investigation or theoreti-cal construction . . . to the devalued realm of the ontic and leaves us instead with the 'empty, formulaic avowal of some indeterminate authority'.[15]

According to this argument, that Habermas and McCarthy endorse, the empirical and normative questions elicited by means of the social sciences' critique of metaphysics are lost to the poetic thinking of the Heideggerian philosopher who awaits the return of Being (an issue that will be further explored in terms of world disclosure and rational-discursive thinking in the final chapter).

## 4.3  On philosophy and literature: Derrida

Habermas broadens his position on Heidegger's 'critique of meta-physics' by discussing Derrida's post-structural linguistics. Derrida's position is aligned with Heidegger's critique of metaphysics in a certain sense, with the argument that the spoken word is favoured over the written word in the Western metaphysical postulation of a rational and transcendental foundation (*logos*). Derrida finds a recent example of this tendency in the phonocentrism (and logocentrism) of Saussure's structural linguistics, where the signifier is unproblematically equated with the signified. The illusion thus surfaces that spoken language is a transparent medium of being in which the relation between subject and object is unproblematic. But Derrida argues for a more complex understanding of this relation. He differs from Saussure in denying the assumed transparency of speech as a primary semantic context. With his alternative emphasis on writing, Derrida problematizes the unambiguous identity of meaning and reference. For him, both spoken and written words affirm the traces of the absent – texts are testimonies to the non-identical. Derrida's post-structuralist concept of language investigates meaning in the context of interwoven texts and systems of signs, a strategy that takes the absence of meaning very seriously. The similarity between Heidegger and Derrida, according to Habermas, is that both regard truth (or meaning) as a process related to disclosure and closure – where each text contains its own subtext, each meaning its own nonsense, each literary construction its own deconstruction, and each identity its own *différance*.[16]

The word *différance* plays, according to Habermas, a key role in Derrida's understanding of the differential and temporal nature of the written sign.[17] The point is that an open (differentiated) meaning system ('arche-writing') provides an infinite source or abundance (*supplement*) for all kinds of language use.[18] Differences are thus aspects of a universal text in which the abundance of meaning and the non-hierarchical nature of the text lead to a questioning of the long-standing precedence of logic over rhetoric.[19] It is in this context that the genre difference between philosophy and literature becomes problematical. Habermas writes in this regard: 'even before it makes its appearance, every text and every particular genre has already lost its autonomy to an all devouring context and an uncontrollable happening of spontaneous text production. This is the ground of the primacy of rhetoric, which is concerned with the qualities of texts in general, over logic.'[20] Habermas proceeds to say that Derrida's view of spontaneous text production is strongly influenced by developments in recent American literary criticism, wherein the status of autonomous literary works (as once practised by *New Criticism* and structuralism) is challenged. Critics, such as Miller, Hartmann, De Man and Culler, use the concept of general literature (similar to

Derrida's universal text) to criticize the specialized language of science and philosophy for its lack of metaphor and rhetoric.[21]

In his counter-argument, which is informed by the basic argumentative framework of *The Theory of Communicative Action* as sketched in the previous chapter, Habermas holds that Derrida and his followers neglect the linguistic dimension of productive understanding, where interlocutors engage reciprocally with reference to the meaning of spoken utterances.[22] The problem with an aestheticized understanding of language, one in which rhetoric triumphs over logic, is that it underestimates the normative implications of individualization, critical interpretation, cultural transfer, social integration and the attainment of knowledge on the basis of consensus-oriented linguistic performance.[23] Habermas finds support for his argument in the distinction that literary critics (such as Bühler, Jakobson and Ohmann) draw between poetic and ordinary use of language. He quotes Ohmann on this issue:

> [A] literary work creates a world . . . by providing the reader with impaired and incomplete speech acts which he completes by supplying the appropriate circumstances . . . A literary work is a discourse whose sentences lack the illocutionary forces that would normally attach to them. Its illocutionary force is mimetic . . . Specifically, a literary work purportedly imitates a series of speech acts, which in fact have no other existence. By doing so, it leads the reader to imagine a speaker, a situation, a set of ancillary events.[24]

According to Habermas, the imaginative character of the literary work is removed from the pressure of everyday communicative practice and the sphere of ordinary discourse, leading to the playful creation of a world in which the world-disclosing force of innovative language plays a role.

Habermas deepened his ideas on the relationship between everyday communicative practices and literary texts in his essay on the Italian writer Italo Calvino (one of the rare occasions on which Habermas engages with the work of a novelist). In the case of general or everyday communication, speech-acts function in contexts of action in which participants cope with situations and have to solve problems. The claims that are made in these circumstances – on the truth of statements, the rightness of norms, the truthfulness of expressions, and the preference for certain values – all concern both the speaker and the one being addressed. In the case of literary texts, speech-acts function in contexts where the burden of acting has been

removed from the reader; the situations that the reader encounters
and the problems that he or she faces are not immediately their own.
Literature, therefore, does not expect the reader to take a position
similar to that which everyday communication invites and expects
from those who are participating. Habermas continues that the validity claims that appear within a literary text have a binding force only
for the persons or characters appearing in the work – they have no
binding force for the author and/or the reader. The transfer of validity in this context is interrupted at the boundaries of the text; it does
not extend, via communicative relations, all the way down to the
reader. The literary situation contributes, in Habermas's view, to the
illocutionary disempowerment of literary speech-acts. The internal
relationship between the meaning and the validity of what is said
stays intact only for the characters in the novel or for those characters who are transformed in the second and third persons – but it is
not relevant for the real readers.[25]

In his discussion of Derrida (and Calvino) Habermas makes clear
that fictive elements, metaphors and rhetorical strategies do not
suspend the illocutionary power of everyday language. Against this
background, Derrida's generalization of the rhetorical and poetical
power of language (his aestheticization of language) does not address
the tension between the world-disclosing or poetical function of
language, on the one hand, and the prosaic, inner world character
or literal function of language, on the other.[26] Derrida's aestheticism
is, according to Habermas, blind to the fact that everyday communicative practices make learning processes possible. These learning
processes develop an independent logic that transcends local limitations. They are processes that curtail rhetoric polysemy and enable
judgements in the light of criticizable validity claims. In short,
Habermas argues that Derrida's deconstruction, like Rorty's pragmatism, neglects mutual understanding with regard to differentiation
among the objective, social and subjective worlds. By collapsing problem solving in a generalized manner similar to the world-disclosing
ability of literature and the linguistic function of poetics, Derrida
(and Rorty) overlook the complex relationships between ordinary
and differentiated language forms. The problem with Derrida's Nietzschean and Heideggerian turn is, for Habermas, that it abandons the
need, in literary criticism and philosophy, to differentiate (and
properly mediate) between expert cultures and the everyday world.[27]

Habermas holds that both philosophy and literary criticism use
illuminating metaphors in the process of problem solving. Literary
criticism, for example, has been institutionalized in Europe since the

eighteenth century as a specialized, differentiated discourse of taste – a tradition which judges literary texts by criteria such as 'artistic truth', aesthetic harmony, exemplary validity, innovative force and authenticity. In this sense literary criticism has an internal logic similar to those of theoretical and practical discourses. In the next significant move, Habermas holds that literary criticism does not belong exclusively to an expert culture; it is also mediated by the everyday life-world. Aesthetic criticism thus has a unique mediating function in musical, visual and literary works. It mediates between the experimental content of a work of art and ordinary language use. The communicative function of a language act does not remove fictive elements from life practices. The world-disclosing function of literary language use is not totally independent of regulative and informational functions. In short, both philosophy and literary criticism (as theoretical enterprises) have, for Habermas, a dual obligation. Although, on the one hand, they are characterized by universal and powerful theoretical strategies that maintain intimate links with the sciences, they are not, on the other hand, merely esoteric components of an expert culture, but are intimately linked to the life-world and common sense (*sensus communis*). It is thus possible, from Habermas's perspective, to hold that literary criticism and philosophy attempt to transfer the content of expert cultures, in which knowledge is accumulated on account of one aspect of validity, to everyday practice, in which all linguistic functions and aspects of validity are interwoven.

Habermas ends his discussion of Derrida's post-structuralist philosophy of language by referring to the rhetorical power of both literary criticism and philosophy. He writes: 'Literary criticism and philosophy have a family resemblance to literature . . . in their rhetorical achievements. But their family relationship stops right there, for in each of these enterprises the tools of rhetoric are subordinated to the discipline of a distinct form of argumentation.'[28] The implication of this quote is that when the problem-solving nature of literary criticism and philosophical work is placed on a par with literature, it becomes unproductive.[29] Literary-critical judgements, for example, lose their force when they move from the aesthetic-experimental context to the critique of metaphysics. In the false assimilation of the one endeavour to the other, both philosophy and literary criticism are robbed of substance. Habermas concludes: 'Whoever transposes the radical critique of reason into the domain of rhetoric in order to blunt the paradox of self-referentiality, also dulls the sword of critique of reason itself (*läßt die Klinge der*

*Vernunftkritik selber stumpf werden*). The false pretence of eliminating the genre distinction between philosophy and literature cannot lead us out of this aporia.'[30]

## 4.4   Postmodernity and genealogy: Bataille and Foucault

Habermas continues his discussion of postmodernity with the argument that Bataille and Foucault also provide a radical (Nietzsche-influenced) critique of modern Western reason. In contrast to Heidegger's ontological and Derrida's language-deconstructive critique of Western reason, Bataille and Foucault advance a more empirical-anthropological and historical argument in their criticism of a subject-centred reason that dominates nature, society and the individual. It is at this point that their thinking reveals its affinity to Nietzsche with the argument that modern reason is a perverse, disguised 'will to power'. In this context the task of critique is to disclose the naked power of reason. In Bataille's anthropological-historical approach the 'other of reason' is investigated – those elements that go beyond a calculable and manipulated world. In Bataille's alternative, which Habermas sees as related to Surrealism, all forms of unity and rationality are exploded in a Dionysian play of orgasmic dance and intoxication. In this process a heterogeneity of suppressed and destructive forces are released – refuse, excretion, dreams, erotic indulgence, aesthetic experiences, violence and derangement.[31] Habermas links this argument to an aestheticization of life: 'In this concept, Bataille condensed the basic experience of the surrealist writers and artists who wanted shockingly to proclaim the ecstatic forces of intoxication, of dreamlife, of the instinctive and impulse generally, against the imperatives of utility, normality, and sobriety, in order to shake up conventionally set modes of perception and experience.'[32]

Bataille's anthropological-economic studies lead, according to Habermas, to a position where all forms of historically embodied sovereignty fall prey to unfree consumption practices. The point is that, since the earliest social structures, certain taboos regarding the sovereign surplus of nature – such as death and sex – have been erected. World religions, for example, removed the erotic, destructive and ambiguous dimensions of society in a prescriptive manner. This move paved the way, according to Bataille, for ethical and cognitive rationalization wherein the rational acceleration of economic growth explodes in the catastrophic forms of wasted consumption – war, civil violence and environmental destruction. Bataille's point is that cognitive and instrumental rationalization can be countered only if society enters into a relationship with its sovereign surplus.[33] Habermas, though, holds that Bataille's heterogeneous argument ignores the modern rational ability to integrate disparate elements in a systematic way. Celebration of the 'sovereignty' that the unrestricted subject has in relation to the sacral power of nature is, for Habermas, an overly romantic and Marxist protest against consumption and reification. In Habermasian terms, the problem is that Bataille's ignorance of communicative reason makes it impossible for him to distinguish between regressive and emancipating versions of sovereign heterogeneity. The use of transgressive-erotic language, together with the idea of non-communicative and aesthetic shock value, contributes, in Habermas's view, to the instigation of a mystical experience and a silence beyond the destruction of the subject. Bataille's dialectic of general economy and the regeneration of pure sovereign force is therefore, like Nietzsche's thought, trapped in a totalizing critique of reason.

In his critique of Western reason, the early Foucault adopts, according to Habermas, Nietzsche's concept of the 'will to power', where meaning becomes a discursive and rational power system dominating reason, politics, institutions and individuals.[34] In Foucault's genealogical model the achievements of reason (e.g. freedom, justice, truth and logic) are traced back to the violent arbitrariness of power systems. This view neutralizes, for Habermas, the role of language-orientated communication in modern societies. In *The Archaeology of Knowledge* (1969), for example, Foucault explains, contra Habermas, that descriptive validity claims and discourses are a regulative function of the power system. This regulative function is the empirical consequence of power relations without any ideal claims to truth, falseness or the essential.[35] Habermas continues that Foucault wants to break the hold of modern natural and human sciences by means of a strategy that is quite similar to that of Horkheimer and Adorno – where the aim is to go behind the façade of scientific universality and objectivity in order to counter the ever-growing proliferation of modern techniques and manipulative practices such as detention strategies, behaviour conditioning, statistical measurement, classification and controlled therapy, which are extended by modern schools, factories, households and individuals.[36] Foucault's alternative to these power systems (as will be further explicated in the next chapter) is to open the space for new kinds of aesthetic relationships to oneself and others – an aesthetics of existence.

Because he links Foucault to Horkheimer and Adorno, it is quite understandable that Habermas will criticize this position. First, he faults Foucault's use of a 'totalizing critique' of reason by means of the 'other of reason' – a motif that also runs through the arguments of other postmodernists. Secondly, Habermas argues that Foucault's transcendental-historiographic interpretation of genealogy cannot escape the performative contradiction that the critique of reason originates in reason itself. Habermas continues that although meaning, validity and values are eliminated in Foucault's genealogical critique, normative concepts such as 'domination' and 'oppression' are still used critically. Foucault's involvement with contemporary political issues is a further indication, for Habermas, that he could not discard a discourse of civil liberties and democratic reforms. Thirdly, Habermas questions Foucault's socio-theoretical interpretation of modernity. The point is that the phenomena of modern culture and society are levelled on Foucault's 'plateau of power'. In this process, the inner development and learning processes of justice and morality, which have, according to Habermas, an emancipating and not just a dominating aspect, disappear. It is precisely the ambiguous nature of modern rationalization processes, their accomplishments and failures, that Foucault misses in his philosophical work. True to his philosophical programme in *The Theory of Communicative Action* (as argued in the previous chapter), Habermas defends a critical reconstruction, rather than a total critique, of the Enlightenment, whereas Foucault's totalizing critique runs into the same dilemma as Derrida's deconstructive assimilation of the genre difference between philosophy and literature.

Habermas concludes his argument by claiming that Foucault reduces social solidarity to creative self-confirmation in a manner that is reminiscent of Nietzsche and Derrida's reduction of intersubjective communication to rhetorical and poetical creativity. The dilemma here for Habermas is that the processes of individualization and socialization are placed outside the parameters of communicative reason. Habermas proceeds that his theory of communicative reason doesn't establish a transcendent reason beyond the everyday life-world. Language use in such a context is time-bounded and dependent on empirical processes wherein the logical and normative rules of everyday language use are not fixed abstractly, but in which the validity claims of communicative action succeed only on the basis of intersubjective and historical examples. The paradox of free and conditioned human nature is most properly addressed, according to Habermas, within the expanding horizon of shared communicative meaning. Such horizons are never transparent to the mind, because they have implicit performative abilities of 'know-how' that escape control.[37] With this argument regarding the restrictions of empirical-historical factors, Habermas wants to indicate that communication does not always proceed smoothly. In his concept of the communicative differentiation of rationality types, for example, he does not attempt to establish a comprehensive, absolute concept of reason.[38]

## 4.5   A postmodern critique of Habermas's aesthetics

This section marks the start of a critical engagement with Habermas and the role of aesthetics in his work. The question is whether Habermas provides a fair picture of the discourse of (post)modernity in the broader framework of the second phase of his aesthetics. Is his portrayal of the main elements of postmodern critique – the totalizing critique of reason, the radical deconstruction of the Enlightenment project, the abandonment of the nostalgic search for unity and totality, and the overcoming of the tyranny of representational thinking and universal truth – correct? In order to address these issues, I will confront Habermas's position with the perspectives of (i) Lyotard (a thinker whom he, interestingly enough, doesn't address in his *Philosophical Discourse of Modernity* or in any subsequent studies) and (ii) the work of some other postmodernists.

(i) Lyotard treats postmodernism not exclusively in terms of the 'will to power' or 'instrumental reason', but also in terms of the 'principle of legitimacy'. The crisis of modernity lies for him in its appeal made on the basis of obsolete meta-narratives of science, morality and art. The scientific paradigm functions for Lyotard as the privileged meta-narrative of modern reason *par excellence*. It is a discourse of the greatest legitimacy (*strenge Wissenschaft*), which is continuously in conflict with 'softer practices' wherein a measure of relativity and indecision prevails. With reference to science and other meta-narratives, such as the emancipation (*Aufklärung*) of humankind, the teleology of the Spirit (Idealism), the hermeneutics of meaning (historicism), and autonomous art, Lyotard writes: 'simplifying to the extreme I define postmodern as incredulity toward metanarratives'.[39] In a significant move, Lyotard pleads for an abandonment of the nostalgic search for unity and totality, in order to enable aesthetic experimentation and the heterogeneous interplay of language games, action and life forms.[40] Lyotard thereby opens a debate between his version of postmodernism and Habermas's version of the philosophical discourse of modernity.[41] Lyotard's first point of criticism is that Habermas supports a subtle ideal of totality and universality in his social philosophy and aesthetics – this argument is offered, despite Habermas's own critique of totalization in scientific objectivism.[42] Secondly, Habermas's project is portrayed as a reconstruction of a universal requirement for possible understanding. This is done on the basis that all participants enter a 'contract' regarding the meta-prescriptions of all language games by locating the *telos* of dialogue in consensus. Lyotard, though, finds consensus too strongly linked with the modern idea of ethical unity, final truth, and aesthetics of the beautiful.[43] Hence his question: what type of unity is at issue in Habermas? Is it an organic unity, as in Hegel, or a synthetic unity of heterogeneity, as in Kant's third Critique?

Thirdly, Lyotard criticizes Habermas's model of rational differentiation.[44] He uncovers a totalitarian strategy behind the attempt to mediate between modern culture spheres:

> Habermas considers that the remedy for this splintering of culture and its separation from life can only come from 'changing the status of aesthetic experience when it is no longer primarily expressed in judgments of taste', but when it is 'used to explore a living historical situation,' that is, when 'it is put in relation with problems of existence.' For this experience then 'becomes a part of a language game which is no longer that of aesthetic criticism'; it takes part 'in cognitive processes and normative expectations'; 'it alters the manner in which those different moments refer to one another.' What Habermas requires from the arts and the experiences they provide is, in short, to bridge the gap between cognitive, ethical, and political discourses, thus opening the way to a unity of experience . . . Is the aim of the project of modernity the constitution of sociocultural unity within which all the elements of daily life and of thought would take their places as in an organic whole?[45]

With this statement Lyotard seems to suggest that Habermas is insensitive to the heterogeneity of language games. As an alternative, Lyotard defends a steering away from Habermas's supposed Hegelian-inspired totalizing of social experience in order to reach the 'heterogeneous mind[s]' of Kant, Wittgenstein and a few French thinkers 'who do not have the honor to be read by Professor Habermas'.[46]

What are the aesthetic implications of these three points of criticism? Lyotard misses the same sensitivity to heterogeneity in the kind of aesthetic attempts that subdue artistic experimentation in the name of orderliness, unity, identity and popularity. He describes art movements such as Realism and neoclassicism as being responsible for providing those images, narratives and forms that the 'Party' demands. This kind of power-political attack on artistic experimentation succeeds, according to Lyotard, where the judgement of a particular work corresponds with established and prescribed aesthetic rules.[47] A priori criteria are thus imposed on the aesthetic object and the public. In his alternative, which seem at the first glance to advocate some notion of autonomous art, Lyotard defends artworks that use techniques to represent the non-representable. 'To make visible that there is something which can be conceived and which can neither be seen nor made visible: that is what is at stake in modern painting.'[48] On the other hand, Lyotard also uses the Benjaminian argument that reproduction techniques destabilize any form of narrative or pictorial realism. It is thus possible for artists and writers to constantly question the inherited rules of artworks and literature. In this sense such artists are destined to have little credibility in the eyes of those concerned with 'reality' and 'identity'.[49] Lyotard's position can thus be linked with an avant-garde and postmodern rebellion against the modern idea of aesthetic purity and prescribed rules, and so finds a natural link with Dadaism, Surrealism, postmodern architecture and the pop culture of the 1960s.[50]

Lyotard proceeds that it is the Kantian notion of the sublime that provides the impetus to avant-garde and other postmodern art movements.[51] The sublime could be described as the tension between the wish to conceptualize and its frustration. The sublime prevents any stabilization of taste by stressing its non-representative nature. Lyotard also uses the image of the sublime (as negative representation that avoids figuration or representation in a painting) to describe the task of the intellectual or philosopher:

A postmodern artist or writer is in the position of a philosopher: the text he writes, the work he produces are not in principle governed by pre-established rules, and they cannot be judged according to a determining judgment, by applying familiar categories to the text or to the work. Those rules and categories are what the work of art itself is looking for. The artist and the writer, then, are working without rules in order to formulate the rules of what will have been done.[52]

Lyotard sees the role of the philosopher in these public aesthetic terms as an alternative to transcendental Idealism (Hegel) or the moments of reconciliation in communicative reason (Habermas). He continues, in dramatic style, that it is Kant who has indicated the high price of 'the nostalgia of the whole and the one, for the reconciliation of the concept and the sensible, the transparent and the communicable experience. Under the general demand for slackening and for appeasement, we can hear the mutterings of the desire for a return of terror, for the realization of the fantasy to seize reality.'[53]

(ii) Other contemporary French thinkers such as Derrida, Lacoue-Labarthe and Nancy also undermine the traditional trust in the self-referential, organic, idealistic and formalistic work of art.[54] Derrida, for example, plays with the concepts of *ergon* (work) and *parergon* (frame) to emphasize their mutuality. In this context the distinction between art and non-art does not make sense to Derrida. When art as institution contradicts the false whole of the individual work, it is not autonomous. Art for art's sake is thus merely a variation on the theme of 'aesthetic ideology'. Lacoue-Labarthe and Nancy, on their part, trace the idea of 'aesthetic ideology' back to its roots in Romanticism: 'it is an aesthetic that is understood to be the culmination of Idealist philosophy, or perhaps even Western metaphysics as a whole, and not its abstract negation. Bourgeois culture at its height rather than at its moment of seeming decay is thus taken as the point of departure for aestheticized politics.'[55] Lacoue-Labarthe and Nancy criticize the following aspects of Romantic art: the part as anticipated by the whole, the artist as a self-creating genius, and the critic as having superior knowledge.[56] Such a concept of art amounts, for them, to a search for essential forms, a kind of quasi-religious metaphysics of art, a 'literary absolute' or *eidos* aesthetic – a movement wherein all differences, contradictions and ambiguities are resolved. As Europe's first self-conscious intellectual avant-garde, the Jena Romantics introduced an aesthetic meta-narrative. But, finally, the failure of the dream of the organic artwork also defeats the inflated image of the (aesthetic) subject.

In a similar manner, De Man links the ideological nature of aesthetics (*eidos* aesthetic) to Schiller's work. He argues that art becomes ideological when life is transformed into the aesthetic state according to the aesthetic political programme of an organic work of art.[57] This is clearly stated in De Man's Kleist essay, in which he cautions against the 'hidden violence' of aesthetic education.[58] The violence at issue is the cultural impulse, particularly in language, that makes forced totalization possible. In another essay on Kant and Schiller, De Man even finds support for his argument by quoting from

Goebbels's novel. Jay writes: 'Although in many ways appreciative of Kant's resistance to metaphysical closure and epistemological over-reaching, de Man nonetheless identified in him the potential to sanction, however unintentionally, a sinister tradition . . . In other words, for all their emancipatory intentions, Kant and even more so Schiller spawned a tradition that contained the potential to be transformed into a justification for fascism.'[59] In the previous chapter I indicated that postmodern thinkers also view with suspicion Habermas's concept of 'normal language use'.[60] The point is that a preference for transparent language can extinguish human sensitivity to the other. In contrast to a formal use of language, humour, irony, metaphors and aesthetic expression provide humankind with the tools to engage with the settled ideas of the world.

Despite subtle differences amongst the various postmodern positions that have been presented in this section, they share the following common features: all struggle against bureaucratic control, unrestrained economic growth, limited self-expression and disciplinary compartmentalization.[61] From a philosophical perspective, the impulse to systematic exclusion, social homogeneity, categorical purity, objectivity and limited differentiation is criticized. In an attempt to limit such 'metaphysical illusions', Lyotard's concept of heterogeneity is related to Derrida's approach of literary deconstruction and Foucault's concept of genealogy. Like Adorno, these thinkers are especially critical of any kind of identity thinking.[62] It is interesting that Habermas's defence of communicative rationality and his reconstruction of the discourse of modernity are interpreted from these perspectives as a kind of thinking that restricts heterogeneity. Consequently, Habermas's version of the philosophical discourse of modernity is questioned. His hopes of uncovering the forgotten tracks and traces leading to the kind of rational concept that he defends in *The Theory of Communicative Action* become contentious. It is an open question, though, whether Habermas's interpretation of the philosophical, social and aesthetic roots of modernity leads to a homogenized or totalized position, as some postmodernists state. This issue will be explored in the next chapter, when various critical perspectives on Habermas's aesthetics will be discussed.

## 4.6 Summary

The aim of this chapter has been to show how Habermas's position in the second phase of his aesthetics became consolidated in his debate with postmodern thinkers. In this process his reconstruction of the philosophical discourse of modernity can also be interpreted as a refinement of the arguments in *The Theory of Communicative Action*. One of the foci of communicative reason is the presence of criticizable validity claims in language. On the basis of different claims and their relationship to the world, the differentiation between learning processes in science, law and art is constructed – a differentiation that does not exclude the possibility of communication between these spheres. In the previous chapter it was indicated that Habermas's model of communicative reason is supplemented by a concept of societal rationalization and the distinction between life-world and system, where art receives a role in both the intersubjective life-world and the bureaucratic systems of the culture industry – a move that accommodates both autonomous and popular art. These arguments have been contextualized in this chapter through Habermas's reading of the philosophical discourse of modernity and his critical case studies of Nietzsche and his followers. Whereas Hegel's counter-discourse of modernity still remains within the basic framework of modern reason (and left- and right-wing Hegelians follow Hegel by staying within the broad parameters of this debate), it is only with Nietzsche and his postmodern followers, according to Habermas, that an anti-discourse is inaugurated. Only with Nietzsche's aesthetic alternative is there a move beyond the confines of Hegel's counter-discourse.

It is quite understandable that Habermas's model of communicative reason plays a central role in the development of an alternative to postmodernism. In this process the position of postmodern thinking and postmodern aesthetics on rationality are problematized from Habermas's perspective: Nietzsche's 'quasi-messianic expectation of art', for example, traces aesthetic experience back to an archaic past, thereby dismissing the critical faculty to appreciate and judge art from the perspective of rational argumentation or procedural rationality. Heidegger's poetic transcendence of propositional truth and conceptual thinking ends, according to Habermas, in an aesthetic ontology that causes being to become unspecified. The idea of the indeterminate normative dimension in language leads Derrida, on his part, to suspend the genre difference between philosophy and literature. But Habermas remains sceptical about whether the 'foundational philosophy of Western culture' and the 'tyranny of logocentrism' can be liberated in such a way. He continues that in Bataille's works aesthetic experience is radicalized to such an extent (and very like in Surrealism) that his concept of heterogeneity implies the aestheticization of life – 'sovereign and aesthetic surplus'. To this position, according to Habermas, Foucault adds his voice that an 'aesthetics of existence' is the answer to the crisis of modern reason.[63] Finally, Lyotard sets his aesthetically informed concept of heterogeneity against the 'hidden totalization' present in Habermas's model of argumentative reconciliation.

Habermas's alternative to these aesthetic proposals, discussed as the second phase of his aesthetics, is to propose a communicative reconstruction of the philosophical discourse of modernity – with reason as the unforced intersubjectivity of mutual understanding and reciprocal recognition. Hegel's portrayal of the reconciling, healing force of reason in social and aesthetic modernity is thus translated in Habermas's model into the unforced intersubjectivity of rational agreement. In many ways Habermas sees himself, in the discourse of modernity, as continuing the young Hegelian path of practical philosophy. His position provides an alternative to the post-Nietzschean and postmodern positions, where the singular, particular, 'exceptional' and 'other' take precedence – things that are accessible only by means of aesthetic, mystical and archaic experiences. Habermas, by contrast, has a more social, interactive model of reason. Within the paradigm of communicative reason decentralized subjects participate in social interaction through the mediation of language and validity claims. Even though Habermas accepts that the consciousness paradigm has been exhausted, and even though he sets reason in the concrete situation of historical, social, physical and linguistic phenomena, he maintains that the defects of the Enlightenment can be remedied only through further enlightenment. Against this background, a totalized critique of reason and concurrent aestheticization of life, as postmodern thinkers propose, undermine for Habermas the critical and aesthetic potential of reason. It is the complexities of this issue that will be critically examined in the next chapter, where various critiques of Habermas's aesthetics will be considered.

# 5

# Critical Perspectives on Habermas's Aesthetics

Having sketched Habermas's aesthetics, in terms of two phases, it is now necessary to turn to a critique. I will do this in the following way. First, I will investigate the status of aesthetics, and more specifically the rationality of aesthetics, in Habermas's theory of communicative reason. Important issues in this regard are the restriction of the validity of art to the subjective judgement of the author or creator and Habermas's distinction between 'normal' and 'abnormal' language use (section 5.1). The critique of the formal and abstract nature of Habermas's theoretical project that emerges here will be further elaborated in section 5.2, where the issue of nature enters the picture. Foucault's concept of the *aesthetics of existence* and Whitebook's psychoanalytic concept of *nature* are important in this regard. This problematic is situated, amongst others, in the context of the tension between discursive reason and practical, embodied intuition. Merleau-Ponty, for example, describes the body as an original unity of predispositions, habits and intentions that leads to intentional and expressive socializing; whereas Habermas seems to see the body as a non-reflexive, mechanical and linguistic behavioural system.[1] Thirdly, Habermas's concept of social rationalization will be examined via a linkage between his restriction of the validity of art to the creative subjectivity of the author or creator to a kind of subjective production aesthetics. An alternative reception aesthetics – which implies a more communicative understanding of the nature of aesthetic experience – is proposed. To this idea the concept of post-avant-garde art is added – a move that opens a more appropriate mediation between art and life (section 5.3). Finally, I offer two possible interpretations of the ongoing debate between Adorno and Habermas (section 5.4).

## 5.1   The role of aesthetics in communicative reason

Habermas's restriction of the aesthetic to the subject's inner nature, in his theory of communicative reason, has been noticed by a number of his commentators and interlocutors. The interesting point here is that, despite Habermas's emphasis on intersubjectivity, he restricts the validity of art and aesthetic judgements to the subjective sphere of the author or creator. This subjective *impasse* implies that aesthetic judgements are not fully part of the intersubjective sphere of formal discourse.[2] This dilemma leads to a situation whereby Habermas is criticized for not mediating sufficiently between the pre-discursive horizons of aesthetic judgement and taste, on the one hand, and the formal argumentation of discursive reason, on the other. For Ingram, such mediation presupposes the role of intuitive reason.[3] In the philosophical tradition stretching from Plato to Hegel, according to him, dialogical analysis is only one aspect of rationality. Another important aspect is the intuitive power of synthesis or practical reason. Plato's concept of *poēsis* (the metaphorical agreement between heterogeneous experiences) and Aristotle's concept of *phronēsis* (the application of general rules of behaviour in particular, everyday practice) are such examples for Ingram. Both include art and taste – in other words, the aesthetic establishment of certain models of communication and virtues that the Greeks considered as essential for full human development.[4] Martin Jay has also remarked that it is not altogether clear how aesthetic rationality is mediated with other forms of rationality – in Habermas's differentiation between cognitive-instrumental, moral-practical and aesthetic-expressive rationality spheres (in each of which experts use a particular logic). Against this background, Jay offers three tentative, and interesting, alternatives to the restriction of the aesthetic sphere in the second phase of Habermas's aesthetics.

First, Jay refers to an early essay of Habermas, 'Between science and philosophy: Marxism as critique' (1963), in which Habermas favours allegory over classical symbolism, but without elaborating. Secondly, Jay mentions Benjamin's philosophy of language, and more specifically semantic art potential, as a remnant of the original mimetic-expressive relationship between language and nature. He then asks the following questions about language: is it a kind of rationalized mimesis?[5] Or are the elements of correspondence in language wrested from the primordial state of undifferentiated immediacy? Although Jay is not fully convinced by Habermas's formal linguistic alternative, he is very tentative about the status of Benjamin's Romantic onomatopoeic theory of language. Thus he suggests, thirdly, that the relationship between language and nature in Habermas could be creatively addressed by incorporating ideas from Suzi Gablik's *Progress in Art*, where she argues that non-representational modern art has a cognitive advantage over Piaget's formal-operational model.[6] Even though Jay does not further elaborate on Gablik's argument about the mediation between artistic rationality and everyday life and her Benjaminian emphasis on mimesis, he nevertheless holds that Habermas should provide a more explicit explanation of the nature of aesthetic-expressive rationality in his defence of modernity.[7] The relationship between cognitive-instrumental, moral-practical and aesthetic-expressive rationalities and their respective reintegration into the life-world are difficult to comprehend, due to the unknown nature of aesthetic rationality in Habermas's proposal. Jay concludes that although Habermas has spent a huge amount of intellectual energy in developing a communicative concept of rationality, his reflections on aesthetics, and its communicative potential, remain relatively underdeveloped.[8]

It should come as no surprise that the restricted role of aesthetics in Habermas's formulation of a theory of communicative reason can be linked to his formal, abstract pragmatic analysis of language. A pivotal aspect of this view of language is the distinction he makes between 'normal' and 'abnormal' (or secondary) language use.[9] In this context, the following questions surface: does the concept of 'normal' language do justice to the imaginative and creative nature of language? And what role is there for poetry, humour and irony in 'normal' language usage? Derrida's literary-philosophical way of writing, which freely uses forms such as irony, can be cited against Habermas, according to Norris, as an example of interdependent or interwoven discourse of free mixing. In addition, Habermas's preference for serious, clear language usage and categorical distinctions can extinguish human sensitivity to domination. It is precisely at this point that humour, irony, metaphoric language usage and aesthetic experience could supply the space and tools to fight the established views of the 'subject', the 'other' and the 'world'. Another implication of Habermas's distinction between 'normal' and 'abnormal' language is the fact that the ('normal') language of communicative action is portrayed as the primary mechanism of social integration (in modern societies), whereas 'abnormal' language is of a secondary nature. As Cooke indicates, when 'normal' language is preferred over 'abnormal' language, then it implies that language oriented towards understanding is the original version, while other language modes (such as figurative, symbolic and more generally indirect modes of language use, on the one hand, and strategic or more generally instrumental modes of language use, on the other) are parasitic on it.

Apart from the interesting point that Habermas's formal view of language groups poetic and strategic language together without qualification, Cooke seems to suggest that we understand symbolic and strategic language use only because we already understand language when it is used communicatively. This is like saying that we understand the non-literal use of language only because we already know what it is to use language literally.[10] The formal nature of Habermas's language theory further implies that the speech-acts of aesthetic-literary discourses are detached from everyday contexts of action. Hence they have no illocutionary force or binding effect on the recognition of validity claims – and the added implication is that those speech-acts that function primarily to create, disclose or articulate thus do not, by virtue of this very fact, fulfil functions of reaching understanding (*Verständigung*). Cooke therefore states that if the world-creating and world-disclosing dimensions of linguistic activity are neglected (an aspect that will be fully examined in the next chapter), this leads to an impoverished notion of communicative action. In following Pratt, Taylor and Seel, she proceeds by indicating that a broader conception of communicative action would have the advantage of being conceptually open to modes of language use that articulate and disclose, rather than co-ordinate, action.[11] The idea that everyday language use refers to more than three validity claims simply means that Habermas's proposal will have to be understood in a more multi-dimensional way.

In responding to the kind of criticism that has been offered in this section, Habermas has said that the categorical distinction between normal (literal) and abnormal (non-literal) language use is harmless and serves only theoretical purposes. Accordingly irony, humour and fiction in normative language usage are based on category mistakes between the validity claims of being/illusion, is/ought and essence/appearance. Habermas thus restates his standpoint whereby normal language is preferred by stressing its co-ordinating role in human action. It is thus clear that he does not want to give up his position that the creative power of poetry, fiction, music and painting 'do not as a rule take over functions of co-ordinating action'.[12] Habermas adds that the radical effect of the aesthetic experience on thought and action must still be seen as coherent with the relative

autonomy of the aesthetic sphere in the modern world. With autonomy (a theme that was addressed earlier and will be further
explored in section 5.3) Habermas indicates that the aesthetic validity of a modern artwork differs from its theoretical and normative
validity – aesthetic sincerity is differentiated from scientific truth and
normative correctness. Habermas then restates his position that the
ability to differentiate separates a modern world-view from a pre-
modern one. If this point on differentiation is taken, it still remains
an open question, though, whether the formal-discursive dimensions
of communicative reason do in fact allow space for the communication of formal and expressive language elements. Inevitably, the
provocative question in Habermas's Benjamin essay surfaces again in
this context: what becomes of happiness in his formal proposal
of communication?

## 5.2   Habermas and the de-linguistification
of (inner) nature

Habermas's defence of formal language use (which is the result of
his differentiated model of reason) can also be problematized in
terms of its separation from inner and outer nature. In this regard
it is relevant to consider the positions of (i) Foucault and (ii)
Whitebook.

(i) One of the central themes for Foucault is the position and
meaning of the embodied subject who is the victim of modern power
networks.[13] In terms of this argument, the historical subject is progressively separated from his or her inner nature, thereby becoming
a victim of the network of 'normalizing bio power'. It is quite understandable that such an argument will be critical of Habermas's
concept of the 'subject' for ignoring the history of its own pre-
rational and corporeal otherness. As an alternative, Foucault constructs a model in which the reflexive and embodied self is open to
his or her own body and pleasure. Such a subject doesn't interpret
the body and its demands as the object of knowledge or legal regulation, but as the object of *aesthetic* self-creation. Foucault traces the
elements of such an interpretation of the subject back to the Stoics,
who moved from the urban *technē* of existence to another form of
*technē*, the *bios*, as material for an artwork or as aesthetics of existence. In addition to the aesthetic perspective of the *bios*, Foucault
also focuses on the Stoic idea of a '[s]trong structure of existence

without any relation with the juridical *per se*, with an authoritarian system, with a disciplinary structure'.[14]

Foucault finds the modern equivalent of a Stoic-influenced aesthetics of existence in Baudelaire's description of the dandy as an individual who creates a work of art from his body, behaviour, passions and existence. Such an account of the self is motivated by an interest in the body, pleasure and the aesthetic form, as opposed to a social or political interest. In his essay 'What is enlightenment?', Foucault writes: 'The deliberate attitude of modernity is tied to an indispensable asceticism . . . what Baudelaire, in the vocabulary of his day, calls dandyism . . . the dandy who makes his body, his behavior, his feelings and passions, his very existence, a work of art.'[15] Foucault thus provides an alternative model of subjectivity (one in which things like the body, spontaneity and expressiveness play a central role) to the intersubjective-formalist one that Habermas defends (one that seems to interpret inner nature as a sphere of passive subjectiveness).[16] In a follow-up, Foucault makes an ethical appeal to his notion of the aesthetics of existence. Self-control is important in this regard – 'the kind of relationship you ought to have with yourself, *rapport a soi*'. It further implies a continuous process of aesthetic self-creation and self-articulation. The primary motive is the will 'to live a beautiful life and to leave to others the memories of a beautiful existence'. Such an ethics of active self-creation is, according to Foucault, missing in most modern subjects.[17] But this raises the question: does Foucault's aesthetics of self-creation not end in a form of asocial asceticism such that the provocative construction of access to the self's pre-rational bodily otherness may alienate intersubjective relations? And how can an aesthetics of existence be linked to collective political action?[18] Without denying the importance of these questions, Foucault's aesthetics of existence still challenges us, contra Habermas, to think about self-creation as a process in which aesthetic criteria contribute to the reasonable, acting subject. This is an important point, because the aesthetic self (in its openness to the 'other') is allowed to play a role in all aspects of everyday life. The aesthetic significance of this position is that the needs of human beings are addressed without inhibiting their knowledge and moral-political judgement about certain social and technological infrastructures.[19]

(ii) In his psychoanalytic studies, Whitebook shares Foucault's concern with the social relevance of inner and outer nature. Whitebook revisits Marcuse's essay 'On hedonism' (1938), where 'inner nature' is clarified in terms of the tension between rationalism and hedonism (*eudaemonia*). An important aspect of this essay is the positioning of collective, objective, universal truth against the contingency and transient nature of individual human existence. This could also be described as the tension between rationality and the individual claim to happiness – beyond class struggles and scarcity. The call for hedonism is thus a claim about the biologically embodied individual – that is, a claim to happiness against the demands of the collectivity.[20] Like Adorno's, this position is the result of a certain reading of Freud where id psychology is defended against revisionist ego psychology. Id psychology serves in this context as the basis for studying the disharmony between the instinctive substratum, the seat of happiness, and the repressive ego. For Marcuse, according to Whitebook, only a revolution of the instincts can lead to happiness – only the utopian combination of the emancipated instincts and aesthetic rationality can solve the riddle of history. Whitebook uses Marcuse's essay as a critical reminder of the disharmony between reason and instincts, a line of thought that Habermas, like ego psychologists, does not continue. Whitebook then sets the differences between the first generation of Critical Theorists and Habermas on psychoanalysis in the context of recent empirical studies on rationalization and individualization. Important in this regard is the phenomenon of the 'new patient' who suffers from a feeling of emptiness, isolation and futility, pre-oedipal anger, primitive seclusion, rejection and fragmented fear about his or her self-image.

Whitebook argues that certain aspects of capitalist evolution have had an immense, disruptive impact on the individual psyche and family patterns in the life-world. This has led to the narcissism of the 'new patient' in terms of a heightened drive for material success, power and status; a progressive fetishism with youth, health and glamour; an attempt to escape from illness, ageing and any form of weakness; and a repressive desublimation of sexuality associated with an inability to maintain permanent relationships of emotional depth. At this point the following position of the first generation of Critical Theorists becomes important for Whitebook: only reconciliation between reason and inner and outer nature harbours the promise of escape from the aporia of the dialectic of Enlightenment. Against this background, Habermas's concepts of autonomy and self-development and his version of institutional regression and anomie are obviously questioned.[21] In short, how does Habermas accommodate inner and outer nature in his theory of communicative reason? In asking this question, Whitebook clearly displays scepticism regarding whether the tension between society and inner nature can be harmoniously resolved by the linguistification of society. He thus portrays the linguistification of the social (Habermas) as a kind of 'filter' through which inner nature becomes intersubjective. Here Habermas's project is placed against an important aspect of Freudian psychoanalysis – the role of the body in the study of the drives (*Triebslehre*).[22] It seems to be the case that happiness and the good life, which are normally linked to inner nature, are not as important in Habermas's formal-linguistic approach as they were in the case of Marcuse and Adorno.[23] With regard to outer nature, Whitebook argues that it is interesting that Habermas interprets it as an object of instrumental rationality and the domain of the natural sciences.[24]

In response to Whitebook's criticism, Habermas replies that his communicative model does not lose inner nature (and aesthetic experience) in a cultural mist. On the issue of reconciliation between internal happiness and moral judgement, Habermas draws a sharp distinction between autonomous duty, on the one hand, and the ego's communicative access to its inner nature, on the other. Thus he concedes that particular life forms and histories have a context or horizon that cannot be objectified *in toto*. Happiness, as opposed to justice or knowledge, does not appeal to general structures – it relates to particular constellations of experienced practices, value orientations and traditions, and it is always historically unique. Habermas thus agrees with Whitebook that it is difficult to set a clinical intuition about the 'good life' in a universally binding morality.[25] Nevertheless, he maintains that communicative access to a good life provides better possibilities than an Adornian access to the id.[26] In the relationship between universal moral norms and the ethical life-world, practical reason asks for the application of abstract, general norms in particular situations. Without such a move, according to Habermas, the psychological imperative to translate morality into an ethical life disintegrates – without 'proper' life forms to embody moral principles, the social circumstances for their concrete existence disappear.

What is there to learn, especially from an aesthetic point of view, from the debate between Whitebook and Habermas? Both agree that if the mastery of nature is a *telos* of the Enlightenment, then it leads to reification and the destruction of non-renewable sources of meaning. In this sense modernity is defended against a radical critique of the Enlightenment. The uniqueness of Whitebook's position, though, is that he returns to the first generation of Critical Theorists in addressing these issues. Thus he asks provocatively whether Habermas's communicative model is an improvement on *Dialectic of*

*Enlightenment?* Whereas Adorno, Horkheimer and Marcuse emphasize the underlying Freudian and post-Marxian dimension of the
unconscious, motivational processes and the id, Habermas moved
away from Freud to the communicative implications of Piaget and
Kohlberg's developmental psychology. Whitebook writes: 'This does
not say that one should mystify the unconscious or the drives as the
special repository of truth . . . It is to say, however, that we cannot
defend the project of modernity – which must be defended – at the
price of sacrificing the naturalistic tradition that runs from Feuerbach
through the young Marx and Freud to the early Frankfurt School.'[27]
The issue here is whether it is better to describe the interconnection
between inner nature and theory in psychoanalytic or developmental psychological terms. By considering the materialist motives that
Freudo-Marxism derives from a theory of motivation, Whitebook
asks: does Habermas sacrifice happiness at the cost of the normative
dimension? Does he prefer justice to happiness? Habermas's view of
formal rationality runs the danger, according to Whitebook, of separating form and content, morality and happiness. But Whitebook, like
Jay, wants to retain the link between meaning and the natural
element of human existence.

## 5.3   The role of aesthetics in social rationalization

I have already indicated (in chapter 3) that Habermas's theory of
communicative reason has four components: a theory of communication and rational argumentation (of which the aesthetic implications were investigated in the first two sections of this chapter), a
theory of social rationalization, the concepts of life-world and system,
and finally a position on modernity/postmodernity. In this section the
last three of these aspects will be revisited, by studying (i) Keulartz's
and (ii) Bürger's interventions.

(i) Keulartz offers an interesting position on Habermas's aesthetics.
In the first step of his argument he indicates that whereas the communicative relationship between artist and public has a significant
role to play in Habermas's *The Structural Transformation of the Public
Sphere* (formulated as the first phase of his aesthetics in this study),
it disappears in *The Theory of Communicative Action* (the second
phase of his aesthetics). The point is that the intimate link between
a concept such as 'equality' and the aesthetic-literary 'public sphere'
(in his early work) disappears in Habermas's later work on commu-

nicative reason, where aesthetics is interpreted as a model of production aesthetics that cancels the communicative space between
artist and public. The model of production aesthetics is, according to
Keulartz, steered by Habermas's theory of social evolution and cultural differentiation. (It is also linked, according to him, to certain
events in the 1960s, such as the aporias of orthodox Marxism, the
labour movement and the failure of Surrealism).[28] According to the
differentiation argument, metaphysical-substantive reason is replaced
by modern reason, which is divided into spheres that can be proce-
durally mediated only by means of cognitive-instrumental, moral-
practical and aesthetic-expressive rationality. Habermas writes: 'From
this point on, there are also internal histories of science, of moral and
legal theory, of art – not linear developments, to be sure, but learning processes nonetheless.'[29]

Habermas's theory of differentiation has, for Keulartz, two perspectives on reality: the outer world (divided into the objective world
of things and the social world of norms) and the inner world (the
subjective world of intentions and needs).[30] The point is that validity
claims in the inner world are presented not in the medium of discourse, but in an asymmetrical kind of therapeutic critique (which
implies sincerity of intentions) and aesthetic critique (authentic
needs that promote or inhibit a good life). Keulartz therefore asks
why the shift from a philosophy of consciousness to a philosophy of
intersubjective communication is not reflected in the inner world.[31]
Accordingly, the reconciliation offered by therapeutic and aesthetic
critiques is only possible on the basis of the reunion of subject and
object – a self-reflexive process in which consciousness enters into a
relationship with itself (a position that comes very close to the philosophy of consciousness of German Idealism).[32] Such a model of production aesthetics has, according to Keulartz, important implications
for art critique. Whereas the art critic (*Kunstrichter*) has a role equal
to the public in the model of the literary public sphere (in *The Structural Transformation of the Public Sphere*), he seems to have a different role (in the *Theory of Communicative Action*) when the critic must
open the public's eyes. This latter position is not one of intersubjective critique, but is more akin to contemplation, sympathy and
empathy – a situation in which the bond between the public and the
artist is disentangled. Here the critic loses his mediation role and
becomes part of the process of art production. According to
Keulartz, Habermas uses the concept of subjective genius and the
metaphor of birth to describe his position here.[33] '[T]he talented artist
could lend authentic expression to those experiences he had encoun-

tering his own de-centred subjectivity, detached from the constraints of routinized cognition and everyday action.'[34]

In the second step of his argument, Keulartz holds that whereas the communicative significance of art is excluded in Habermas's concept of inner world rationality, it is present in his discussion of mass culture. Habermas argues that the ideological grip of the culture industry on the subjective consciousness is overestimated, and that a blind eye is turned to the communicative infrastructure of the life-world of the receiver. If this aspect of Habermas's thinking (which is influenced by Benjamin) is taken seriously, according to Keulartz, then the production aesthetics of his 'aesthetic critique' should be supplemented by a reception aesthetics related to his view of mass culture – a move that corresponds to the paradigm shift from a philosophy of consciousness to communicative reason.[35] The challenge is thus, to transform the subject–object model of aesthetic critique into a subject–subject model of the culture industry. In reception aesthetics the communicative and dialogical relationship between creator or artist and public is central. The role of communication in reception aesthetics can be elaborated through questions such as: what attitude and manner of identification are expected of the reader/viewer/listener? What skills must he or she have to receive the work adequately? To what extent is a particular socio-historical public able to respond critically to an implied and intended reception? What happens if a particular work is not received adequately – in other words, if the implied and the real public overlap only partially? Does the artist tap his or her own resources as a basis for reception, or does he or she acknowledge the interests of the public in his or her creations? Which motives and considerations determine the nature and direction of the process of feedback? What are the roles of the market, art critique and art theory?[36]

In posing these questions, Keulartz is suggesting that the validity of art should no longer be restricted to the individual (of production aesthetics), but should be placed in a model of communicative interaction between creator and public. This is the context of reception aesthetics and the avant-garde. The avant-garde, according to Keulartz, plays a mediatory role between autonomy, on the one hand, and the variety of realistic and engaged schools, on the other. Such a view of art, wherein the aesthetic-expressive aspect is balanced by the cognitive and moral practical aspects, could lead to a renewed integration of Habermas's three moments of the evolutionarily divided reason.[37] It is at this point that Keulartz requests a more favourable interpretation of the avant-garde than *The Theory of Communicative*

*Action* (the second phase of Habermas's aesthetics) allows. The point is that realist and engaged schools of art produce communicative possibilities that show similarities with the model that Habermas depicted earlier in *The Structural Transformation of the Public Sphere* (the first phase of his aesthetics). In an attempt to be more concrete, Keulartz refers to contemporary literature with its experimentation with new subcultural or anti-cultural identities, in which the identification with women, servants, prostitutes, patients, fools and punks is creatively linked with discourses on women, gay and punk movements. In this sense it means a return to *The Structural Transformation of the Public Sphere*, where identification and rational discussion are interdependent. Literature serves in such a context as a medium for self-enlightenment about heterogeneous groups which are the victims of social discrimination. Kunneman and Keulartz describe this phenomenon, in a similar way to Honneth, as 'identity discussions' – where there is a struggle, under symmetrical, communicative circumstances, to agree on claims of sincerity and authenticity.

Kunneman proceeds that such identity claims form a unity of discursive and active elements. The experimentation with alternative forms of self-expression and experience is of central importance for arguments about the efficiency of the identity model through which self-experience and expression are structured.[38] This is a kind of aesthetic experience and learning that people gain in the sphere of discussion groups and identity discussions. By identifying with characters in novels and dramas, readers or viewers are able to experiment with particular identity formations and the interpretation of needs. It is thus possible to emphathize with feelings in a particular situation, and so be able to enter or break particular relationships. Such experiences can be discussed in public debates about the advantages and disadvantages of particular identity formations and interpretations of need. Against this background, Keulartz restates the argument that the replacement of production aesthetics in Habermas's work by a communicative idea of identity discussion (or a similar concept connected with reception aesthetics) could strengthen the focus on the aesthetic experiences of the public and their interdependent relationships.[39] In this way a paradigm shift from the philosophy of consciousness is performed in the sphere of art and culture, thereby fulfilling the conceptual promise of the first part of *The Structural Transformation of the Public Sphere*.

(ii) Whereas Keulartz refers to the avant-garde in passing, Peter Bürger has worked more specifically on this topic. The avant-garde, to him, refers in the first place to art as institution[40] – 'the productive and distributive apparatus and . . . the ideas about art that prevail at a given time and that determine the reception of works'.[41] According to this understanding, the aims of art are combined with the aesthetic norms of production and reception. A more specific meaning of the term refers to those ideas – for example, autonomous art – which govern the production and reception of artworks in bourgeois society. Bürger continues: '"the avant-garde movements" first made recognizable certain general categories of the work of art; the aesthetician must understand the development of art in bourgeois society.'[42] After this description of the 'autonomy of art', Bürger interprets it as an ideological category of civil society which disguises its actual historical evolution, when 'the relative dissociation of the work of art from the praxis of life in bourgeois society . . . becomes transformed into the (erroneous) idea that the work of art is totally independent of society'.[43] He traces this concept back to Kant and Schiller, for whom art does not serve any more as a cultic object of religion or a self-portrait of aristocratic society, but as a portrayal of bourgeois self-understanding that lies outside the praxis of life. In place of the collective production and reception of sacrosanct, royal art comes the individual production and reception of art. Finally, art's separation from life is brought to completion by aestheticism in the latter half of the nineteenth century. It is only with the twentieth-century avant-garde, according to Bürger, that the relationship between individual creation and collective reception is creatively problematized.[44]

With this reconstruction of the aesthetic sphere, Bürger develops a critique of autonomous art. His point is that autonomous artworks ignore the institutional framework in which they are embedded. Hence only one type of art is normative, while other forms, such as popular art and literary realism, are rejected. Bürger writes that '[t]he meaning of the break in the history of art that the historical avant-garde movements provoked does not consist in the destruction of art as an institution, but in the destruction of the possibility of positing aesthetic norms as valid ones'.[45] The avant-garde's criticism of the aestheticism of autonomous art is aimed at its social impotence. This, according to Bürger, is the case with Adorno's understanding of art, where autonomy determines the function of art – ideology critique is thus accomplished at the cost of functional analysis.[46] Consequently there is the danger that the socio-historical background of the artwork and its reception disappears. At this point Bürger defends the theoretical implications of the avant-garde wherein normative (value) analysis is replaced by functional analysis of the artwork in the changing art institution.[47] Bürger's concept of the avant-garde is further critically inclined towards Adorno's concept of aesthetic truth. This is due to the difficulty of distinguishing between the historical significance (*Sinn*) of art and its contemporary relevance (*Deutung, Gehalt*). In Bürger's alternative 'institutional sociological' and functional analysis, *Sinn* and *Deutung* are placed in a dialectical relationship. Such a sociologically informed understanding of art allows one, for example, to contextualize Goethe's drama in the contemporary literary institution. The interpretation of individual works thus becomes a *Bedeutungsproduktion* (production of meaning) that self-consciously presupposes a historical experience and a conception of literature different from those of Goethe and his time.

But Bürger acknowledges that the avant-garde attack on autonomy has limits. He questions the integration of art with the praxis of civil society, and the related issue of the phenomenon of the culture industry.[48] These issues are problematized by the post-avant-garde, which views art as a partially independent development from other institutions in civil society. It has, relatively speaking, a more independent role to play than the mere production and reception of mass culture. In this process autonomous art both affirms and critiques the society to which it belongs.[49] In short, this acknowledgement of the limits of the avant-garde places Bürger's concept of the post-avant-garde closer to Adorno's aesthetics. It is also in this context that Bürger comments on Habermas's aesthetics.[50] First, he finds Habermas's notion of the autonomous development of science, morality and art to be an inaccurate portrayal of the structural differences between these spheres. In Bürger's view, Habermas underestimates the power of modern instrumental reason in the process of the mediation between science and everyday life. 'While autonomous art carries with it the idea of its selftranscendence this cannot be said to be true of science in the same way.'[51] Bürger claims that Habermas's hope of an equal share for each of the mentioned spheres in a reintegrated rationalized life-world is unrealistic. Secondly, he argues that there is an ambivalence between the growing differentiation of separate value spheres in modernity, on the one hand, and the pursuit of reintegration in the life-world, on the other. 'In fully developed bourgeois society "autonomy" and "use" of art have increasingly come to oppose each other. They will not be so easily reconciled as Habermas's construction of modernity suggests.' Finally, there is the danger that autonomous art will overlook the semantic potential that stems from art's original expressive mimetic relation to nature. On this score Bürger finds Habermas's critique of the aestheticism of Surrealism and the avant-garde too harsh. 'Even the failure of the demand for sublation should not be regarded as a mistake without results. On the contrary. If it is possible today to think of free productivity for everyone, then it is certainly due to the fact that the avant-gardists questioned the legitimacy of the term "great art work".'[52]

In summary, Bürger shares certain critical views with Jay and Keulartz on Habermas's treatment of aesthetics. All of them find a lack of aesthetic experience in his model of rational differentiation. Bürger judges, from the perspective of the avant-garde, that the position of art in Habermas's differentiated model does not contribute to a liberated life praxis. All these critics of Habermas seem to indicate that art has a too restricted role in his model of differentiation, thus leading to a situation where it cannot be translated into communicative reason. For Bürger such a view of art ignores the reality of art as an institution. In the place of autonomous art, whether in the form of Adorno's or Habermas's qualified version, a great number of varying materials, styles and traditions are here to stay, Bürger claims. He writes: 'Whether this condition . . . still permits an aesthetic theory at all, in the sense in which aesthetic theory existed from Kant to Adorno, is questionable.'[53] Zuidervaart, on the other hand (as indicated in chapter 3), holds that the avant-garde's 'total onslaught' on autonomous art reveals, ironically, a more complex normativity – namely, art as a network of criticizable norms beyond autonomy.[54] Jay, for his part, asks whether the differentiation between the modern value spheres can be mediated in a non-colonizing manner, thereby averting the discredited dream of a perfect harmonious, rational totality. In short, how is reconciliation to be accomplished in the sphere of the life-world?[55] He restates the caution (also that of McCarthy and Ottmann) that a too sharp differentiation of cultural spheres will end in an animosity between humankind and nature – a point that Habermas seems to realize in the following remark: 'I do not regard the fully transparent society as an ideal, nor do I wish to suggest any other ideal.'[56] On the other hand, Habermas argues that communicative ethics cannot be equated with inorganic nature, because a naturalistic ethics can easily disintegrate into a discredited religious or metaphysical world-view. He therefore defends the view that a communicative non-colonizing interaction is possible between the differentiated spheres and the life-world. Exactly what such mediation should look like, though, especially where the cognitive and aesthetic approaches to nature contradict one another, as indicated in this section, is not clear.

## 5.4  Reading Adorno after Habermas

(i) Most critical positions against Habermas's rational formalism, as discussed in this chapter, suggest a revisiting of Adorno's aesthetics. Moreover, this study has been motivated by the following question: how is it possible that Habermas (as the most prominent member of the second generation of Critical Theorists) developed such a restricted concept of aesthetics as compared to Adorno (the most prominent member of the first generation)? It is in this context that Jay Bernstein and Wellmer, like (see (ii)), Whitebook, reopen the debate with Adorno's aesthetics – a move that implies a rereading of Adorno after Habermas.[57]

On the issue of the differentiation of the autonomous forms of discourse, Bernstein holds that by severing autonomous aesthetics from its mythic, religious, metaphysical and traditional aspects, the internal logic of art becomes damaged. The problem today is that art can only enter into a relationship with society by revoking its own standards of internal validity. Hence art must turns against its own autonomy and the processes of social differentiation. Bernstein writes: 'For Adorno, the cognitive import of the autonomous art is its testimony against differentiation, against formal reason, against modernity.'[58] Art thus offers an alternative to instrumental reason in the form that the particular is mediated by the universal nature of conceptual reason. Art is not only particular, it is also an attempt to establish a 'non-conceptual unity' of elements.[59] In both its universal and its particular moments, the appearance of art claims knowledge. Through aesthetic semblance the differentiation of reason (in terms of truth, normative correctness and expression) is bridged. In this sense art harbours for Adorno an archaic unity of logic and causality.[60] This point serves as a model for an alternative form of praxis; it gives shape to things in a manner that differs considerably from instrumental reason.[61]

Against this background, Bernstein argues that art is doubly excluded, from the conceptual understanding of theoretical reason and the intuitive nature of practical reason. Art answers only non-discursively. 'Art seeks to give an answer, but since that answer is mimetic rather than judgemental it is in a sense a non-answer. This accounts for art's becoming enigmatic.'[62] Art stresses the sensual, particular, a-conceptual nature of reality. Philosophy, on the other hand, describes the a-conceptual conceptually. This aporia leads to the dialectic of art and philosophy: art without philosophy is blind, and philosophy without art is empty. Closely related to this aporia, according to Bernstein, is the idea of truth content.[63] The point is that philosophy or argumentative reason cannot decide in isolation the validity or invalidity of art.[64] Philosophy may enhance one's understanding of artworks up to the point where their claims become clear, but beyond that one must return to the autonomous artwork itself. Bernstein thus underwrites Adorno's position that '[a]ctually, only what does not fit into this world is true'.[65] He portrays Adorno's position as one where the internal authenticity, truth and validity of works of art testify against universal and instrumental reason, and points to an alternative view of the truth concept.[66] In short, art articulates a meaning that is beyond meaning. This is, according to Bernstein, what is meant by the antinomy of art. He then positions Adorno's utopian, ecstatic aesthetics against Habermas's communicative alternative. The question is whether Adorno's idea of subjective reconciliation traps him within a philosophy of consciousness which underestimates the communicative possibilities of reception aesthetics.

The issue is: should the Adornian paradigm of mimetic reconciliation be replaced by Habermas's communicative model of dialogue and democratic intersubjectivity – 'socialization without repression'?[67] Bernstein responds by quoting two qualified statements by Adorno on autonomy: 'the process enacted by every art work – as a model for a kind of praxis wherein a collective subject is being constituted – has repercussions on society'. And, 'Enshrined in artistic objectification is a collective We. This We is not radically different from the external We of society. It is more like a residue of an actually existing society of the past. The fact that art addresses a collectivity is not a cardinal sin; it is corollary of the law of form.'[68] On this reading, Adorno is portrayed as being mindful of the capitalist reification of subjectivity and open to the solidary nature of substantive reason. Bernstein writes: 'The law of form in autonomous art addresses us because in it empirical form and logical form are not differentiated; a form that is quasi-empirical is precisely one which is not universal, hence if true and purposive such a form could only be our form, the form of the praxis of a substantially joined collectivity.'[69] With reference to the differences between the Adornian 'We' and the Habermasian notion of intersubjective communication, Bernstein challenges Habermas's differentiation between truth by normative correctness and aesthetic truthfulness. The point is that art's ability to reveal truth is thwarted here. In his Adornian alternative, Bernstein conceives of aesthetic rationality as a type of reason that presupposes critical solidarity – where the particular and the universal, empirical and conceptual forms, are reconciled, and where otherness and differentiation are accepted. To summarize, Bernstein describes Adorno's contribution, between modernity and post-modernity, as an attempt that implies not consensus or universal truth, but critical solidarity.[70] It is a perspective devoid of the elements of transparency, homogeneity, surplus and enlightened rationality.

(ii) Wellmer, for his part, positions himself in a *Kraftfeld* (field of tension) between Adorno and Habermas by considering the Adornian concepts of instrumental reason, aesthetic reconciliation and truth. Wellmer describes Adorno's mimetic alternative to instrumental reason as a trans-discursive philosophy – where both art and philosophy play a mimetic role which frustrates instrumental thinking. Mimesis functions in this context as a model of reconciliation, redemption, synthesis and peace. It refers to sensually communicative and expressive interaction between living beings. Through mimesis art and philosophy provide a clue to the 'redemption of the flesh', such that natural elements (inner and outer nature) are liberated from the violence of identity thinking. Mimesis can thus be described as a utopian combination of sensualism, on the one hand, and an eschatologically aesthetic reconciliation that acts as 'a preview of a reconciled relationship among people, things and natural beings', on the other.[71] Mimesis as reconciliation (and as synthesis and peace) in art and philosophy does not only destroy instrumental reason, it also unites the mimetic with a 'rational' moment. In contrast to identity thinking, art and philosophy thus achieve a synthesis that peacefully respects the particular. Wellmer links this aesthetic-philosophical understanding of reconciliation with Adorno's concept of truth. Important here is the aporetic relationship between art and philosophy, leaving each sphere with only partial access to truth. In art, truth emerges sensually, not discursively; it thus needs the conceptual and interpretive power of philosophy.[72] Philosophy's inability to conceptualize non-conceptual reality, however, leads to the 'blind immediacy' of aesthetic perception and the 'empty mediacy' of philosophical thinking. Only in combination are art and philosophy capable of articulating truth. Wellmer holds that such a combination involves two aspects of truth: namely, aesthetic truth (truth[1]) and objective philosophical truth (truth²).[73] Adorno judges truth[1] as a form, according to Wellmer, whereby aesthetic experience is transformed by philosophical insight. The unravelling of the truth content of a particular artwork is thus also an attempt to establish general truth.[74] Each artwork is thus seen as a Leibnizian monad, a unique reflection of reality. Removed from public communicative interaction, it is regarded as a model of aesthetic reconciliation and truth. Wellmer concludes that the actual function and import of a particular work are assimilated in a utopian generalization of 'true art' with little direct influence on the social and historical situation in which the artwork's truth content carries its meaning.[75]

At this point Wellmer develops the central aspects of Adorno's aesthetics – the critique against instrumental reason, mimetic reconciliation and truth – in a communicative direction.[76] Wellmer, like Habermas, accepts that aesthetic and instrumental rationality are part of the same historical development and differentiation of reason, which make it impossible to reverse this process by replacing instrumental rationality with aesthetic-expressive rationality. Such an attempt at social transformation reduces rationality to only one language game – aestheticism.[77] Habermas's communicative model of plural reason indicates, for Wellmer, openness between discourses in a highly differentiated society that goes beyond the idea of a substantive reason.[78] Wellmer thus develops Adorno's concept of aesthetic reconciliation in a communicative direction, where the subject–object paradigm of Adorno's philosophy of consciousness is replaced by the subject–subject paradigm of communicative action.[79] The utopian dimension of aesthetic reconciliation is thereby placed in the sphere of discursive reason. In this context the artwork is interpreted as a medium of communication (following Habermas's linguistic turn), and not as a model of reconciliation (Adorno and Bernstein). Wellmer writes:

> The aesthetic synthesis represented by the work of art, even if we concede to Adorno that it contains a *promesse du bonheur*, can hardly be understood as a model of dialogic relationship between individuals, who recognize each other in their individuality, as equals and as absolute others both at the same time. If beauty is a promise of happiness, of reconciliation with our internal and with external nature, the work of art would be a medium of this transcending experience rather than a model of reconciliation itself. For at least the moral 'synthesis' of dialogic relationship can only be mediated, but not brought to appearance by the aesthetic synthesis of the work of art. Even if, as Adorno stresses, the subject, which comes to speak in the work of art,

is a 'we' (and not the individual artist), this collective subject speaks with one voice, speaking to itself, as it were; i.e. the rules of 'synthesis' of this trans-subjective speech cannot possibly prefigure the open rules of a dialogue with many voices. Aesthetic synthesis is no possible model for a state of society free from repression.[80]

In a creative follow-up, Wellmer links this communicative view of art with Adorno's concept of aesthetic truth.[81] In this context Koppe's language of pragmatic differentiation between 'apophantic', 'moral-practical' and 'endeetic' truth is used – a differentiation that broadly corresponds to Habermas's distinction between cognitive-instrumental, moral-practical and aesthetic-expressive rationality.[82] Such a differentiated concept of truth offers, according to Wellmer, an advantage over Adorno's particular emphasis on the objective truth of art. In place of Adorno's integration of aesthetic validity (truth[1]) and objective truth (truth[2]) comes a more differentiated version. Wellmer writes:

> For Adorno, the two planes of analysing the concept of art on the one hand and appropriating the specific, concrete truth of art on the other coincide; and it is only because this is so that he is bound to conceive of aesthetic cognition as philosophical insight, and of the truth of art as philosophical truth. In this way it is the apophantic dimensions of the truth of art which ultimately comes to dominate the picture.[83]

Truth is thus ascribed to art metaphorically, in that aesthetic truth relates to the possible truth potential of an artwork, rather than its literal truth.[84] The *truth of art* is related to aesthetic discourse and aesthetic experience. If the disclosure of the work of art (truth potential) and its success (aesthetic validity) are disputed, aesthetic discourse is employed. Wellmer writes:

> Aesthetic discourse is the mediating instance between the apophantic metaphors . . . and questions of aesthetic rightness. The experience of participants, though, . . . can only be mobilized for discussion and transformed into arguments within the three dimensions of truth, truthfulness, and moral and practical rightness simultaneously. Both the truth-potential and the truth-claim of art can thus only be explained with recourse to the complex relationship of interdependency between the various dimensions of truth in the living experience of individuals, or in the formation and transformation of attitudes, modes of perception, and interpretations.[85]

It is interesting that although Wellmer offers a communicative transformation of Adorno's aesthetics, he also criticizes some elements in Habermas's model of rational differentiation. First, he notes the restriction of 'aesthetic rationality' to the subjective sphere in Habermas's philosophical project (a theme that has been mentioned with regularity in this chapter). Wellmer quite clearly judges the aesthetic sphere important for thinking about moral agency and individuation – an idea that draws on Adorno more than Habermas.[86] In this sense a flexible form of 'ego-identity' is defended, which extends the reflexive boundaries of subjectivity such that moral subjects are situated within a non-formalist framework. In such a model of the relationship between the cognitive and expressive spheres the following aspects are emphasized by Wellmer: the interrelatedness of validity spheres, the importance of interpretations and judgements of all kinds, and the need for a horizon where plural values and needs can become part of rational arguments and discourse ethics. Wellmer continues that such a position can be defended without falling back into a metaphysical view of reason and truth. Such an alternative implies the possibility of learning – that is, building ourselves up through judgements and exercises that force us to change rational perspectives. In this process the perspective of a reconciled world vanishes, allowing the present to be taken with its 'pathologies, irrationalities, psychological blocks and inhumanities which may be empirically observed'.[87] Wellmer thus develops a proposal that goes beyond an aporetical view of the other of reason (Adorno) or the scientific overtones of communicative reason (Habermas). In place of a scientistic rationality comes a fallibilistic, plural, and open concept of rationality.

In his mediation of Adorno's concerns with Habermas's communicative model, Wellmer constructs a less formalist view of rationality. Whereas Habermas's discourse ethics is overly linked to a cognitive model (wherein the core is a consensus theory of truth in the domain of rational discursiveness), Wellmer defends a fallibilist interpretation of truth.[88] The point is that rationality and communicative truth are not the same. Consensus theory cannot provide us with the principles of a universalizable discourse ethics. Wellmer opts, rather, for a model of universality that works negatively. When we encounter an exception, this difference reveals a tension. Interpretations (not prescriptions) of conflicting situations are the only possible path to the rightness of action. Consensus should be the result of valid choices, not both the starting point and the result. The basis of the norm rests mainly on the possibility of stressing arguments, which, in a way, would display an ethics of dissensus, rather than consensus. At this point Wellmer emphasizes the importance of the interpretation of the situation – and hence judgement.[89] Wellmer's proposal of justification and the application of judgement therefore open interesting possibilities. On his proposal, artworks are no longer generalized in a utopian way (Adorno) or reduced to the subjective sphere (Habermas). The challenge, rather, is to provide a creative reading of this tension. In the process he acknowledges that Adorno didn't deal with truth as pure correspondence of facts, or mere truth in an existential or pragmatic sense. There is, though, a dimension in his work that mediates between theoretical interpretations and social and historical situatedness, thereby emphasizing the importance of social consciousness for aesthetic truth and the necessity of opening aesthetics to critical testing, thus countering a rigid methodology.[90] Zuidervaart has formulated this point by stating that Adorno's complex genius is 'his refusal either to divorce aesthetic norms from a larger sociohistorical process or to accept whatever aesthetic norms have taken shape in the sociohistorical process'.[91] If this aspect of Adorno's aesthetics is accepted, the idea of a totalizing critique of reason can be replaced by a plural reconstruction of rationality. In bridging the gulf between aesthetic utopia and historical society, artworks function as a medium of intersubjective communication, as Wellmer has indicated, rather than as a model of utopian reconciliation.[92]

## 5.5   Critical summary

In the critical responses to the two phases of Habermas's aesthetics, a number of important issues have emerged in this chapter. First, Jay (and many of the other critics mentioned in this chapter) mentioned the problematic status of aesthetics in Habermas's model of rational differentiation. The point here is the restriction of aesthetic validity claims to subjective experiences. This implies that only subjective aesthetic experience has the potential to disclose truth in the complexity of lived experiences. Although Habermas acknowledges that such experience could potentially affect the cognitive and moral dimensions of life, he still translates aesthetics into a formal understanding of linguistic intersubjectivity. The implication of such a move (as Keulartz indicates) is that the 'truth of art' is restricted to the subjective judgement of the author or creator in production aesthetics. Jay, Foucault and Whitebook also add their critical voices against the limitation of rationality to the sphere of formal discourse. They all find the absence of a sufficient mediation between the pre-discursive horizons of aesthetic judgement, taste, inner and outer nature, on the one hand, and the formal argumentation of discursive reason, on the other, to be a major deficiency in Habermas's proposal.

Secondly, and related to the previous point, Habermas's formal view of language has been criticized. The point of contention is that 'normal' or everyday language use functions for Habermas as the primary mechanism of social integration in modernity. Everyday language is thus the original mode of language use, leaving other uses of language – such as figurative, symbolic and strategic modes of language use – parasitic on it. This implies that we can understand poetic language use only because we already understand normal language use. Moreover, those speech-acts that function primarily to create or disclose do not reach everyday understanding (*Verständigung*). This point (which Habermas makes against Derrida, as indicated in the previous chapter) entails that the generalization of the rhetorical and poetic power of language (i.e. language aestheticization) does not consider adequately the strained polarity between the poetic and world-disclosing function of language, on the one hand, and the prosaic inner-world function of language, on the other. But it is an open question whether neglecting the world-disclosing dimensions of linguistic activity impoverishes the notion of communicative action and reason. In the next chapter I will argue that it is this issue that prevents Habermas from assigning to aesthetics a reasonable role in his argumentative-communicative architectonics.

In the third place, all the perspectives offered in this chapter are, in their respective ways, critical of Habermas's communicative model of rational differentiation. In this connection, the following questions emerge: how does communicative reason mediate between the differentiated modern value spheres of cognitive, moral and aesthetic reason? How communicatively open are these spheres to one another? Habermas seems to suggest that the aesthetic sphere is part of a dialectic of the Enlightenment wherein modern aesthetic discourse should not be reduced to the autonomous beautiful, on the one hand, or the de-differentiated sublime, on the other. The critical point, though, is that if aesthetic experience is used to shed light on individual problems, situations and the striving for solidarity, then aesthetics is not an autonomous language game, but part of everyday communicative practice. In this way, evaluative language use and interpretation of needs are not only renewed, but the way in which they are related to cognitive and normative approaches is also transformed. Modern art thus contains a utopia, to the extent that the mimetic forces that are hidden in works of art are extracted in a

balanced, non-twisted everyday intersubjectivity.[93] For critical interlocutors like Jay, Whitebook, Keulartz, Bürger and Jay Bernstein, it is
not clear what such a balanced intersubjectivity entails. The question
is whether there is still a constructive role for art if the aesthetic
sphere is translated into the formal language of argumentative intersubjectivity.[94] It is in this context that Bürger questions Habermas's
understanding of autonomous and popular art and offers his alternative of the post-avant-garde. The point here is also the ambiguity of
Habermas regarding certain standards in aesthetics (autonomous art)
and his position on popular art.

In his Benjamin essay, for example, Habermas criticizes the indi-
vidualizing dimensions of autonomous art by pointing to the collective reception forms of architecture, popular art and music. In this
sense disinterested contemplation, artistic autonomy and absolute
artistic normativity clash with the reality of popular art.[95] On the
other hand, Habermas argues that the false *Aufhebung* of art in life
and the rational in the natural, both being forms of aestheticism,
make the mediation between art and life impossible. In short, while
it is possible to accept the historical differentiation between aesthetic
and instrumental rationality as irreversible, it is also legitimate to ask
whether Habermas's communicative alternative of popular art forms
succeeds. This is where Bernstein and Wellmer's contributions are
important. Whereas Bernstein defends a form of Adornian aesthetic
reason that honours the autonomy of art, Wellmer directs the model
of rational differentiation in the direction of a model of plural rationalities. Wellmer thereby proposes an alternative that goes beyond
Adorno's aestheticization of truth and Habermas's cognitively
informed concept of truth – an alternative that will be further
explored in the next chapter in terms of the rational-discursive and
world-disclosing dimensions of language.

# 6

# The Reciprocity of World Disclosure and Discursive Language

Following on the investigation of the two phases of Habermas's aesthetics (chapters 1–4) and the critical points raised in the previous chapter, this chapter will attempt to offer an alternative to the fate of aesthetics in his work. I will start with Heidegger's contribution of aesthetics as world disclosure in the first section.[1] This interpretation serves as a kind of challenge to Habermas's presentation of Heidegger and Derrida in *The Philosophical Discourse of Modernity* (see chapter 4), without being fully Heideggerian or Derridean. The implications of this qualification will be explored by providing a critical discussion of Heidegger's concept of world disclosure (especially after his *Kehre* – the shift in his later career). It is against this background that Habermas's communicative alternative (with its aesthetic implications) will be reintroduced as a critical counter to Heidegger's version of world disclosure (section 6.2). But Habermas's tendency to neutralize the subversive qualities of novel disclosures by moving these disclosures to the edges of our self-understanding and social practices will be challenged. The argument is that world disclosure articulates a dimension of experience *and a kind of reason* that does not reduce philosophy to social theory and thus serves as a corrective to an over-specialized conception of Critical Theory. Hence it is asked whether there is not a way beyond Heidegger and Habermas by examining the complementarities of world disclosure and rational discursiveness. This question is pursued through a proposal of art as communicative experience (section 6.3). Finally, this proposal is linked to a discussion of the political and aesthetic implications of world disclosure (section 6.4). It is suggested that, far from being irrational and anti-democratic, world disclosure could contribute to a deeper understanding of the plural nature of democracy in our times.

I should first provide some pointers regarding how the concept of world disclosure will be used in this chapter. World disclosure is a process that occurs at two levels. World disclosure 1 refers to the disclosure of an already interpreted, symbolically structured world – that is, the world within which we always already find ourselves. It is a world that shapes us so that we see and question reality through its habitual categories and presupposed categories – a position that Heidegger defends in *Being and Time*. World disclosure 2, on the other hand, refers as much to the disclosure and finding of new horizons of meaning as to the disclosure of previously hidden or unthematized dimensions of meaning. World disclosure thus describes a meaning-creating process where in innovative thinking is capable of making, unmaking and remaking worlds.[2] Poetic language, for example, discloses the world to us in new ways, when novel, successful metaphors connect disparate experiences or objects in a way that breaks old patterns and illuminates new possibilities of seeing, thinking or speaking.[3] This is the definition that Heidegger uses after his *Kehre*. According to Kompridis, world disclosure 2 can produce either unifying or decentring effects.[4] He mentions the work of Taylor, Dreyfus and Gadamer as being concerned with weaving a web that holds our language, social practices and world-views together; whereas Rorty, Castoriades and Derrida seek to distance us from existing patterns of interpretation by pushing us to enlarge and transform our self-understanding and social action. Thus there are similarities with Adorno's emphasis on the decentring power of novel works of art – their power to dishabituate us from moving within already existing horizons of meaning. Heidegger's position on this issue is ambiguous, however. On the one hand, he unifies the heterogeneous aspects of our pre-understanding of the world – by drawing together what is distant into a common space and what is near. On the other hand, like Adorno he decentres this common space in order to create alternative spaces, to make the common uncommon, and to escape from the bonds that bind us.[5]

## 6.1  Truth as aesthetic world disclosure: Heidegger

In *Being and Time*, Heidegger describes language as a medium that pre-emptively prejudices everything occurring in the world. An important epistemological implication of this view is that language cannot revise itself on the basis of the growth of knowledge or learning processes – for language as the 'house of Being' discloses the world in which we think, classify and judge.[6] In the idiom of a philosophy of history, language is a contingent, fateful *Seinsgeschehen* ('Being-happening') into which we are thrown. In *Being and Time* every act of classification by human beings (*seienden*) in the public sphere is possible only on the basis of 'the prior projection of the Being-constitution'.[7] World disclosure thus determines a priori what 'things are', and how they should be understood, thereby 'immunizing' itself against any inner-worldly experience.[8] In his early work Heidegger formulates the concept of truth as disclosure in such a way that it is no longer dependent on either traditional metaphysical or subject-centred foundations. In its place, he offers his analysis of human existence, *Dasein*, which is not the same as the autonomous individual subject and relates to 'being in the world'. Many commentators have pointed out that although subjects still play an epistemological and communicative role in Heidegger's *Being and Time*, the position changes after his *Kehre*, when world disclosure is radically interpreted as an endowment of truth.[9] According to this radicalized version of world disclosure (i.e. world disclosure 2), the subject's contribution to truth and knowledge, as standard of all beings, is downplayed, while the role of Being is highlighted.[10] The traditional assignment of truth to propositional statements in normal language use thus becomes less important.[11]

After his *Kehre*, Heidegger argues, quite differently from Habermas, that a thing appears only within an openness that is not the result of the correspondence of mind and matter, but one that comes before, as a domain of relatedness (*Verhältnis*).[12] In other words, all working, action and calculation remain within an open region in which *Dasein* (beings) can properly take their stand and become capable of being said. The correctness (truth) of statements becomes possible only through openness of *Verhalten* (comportment). Heidegger continues that Western thinking, from its origins, interprets this open region as *aletheia* (unconcealed). He writes: 'If we translate *aletheia* as "unconcealment" rather than "truth", this translation is not merely more literal, it contains the directive to rethink the ordinary concept of truth in the sense of the correctness of statements and to think it back to that still uncomprehended disclosedness and disclosure of beings.'[13] The openness, or open region, where truth and the disclosure of beings take place, is also the ground of freedom, for Heidegger, where man does not 'possess' freedom as a property. Freedom (*ek-sistent* and disclosive *Da-sein*) rather possesses man – a view with interesting implications.[14] The first implication of the open region, as Heidegger argued in various studies after *Being and Time* (and more specifically in his essay entitled 'The origin of the work of art'), is the establishment of the relationship between truth-as-disclosure and aesthetics.[15] In this process aesthetic experience becomes the model of the encounter with the truth of Being – an ontological move that disallows any secular or anthropocentric approaches. In place of critical commentary come responsive gestures.[16] In Heidegger's essay, art is prior to the artist and artwork.[17] The artwork opens up Being.

This opening up or disclosure of a world – that is, the truth of beings – happens in the artwork, and it is kept abidingly in place.[18] For Heidegger the world is never an object that stands before us. In his language, 'the world worlds' and is more fully in being than the perceptible realm in which we believe ourselves to be at home. In the disclosure of the world, all things gain their lingering and hastening, their remoteness and nearness, their scope and limit. True to his sensitivity to etymology Heidegger distinguishes *world* (as described) from *earth* (that which comes forth and shelters). The setting up of a world and the setting forth of earth are two essential features of the work-being of the artwork.[19] The world wants to disclose itself, so in resting upon earth it strives to surmount it. The earth, however, as sheltering and self-closing (*Sich-verschliessende*), always tends to draw the world into itself and keep it there.[20] Truth (*aletheia*) only emerges, therefore, as the rupture between disclosure and closure – the tension between world and earth.[21] In an interesting move, Heidegger broadens the truth character of art to the scientific and social spheres. Science here is not an original happening of truth, but the cultivation of a domain of truth already opened by art.[22] Similarly, the political domain is an opening or site where 'words, things, and deeds come into a definite historical arrangement', and thereby constitute a world. It is at this level that the practices and institutions of the political world and modern democracy are questioned and tested. In this sense an 'other politics' is possible only on the basis of a rearrangement of words, things and deeds. It is important to note that such a view of politics stems from an understanding of action that goes beyond a rational concept of action and the will.[23] Science and politics are thus only possible via world disclosure and by being open to the other of thinking and social action. In short, Heidegger's antipathy towards the public sphere (and democracy) is strongly articulated through (a) the material and historical a priori and (b) the normative character (unrevisability) of world disclosure – both being incommensurable with other projections.[24] It is quite understandable that such a provocative formulation of world disclosure (and its aesthetic and political implications) is subject to criticism. I will critique it with reference to (i) the status of validity claims; (ii) the aestheticization of truth; (iii) Heidegger's attributive use of language and holism; and (iv) the implications of his thinking for the public sphere and politics.

(i) From the perspective of a formal language theory (dealing with the issues of truth or rightness), the problem is that the validity claims of propositional truth are made secondary in relation to Heidegger's pragmatical validity through world disclosure.[25] The problem is intensified through Heidegger's insistence that truth (as disclosure) is plural – a position that disallows any criterion for deciding between different competing assertions, leading to a situation where there are no resources to establish that something is true-in-itself and not just true-in-some-world. Bohman, for example, argues in Habermasian fashion that learning requires what Heidegger seems to deny: the cognitive capacity to consider various points of view with the aim of comparing and co-ordinating them.[26] A one-to-one relation between world disclosure and truth is thus questioned. Seel asserts that Heidegger's imaginative use of disclosure should be kept semantically in the middle of a process of 'finding' a world (world disclosure 1) and 'making' a world (world disclosure 2). By levelling the distinction between disclosing and justifying the world, Heidegger ontologizes truth (as disclosure) beyond *Dasein*'s grasp. Not even a consideration of scientific paradigms is helpful here, because the community is unable to test in what respect assertions or events uncover or conceal things.[27] Both Bohman and Seel seem to suggest that the connection between world disclosure and truth needs to be made more modestly and less immediately. Disclosure is misguided when it is reduced to truth; conversely, the idea of truth is misguided when it is reduced to disclosure.[28]

(ii) Related to the problematic merging of truth and world disclosure is Heidegger's aestheticization of truth – a point that Habermas also makes in his *Philosophical Discourse of Modernity* (as discussed in chapter 4). In his essay on the origin of art, Heidegger even goes so far as to describe all forms of disclosure (artistic, linguistic, political and scientific) as equal and immediate manifestations of one and the same truth. In this process art does not represent a form of truth, it is rather *the* truth through disclosure. The problem is that such a strong aesthetic position, which has some similarities with Adorno's concept of the truth content of art (see chapters 2 and 5), severs all connections between the truth of art and other forms of reason. This argument, according to Kompridis, relies on a specific reading of Hegel's analysis of classical art as 'aesthetics of truth' (in his *Lectures on Aesthetics*). In an attempt to revisit Hegel's position on classical art, Heidegger asks: is art still an essential and necessary way in which truth happens, one that is decisive for our historical existence, or is art no longer of this character? The difference between Heidegger and Hegel seems to be that Heidegger wants to answer this question positively, whereas Hegel claims that classical Greek art was the first and last time that the world was truthfully disclosed by art – hence Hegel's statement that art no longer counts for us (moderns) as the highest manner in which truth is obtained.[29] The critical issue here is that Heidegger's claim that a work of art can found (*stiften*) a world goes too far. It goes too far, for some of his critics (including Habermas), because what art 'founds' cannot unburden or replace the demand for evaluation and justification.[30]

(iii) The absence of a need for evaluation in Heidegger's concept of language is, according to Lafont, the result of his debt to a German tradition of language (Hamann, Herder and Humboldt) which criticizes language as an instrument and defends the constitutive role of language in the world.[31] Humboldt, for example, excludes any possibility of a relation of pure designation (*Bezeichnung*) between a name and its object – based on the view that humans encounter objects in the way in which language leads them to them. Lafont describes such a position as a hypostatization of language – where language prejudices experience to such an extent that the assumption of a relatively language-independent objective world, which forms the basis of the intuition of truth, disappears.[32] She continues that such a 'holistic theory of meaning', which she connects with an 'intensionalistic theory of reference', has the following relativistic epistemological consequences: the transcendental unity of the philosophy of consciousness is split into the particular world-views or world disclosures of the various historical languages; reference and truth become language-immanent dimensions, and are thus relativized in their validity to the different linguistic world-views; and finally, these world-views are prejudiced over against internal learning processes. Lafont therefore holds that this perspective on language (which she also describes as the attributive use of language), like the conception of 'language as instrument', leads to a kind of epistemological reductionism.[33] As an alternative she suggests that the world-disclosing and intentionalistic dimension of language should be balanced by the referential (or designative) function of language – an idea she gets from Donnellan's differentiation between the attributive and the referential uses of language.[34] The point here is that Heidegger assimilates the attributive and referential uses of language, privileging the former.

Lafont defends the position that the referential function of language must transcend specific historical languages. The intimate link between speaking and learning subjects can thus only be re-established on the basis of an understanding of the world-disclosing (attributive) as well as the referential function of language, which should be balanced and not pre-judged from an 'idealistic point of view'.[35] (The interesting question is how Lafont would deal with the debate between Habermas and Derrida. Is Habermas's position one of referential, and Derrida's of attributive language use?). Lafont's criticism of attributive language can also be linked to holism. Heidegger is well known for his frequent reference to the unifying or holistic power of world disclosure, its power to centre a world, to simultaneously animate the nearest and most distant elements – whether they are Van Gogh's pair of 'peasants' shoes' or farm life itself. This is the phenomenon wherein 'the worlds world only as wholes'. Heidegger's critique of modernity, as an epoch in which the world is *de-worlded*, is based on this unyielding holism. Although Heidegger also aims to redeem forms of cognition which do not objectify or manipulate 'the thing' out of its native context, one could ask: should the network of holistic interrelations be so tightly structured? Although there is a need to uncover an undifferentiated idea of wholeness in a disenchanted modern world, such an approach could be seen as incompatible with – even intolerant of – democratic forms of life among citizens.[36] There is the danger that such a defence of holism could become separated from other modes of cognizing and acting, such as judging, arguing, reflecting, testing, experimenting and objectifying. It is thus an open question whether the capacity for world disclosure and the capacity for reason giving are not mutual. This implies that the 'messy process' of justification and criticism cannot be avoided – with profound implications for the public sphere.[37]

(iv) Heidegger's antipathy to the public sphere, by contrast with Habermas, is well known. Heidegger criticizes the everyday drone of contending voices that utilize language only as a 'tool' for mediating claims and actions, and not as the highest mode of participating in Being. Against this thoughtless willing and wanting of everyday life, he sets his version of authentic thinking, which is particularly reluctant to develop conceptual resources that might be useful for every-day ethics and politics. White quite correctly holds that Heidegger's conceptualization of action does not allow a satisfactory compre-hension of the normative tension and interconnection between actors in social and political life. Any emphasis on participants in a dialogue, on something like the I–Thou relation, for example, merely rein-forces, for Heidegger, the disease of everyday subjectivity. Conse-quently, Heidegger has often been charged with advocating a mode of 'mysticism' that merely opens the space for the persistence of anti-democratic sentiments and a 'diffuse readiness to obey'. There is a sense of a responsibility to act that Heidegger, according to White, misses. The consequence of this argument is that such an under-standing of action cannot serve as the basis of a non-authoritarian, democratic approach to politics.[38] Although some commentators have argued that Heidegger's later work provides the basis for a non-authoritarian, postmodern praxis, White's argument remains plausible.[39]

White continues that a praxis or politics that is open to the dis-closure of the other could easily be separated from the discourse about the conventions of everyday patterns of involvement in the public sphere. In this regard Heidegger works with a one-dimensional perspective, in which the acting and normative dimensions of poli-tics are neglected. Can one have a type of politics attuned to making present through disclosure yet not able to initiate a new order of presence? As an alternative, White contends that laws are not per-manently moored in order to make present; they arise, rather, from continually renewed deliberations that carry with them a conscious-ness of the conventionality, fallibility, precariousness and revisability of all political arrangements. Such an approach to a practice of laws, interestingly, stays close to Heidegger's political openness to realign-ing words, things and deeds. In short, there is nothing wrong with describing radical democracy as being tied to the absence of meta-physically grounded principles. But, as White indicates, there is a real difference between such a position and the further implication that such a politics has, as its guiding spirit, action without any guiding principles or conventions.[40]

## 6.2   Truth as rational discursiveness: Habermas

Although Habermas was influenced by Heidegger in his early philosophical career (his doctorate on Schelling's transcendental reconciliation between nature and spirit, for example, stands in the tradition of Jewish and Christian mysticism, as well as a Heideggerian-informed critique of Cartesian dualism[41]), Habermas broke with the Heideggerian tradition when his *Introduction to Metaphysics* (1935) was republished after the war (see section 1.1). It was incomprehensible to Habermas at that time that Heidegger could treat the political and social circumstances of the thirties so uncritically.[42] This, coupled with his interest in the Frankfurt School, persuaded him that the spiritual alienation of the modern era is rather of a social than an ontological nature. It is at this stage of Habermas's career that his studies turned towards a study of the complex trajectory of modern reason and its relation to the public sphere. From that moment on, the guiding motives of his work were a theory of modernity – that is, a reflection on the pathology of modernity from the possible 'viewpoint of the realization . . . of reason in history'.[43] It has already been indicated (in chapter 2) how Habermas's intellectual project can be interpreted as a return to one of the positions of the first generation of Critical Theorists (the outer circle) – the revival of a critical, communicative foundation of social reason in a programme of interdisciplinary social research that guards against the *cul de sac* of a concept of instrumental rationality, on the one hand, and Heidegger's passive awaiting of the disclosure of aesthetic truth after his *Kehre*, on the other.

Habermas's position on world disclosure can be studied by placing it in the context of the major aspects of his theory of communicative reason (with its implications for the second phase of his aesthetics). Habermas's *Theory of Communicative Action* is in many ways the result of his intense disagreement with Heidegger (and Adorno). Without a full discussion of Habermas's argument (as was provided in chapter 3), the following aspects can be noted here. Habermas argues, in the first place, against a philosophy of consciousness – the monological image of a subject-centred mind with a related model of strategic action that is determined by a one-world ontology of objectivity. Habermas's problem with this is that only a model of cognitive-instrumental rationality is available here to judge the 'truth', 'effectiveness' and rationality of action. His alternative to a philosophy of consciousness (which he links with Heidegger and Adorno) is the concept of communicative reason (and action), where subjects are no longer defined as *solus ipse* dealing with the world objectively and instrumentally. Communicative action is modelled not on the polarity of subject and object, but on the intersubjective and dialogical reciprocity of subject and subject.[44] Communicative action is also based on the view that participants have developed a decentred view of the world – such that they have learned to take objective, norm-conformative and expressive orientations towards the objective, social and subjective worlds. In this manner it is also performatively possible, according to Habermas, to make different validity claims as regards different worlds. These dimensions of validity (with their respective standards of truth and falsity and modes of justification) open a differentiated view of rationality. Communicative action is therefore applicable where a speaker performs a discursive offer or speech-act, which can be accepted or rejected by (a) participant(s).[45]

Habermas's defence of communicative reason, as explained, is quite forthright about communicative rationality as the 'consensus bringing force of argumentative speech'.[46] His sociological distinction between the modern cultural spheres of science, law and art also holds that the conflicts in the life-world can only be addressed via the rational reciprocity of arguments. Against this background the obligation to reach agreement is in the first place clearly not a moral (or expressive-aesthetic) one, but a rational-discursive one. In terms of the criticism in the previous chapter (and the remarks on world disclosure in the previous section), it is possible to ask whether Habermas's strong position on the rationality of argument giving and his associated consensus theory of truth leave any room for the world disclosing dimension of aesthetic rationality. His emphasis on the rational-discursive dimension of reason is clearly un-Heideggerian. Whereas the early Heidegger's concept of world disclosure 1 still depends, according to Habermas, on the activity of responsible subjects, his *Kehre* inaugurates an independent entity that regulates 'the grammatical transformation of linguistic worldviews'.[47] World disclosure 2 thus determines the conditions of history, overriding the transforming capacity of social actors. By surrendering the subject to Being, Heidegger creates, according to Habermas, a form of heteronomy wherein validity and normativity become unspecified in the poetic transcendence of propositional truth and conceptual thinking. For Habermas, such a position underplays the autonomy of human thinking and action and the existential concept of freedom. The empirical and normative dimensions of the social sciences' critique of metaphysics are lost to the poetic thinking of the philosopher who awaits the return of being.[48]

In his alternative, Habermas holds that one can be situated within a holistically structured world of meaning and still use its enabling conditions to achieve relative autonomy via reflectively directed speaking and acting. Individuals' ability to raise and contest validity claims initiates learning processes that retroactively alter the previous understanding of the world. In short, Habermas replaces Heidegger's asymmetry between being and beings with symmetry between world disclosure 1 and processes of intersubjective learning.[49] Habermas's position regarding world disclosure 2 can, for its part, be explained by revisiting his debate with Derrida. In this debate Habermas argues against an aestheticization of language (see chapter 4) that does not acknowledge the strained polarity between the poetic and world-disclosing functions of literature, on the one hand, and the prosaic (argument-giving) inner-worldly function of language, on the other. Such an aestheticization of language cannot account for the fact that it is everyday communication that makes learning processes possible – each with its own independent logic that transcends local limitations. Habermas continues that his position curtails rhetoric polysemy and promotes judgements in the light of criticizable validity claims. Derrida (like Heidegger), on the other side, neglects mutual understanding with regard to the objective, social or subjective worlds. The problem with Derrida (and Heidegger) is that they level the world-disclosing dimension of art and literature with philosophy.[50] In his alternative, Habermas argues that philosophy and literary criticism are intimately linked to the universality of the sciences. Like other specialized discourses, such as science, law, morality, economics and political science, they make use of illuminating metaphors only if they satisfy the special purposes of problem solving. In all these cases the literary dimensions of language use are secondary to the distinct forms of argumentation. In short, if the problem-solving nature of philosophy is levelled with literature, it becomes unproductive.[51]

Habermas's position can also be critically challenged from different perspectives. In the first place, his alternative confines world disclosure 2 to the realm of art and aesthetic experience. Although it undoubtedly curbs the excesses of Heidegger's ontological holism, one could argue that Habermas draws too strong a conceptual boundary between the capacity for disclosure as manifested in art and literature, on the one hand, and the capacity for argumentative learning processes of science, law and morality, on the other. It is therefore noteworthy that Heidegger's postulation of an opposition between the ontological capacity to disclose a world and the normative capacity to give reasons is repeated in Habermas's case. Against this background it is not possible for Habermas to interpret the relationship between world disclosure 1 and world disclosure 2 in a reciprocal manner. Habermas's insistence on the exclusive rationality of world disclosure 1 raises the following questions: what happens when arguments fail and the communicative exchange of reasons break down? What happens when the interpretation of our problems continually becomes blocked and stagnates, because the vocabulary in which they are framed is semantically overburdened or exhausted? Do we stop learning, or must we await the next disclosure of being? These questions indicate that Habermas's model of communicative reason and his identification of processes of intersubjective learning with reason-giving practices of argumentation and problem solving (with its aesthetic implications) need to be critically revisited.[52]

Secondly, one of the main aesthetic problems with Habermas's model of communicative reason is that the validity claims of propositional truth and normative rightness are conceptually linked to the idea of universal agreement. This assumption is based on certain forms of argumentation: namely, theoretical discourses (i.e. claims to propositional, empirical and theoretical truth) and practical discourses (i.e. claims to moral validity). Aesthetic validity claims, by contrast, remain bound to particular local contexts, and are valid, if at all, only for those in a particular space and time. Although Habermas recognizes the limitations of this position, he has not attempted to change the relationship between the validity claims of aesthetic works and the sphere of everyday communicative action. Yet this position leads to an overly narrow conception of communicative action, in that aesthetic criticism has no role to play in the idea of universal agreement.[53] Is there an alternative to this position? In the previous chapter, I argued that one encounters serious problems if one restricts aesthetic experiences to claims about subjective sincerity (Jay and Keulartz). If the disclosive potential of aesthetic truth is released, on the other hand, it will not only affect cognitive, moral and expressive dimensions; it will also transform the relationship between them and the self. The point has been made that opening a perspective on some aspect of human or personal situations implies that the artwork's 'truth potential' must be experienced before its validity can be assessed. Aesthetic validity claims are thus justified by reference to the subjective experience of those affected, and cannot be justified directly by reference to facts, theories and arguments – a move that restricts the rationality of 'aesthetic discourse'.

Thirdly, although Habermas's view of aesthetic validity claims may counter exaggerated accounts of meaning-creating innovation, it does so negatively. This contributes to a situation in which Habermas offers no positive account of semantic innovation and the creative change of meaning. Heidegger and Derrida argue in a discursive manner, on the other hand, that the roles played by world-disclosing language are essential to our intellectual and moral progress.[54] Although Heidegger's (and Derrida's) approach may overstate the role of world disclosure 2, it nevertheless teaches us that any theory of rationality that fails to incorporate a positive account of novel experience and creative meaning change is inadequate. By evaluating meaning-creating innovation only, Habermas's procedural model of rationality discards the rationality of meaning-creating innovation. Habermas considers only the rationality of validity-orientated speech and action (the rationality of reason giving), not the rationality associated with disclosing different horizons of meaning. It is at this point that Wellmer's suggestion of a plurality of rationalities becomes relevant. Wellmer defends a concept of reason that does not reduce aesthetics to the subjective sphere; but he allows it a role similar to those of the cognitive and moral spheres. His proposal thus clears the field for the reflexive possibility of thinking about moral subjects in a non-abstract, non-formal manner. By stressing the interrelatedness of validity spheres, Wellmer highlights the importance of all kinds of interpretations and judgements and argues for a horizon in which plural values and needs can become part of rational arguments and discourse ethics.[55] Such a creative reading of world disclosure 2 offers an interesting alternative to the fate of aesthetics in Habermas's work.

Habermas's position regarding communicative reason and the aesthetic implications of world disclosure is closely connected with his understanding of the public sphere and democracy. Habermas holds that public institutions, such as constitutions, provide the means whereby actors are able to maintain, in a historically new way, a collective sense of 'validity' and 'solidarity' which are not possible in traditional institutions.[56] In this sense, communicative reason goes beyond the strong notion of subjectivity that both liberals and communitarians share, by mediating (intersubjectively) between private and public interests. Politically speaking, Habermas translates communicative reason into the language of a differentiated 'network' of communicative arrangements that are discursively open for public opinion and will formation. Basic individual rights provide the conditions under which the forms of communication necessary for a politically autonomous constitution of law can be institutionalized. Such a 'discursive' conception of democracy attempts to tie legitimacy more closely to the quality of deliberation in political processes. Discursive processes, from the most informal to the formal, maintain a sense of validity and solidarity among a 'constitutional community', and allow the law to be structured, not just by the systematic control of the autonomous expansion of 'administrative power', but also by needs arising from the life-world of actors. The point is that a demo-cratic constitutional state is only functioning well when it constantly and continuously 'translates' communicative power into administra-tive power.[57]

For Habermas the concept of democracy is closely related to an understanding of a differentiated state wherein a multiplicity of sites of deliberation and decision making is broadly warranted by com-municative rationality. In this respect Habermas puts greater empha-sis than Heidegger on the conventions of everyday involvement in the public sphere. This position also allows room for world disclo-sure 1. On the other hand, there is little room for a type of politics of world disclosure 2 in Habermas's normative understanding of poli-tics and democracy. Deliberative or discursive democracy requires, for Habermas, a continual and variegated 'interplay' between public spheres emerging across civil society and a broad spectrum of formal political institutions. Against this background, the liberal model neglects, according to him, the need for a social solidarity obtainable by the radicalization of public communication processes, while the communitarian model seeks to constitute such solidarity around notions of community that are too thick.[58] It is clear that Habermas's take on democracy stays close to the theoretical implications of his model of communicative rationality and the obligation to reach con-sensus. The interesting issue, though, is whether this formal model leads to an adequate understanding of democracy. In other words, is there the space for novel disclosures in Habermas's concept of politics, given the restricted place for aesthetic experience in his model of rational differentiation?

## 6.3  The road beyond: art as
## communicative experience

It has been argued (in the previous two sections) that Heidegger's concept of world disclosure and Habermas's concept of rational dis-cursiveness both have shortcomings. In this section I will explore a way beyond Heidegger and Habermas by considering the history of aesthetics (Hegel, Kant and Dewey) briefly, and by taking Wellmer's communicative redirection of Habermas's project (as discussed in the previous chapter) one step further. If one studies Habermas's position with respect to Hegel and Kant's aesthetics, one finds that although he invokes the Kantian differentiation between spheres of reason, he associates the aesthetic with subjective expressiveness. In this respect Habermas stays close to Hegel by keeping aesthetics under the watchful eye of reason – whereas for Hegel it is absolute subjective reason, for Habermas it is communicative reason based on the presentation of arguments. Kant, on the other hand, takes a more radical position than Hegel with regard to aesthetics. In his *Critique of Judgment* aesthetics does not conform to the spheres of science or morality, but has a rationality of its own. Kant therefore cannot reconcile aesthetics with the other spheres so easily as Hegel.[59] This insight is of great importance to thinkers such as Nietzsche, Heidegger and Adorno. But, at the same time, it runs the danger of overstraining the rational element of the aesthetic. It is at this point that Dewey's pragmatic aesthetics and Wellmer's creative reading of Adorno might serve as possible ways beyond Heidegger's overestimation and Habermas's underestimation of world disclosure.

Dewey's contribution, according to Kompridis, is that (contra Heidegger and Habermas) he interprets the activity of disclosure as one type of action on a cognitive continuum, along with other dimensions of intelligent action. Dewey, according to this argument, does not succumb to drawing a too strong cognitive boundary between the capacity for world disclosing and the capacity for giving reasons.[60] Rather, he maintains the mutuality of world disclosure and rational discursiveness – the disclosure of new or hidden horizons of meaning and their discursively tested validity. In this way world-disclosing perspectives are not overburdened with truth claims. In such a context novel disclosures are primarily a happening of meaning, from which potential truth effects may follow, but not without being 'tested and organized'.[61] The following remarks can thus be made, according to Kompridis, on the relationship between Heidegger and Habermas: Habermas is correct that meaning and validity cannot be made identical – at least, not without paying Heidegger's price. Heidegger can also be criticized for advocating a kind of thinking that is more rigorous than the conceptual – for having no ear for speech based on giving reasons (*begrundende Rede*). The problem with Habermas, though, is that he has difficulty hearing speech that is not based on giving reasons. And this will remain a problem as long as such 'speech' is filtered through Habermas's assumption that it represents little more than the discursively mute 'perspective of the outsider'.[62] It is therefore necessary to seek a way beyond the predicaments of both projects.

In grasping world-disclosing experiences as reciprocally structured relationships of doing and undergoing, finding and making, it is possible for Dewey to invoke a more flexible holism than Heidegger and Habermas.[63] It is one in which the active participation and interpretation of speaking and acting subjects are required in order to keep the openness of 'the open' open – a process of novel experience that demands ongoing reflective evaluation. Dewey consequently argues, according to Kompridis, that the decentring and deconstructing dimensions of world disclosure 2 are simultaneously and interdependently linked to a reconstructive moment. Without such a dimension, the transformative content of world-disclosing experience can be neither articulated nor evaluated nor integrated into our self-understanding and our social practices. Dewey describes the processes of deconstruction and reconstruction as a struggle. The decentring effects of disclosure can be handled properly only through the constant activity of reconstructing shattered interpretations of the world in the light of new ones.[64] The interesting aspect of Dewey's philosophy is that novel disclosures of the world and the practices of 'creative democracy' mutually imply one another. Habermas's reluctance, by contrast, to embrace an account of world disclosure 2, in his philosophical and political project leaves him captive to a formal view of reason that runs the danger of closure in terms of occurences in the public sphere.

Wellmer's reading of the tension between Habermas and Adorno (as indicated in the previous chapter) shares similarities with Dewey's interpretation of world disclosure. His argument has two steps: he gives an appreciative reading of Adorno's aesthetics and criticism, followed by an appreciative reading of Habermas's linguistic turn and criticism. What Wellmer appreciates in Adorno is his emphasis on the mimetic element of rationality – that is, those forms of behaviour that are sensually and expressively receptive (and communicative). Wellmer also restates the point that art and philosophy provide a space in which rationality and mimesis can meet.[65] Separated from one another, the immediacy of art and the conceptual mediacy of philosophy can only achieve partial apprehensions of truth. This is the reason why Adorno refers to aesthetic semblance as a picture puzzle or riddle.[66] But Wellmer criticizes Adorno's clear support for art in the tension between aesthetic and philosophical truth. Art remains for Adorno the only sphere of a non-violent synthesis of disparate elements that produces the semblance of reconciliation. This formulation has strong affinities with Heidegger's concept of the truth of art – where Heidegger invokes *aletheia* as the disclosure and closure of truth, Adorno uses the concept of semblance. But eventually, according to Wellmer, Adorno's 'eschatological-sensualist' utopia puts too great a distance between historical reality (praxis) and the condition of aesthetic reconciliation (happiness).[67]

In the second step of his argument Wellmer transforms Adorno's aesthetics in a material and communicative manner. Habermas's linguistic turn and his differentiated concept of rationality are important here. The point is that if the asymmetrical nature of the philosophy of consciousness (Adorno) is replaced by an intersubjective approach (Habermas), art ceases to be exclusively rational and becomes a specific form of rationality – expressive or aesthetic rationality. In place of Adorno's utopian model of aesthetic reconciliation, a post-utopian aesthetic reconciliation is defended, where art serves as a medium for uninhibited communication between individuals in society. Such an 'aesthetic reconciliation of this world' harmonizes, according to Wellmer, 'that which is diffuse and unintegrated, that which is "meaningless", and split off . . . in an arena for non-violent communication which would encompass the opened forms of art as well as the open structures of a no longer rigid type of individuation and socialization'.[68] Adorno's esoteric concept of truth is thus transformed in a model of plural rationalities where 'apophantic-cognitive', 'moral-practical', and 'endeetic-aesthetic' truth all play a role.[69] Such a differentiated, communicative concept of truth offers, according to Wellmer, advantages over Adorno's utopian aestheticization of truth. Although Habermas is one of the influences on Wellmer's reinterpretation of Adorno's aesthetics, he is also criticized.

Wellmer criticizes the cognitivist and scientist residue in Habermas's model of rationality and his consensus theory of truth, because the world-disclosing force of aesthetics is subordinated in relation to argumentative rationality. As an alternative, Wellmer defends equality between the cognitive, moral and aesthetic validity spheres. Such a 'post-utopian philosophy of communicative reason' goes beyond a utopian aestheticization of truth, on the one hand, and a social-theoretical cognization of truth, on the other. Wellmer links his theory of plural rationalities with a fallibilistic theory of truth.[70] This entails that the inherent fallibilism in the 'cautionary use' of truth implies that justification and truth cannot be reduced to one another as Habermas does – the fallibilistic intuition of difference between these terms must be retained, where the 'cautionary use' of the concept of truth expresses a permanent need to critically investigate justifications.[71] In this context rational consensus cannot be a criterion of truth and principle of universalization.[72] In his alternative, Wellmer opts for a model of universality that works negatively – where any exception or difference indicates a certain tension. For Wellmer, consensus should be the result of a valid choice, not both the starting point and the result. He therefore defends an ethics of dissent, rather than consensus. The emphasis is on the interpretation and judgement (not prescription) of situations.[73] Wellmer's model of a plurality of rationalities tries, like Dewey's model, to mediate between world disclosure and discursive reason. By having an inter-related model of validity spheres of truth, he stresses the importance of interpretations and judgements of all kinds, and most of all, of finding a horizon such that plural values and needs can become part of rational arguments and discourse ethics on an equal basis.

In Wellmer's alternative, the perspective of a reconciled world vanishes, allowing the present to be taken with its 'pathologies, irrationalities, psychological blocks and inhumanities, which may be empirically observed'.[74] The world-disclosing force of the aesthetic sphere thus has a role to play by constantly interacting with moral and cognitive perspectives of the world. In this process the extension of the limits of the subject is one of the major contributions of art against reification. The contributions of Gabriele Schwab and Wayne Booth clearly indicate for Wellmer the world-disclosing power of literature, leading readers to questions rather than answers, opening readers to new experiences of otherness, and disrupting previous fix-ities. Wellmer also mentions Kekes's book on morality and pluralism as an attempt to provide an ethics and politics of judgement that could lead to new forms of individuation and socialization.[75]

## 6.4   The political and moral implications of world disclosure

World disclosure, as discussed in the previous section, can be inter-preted as a concept that contributes to a new semantic repertoire, extending the shelf life of current meanings or replacing those that have become inflexible. It has been argued that when values, argu-ments and ways of seeing become fixed, the innovative use of world disclosure can open the cognitive faculties to experience the world in novel, innovative and different ways. This implies that the processes of world disclosure 1 and world disclosure 2, as discussed in the introduction to this chapter, are mutually interdependent.[76] It is thus not necessary to conceive of the contrast between 'world disclosure' and 'validity orientation' in such exclusive terms as Heidegger and Habermas do in their respective ways. Habermas's problem is that he can consider only the argumentative expansion of possibilities for interpretation, meaning and action – a position that neglects the theoretical advantage of the rational potential that emerges with the introduction of a novel horizon of meaning.[77] Heidegger, on the other hand, prejudices world disclosure in terms of either strong forms of innovation or an objective truth event. He thus has an inflated confidence in art, and an equally exaggerated suspicion of everyday life and language use. This perspective, which in certain ways resembles Adorno's concept of the truth content of art, neglects an understanding of the rationality ('logic of discovery') of social and political change.[78] The radical contrast between world disclosure and validity can be avoided if world disclosure is allowed itself to be open to further corrections. World disclosure is thus a non-reductive, infinite, non-teleological process – one in which there is mediation between criticism and creativity, where both the critic and the artist have a role to play as cultural innovators.[79]

Against this background, world disclosure is neither equivalent to nor independent of truth, but a condition for it. It is prior to propositional truth in so far as disclosure enables both true and false statements about the world and us. Such a corrective capacity for disclosure in a culture is a pre-condition not only for truth, but also, and perhaps more importantly, for freedom.[80] Corrective disclosure further enables the possibility of rationality even when hitherto valid criteria, together with the convictions that they have supported, succumb to criticism. Rationality in this context is not an attempt to halt the processes of world disclosure in the short or long run. It is also important to note that world disclosure is not the other of reason – but another voice of reason. Concrete examples of such world disclosure are the impact of the truth potential of an artwork (for example, literature, as Kunneman and Wellmer indicate), on the one hand, or political processes, such as the fall of the Berlin Wall and the end of apartheid in South Africa, on the other. In the latter case a certain historical-political world disclosure shifted all standards of judgement within and outside a community with regard to the past, present and future. Both the fall of the Berlin Wall and the end of apartheid disclosed a world that changed the context of theoretical and practical standards. Citizens of the societies affected were thus faced with a challenge to incorporate into their history something that previously did not belong to it, and thereby to recognize the relevance of historical processes which they previously did not regard as relevant – thus leading to a wide range of hitherto avoided or repressed, but mainly liberating, insights.[81] Disclosure in this way has the potential to lead to a deepened understanding of democracy in the 'fragmented world of the social' (Honneth). It also implies that the democratic universalism of the Enlightenment should not be interpreted as an abstract principle of strict normativity, but rather as an ensemble of shared, second-order practices, meanings and basic orientations – with reference to the habits of rational self-determination, democratic decision making and the non-violent resolution of conflict.[82] It further implies that the moral and political universalism of the Enlightenment, the ideals of individual autonomy and collective self-determination, and the ideas of reason and history all have to be thought through afresh.[83] Against this background, democratic politics should be open to the disclosing power of the different voices of reason – a position that should be equally sensitive to reason giving and aesthetic world disclosure.

Sheyla Benhabib has provided a further interesting nuance to the debate surrounding world disclosure in her critical interpretation of Habermas's discourse ethics. Benhabib links world disclosure to emancipatory concepts of *transfiguration* and *utopia* in the respective pairs of transfiguration/fulfilment and utopia/norm. Transfiguration means, in this context, that the future envisaged by a theory entails a radical rupture with the present, and that in such a situation new, imaginative constellations of the values and meanings of the present must occur. Fulfilment, on the other hand, refers to the fact that the society of the future executes and carries out the unfinished tasks of the present, without necessarily forging new, imaginative constellations out of this cultural heritage. Benhabib continues (in a manner that is similar to Habermas and Honneth's reconstruction of the first generation of Critical Theorists) that the pessimistic argument of Horkheimer and Adorno in the *Dialectic of Enlightenment* – namely, that scientific and technological developments in the nineteenth and twentieth centuries have thwarted the hope of Enlightenment's fulfilment – has shifted their works (and those of Marcuse) from the theme of fulfilment to an esoteric kind of transfiguration. The problem with such a move, according to Benhabib, is that emancipation as transfiguration ceases to be a public project and becomes a private experience of liberation achieved in the non-dominating relation with nature, an aestheticization of life, and in moments of revolutionary eros.[84] At this point Benhabib commends Habermas for

re-establishing the link between the Enlightenment and emancipation in Critical Theory through his concept of a critical public sphere.
His project thus attempts to fulfil the universalistic promise of social
contract and consent theories that, since the seventeenth century,
have always limited particular distinctions such as sex, class, race and
status.

The new nuance that Benhabib brings is the way she links transfiguration (or world disclosure) with debates on personal autonomy
and intersubjectivity. She writes: 'the ego becomes an I only in a community of other selves who are also I's. Yet every act of self-reference
expresses, at the same time, the uniqueness and difference of this
I from all others.' In formulating this view, Benhabib brings in
aesthetic-expressive discourses, because modernity institutionalizes
the discursive evaluation not only of moral and political issues,
according to her, but also of aesthetic and expressive subjectivity.
Benhabib does not agree with the distinction whereby practical discourses are said to be oriented toward the public and universal, on
the one hand, while aesthetic-expressive discourses are oriented
toward what is semi-public, non-universalizable and culturally specific, on the other.[85] She finds this problem in Habermas's restriction
of interpretations of need to the expressive realm alone, while preserving the purity of the normative realm to an analysis of the binding
force of 'normative ought sentences'. Benhabib's criticism (which is
similar to those expressed in the previous chapter) is further developed when she critically questions Habermas's moral view of the generalized other – a view wherein every individual is formally viewed
as a rational being with the same rights, duties and entitlements. The
assumption is that although the other is a being with needs and
desires, it is not the differences, but the commonalities, that constitute humankind's moral dignity.[86] The relationships between individuals are hence those of symmetrical reciprocity. In her alternative,
Benhabib defends a concrete other where every rational being has a
concrete history, identity and affective-emotional constitution. In
Benhabib's interesting alternative to Habermas, the relationship with
the other is thus a reciprocal relationship, where differences com-
plement rather than exclude one another. Consequently, the generalized other cannot just represent the moral point of view, because
relationships of solidarity, friendship and love also have moral implications. Recognition of the human dignity of the generalized other is
therefore just as essential, according to Benhabib, as acknowledgement of the specificity of the concrete other.[87] In Benhabib's creative
alternative on human agency, institutional justice does not represent

a higher stage of moral development than interpersonal responsibility, care, love and solidarity. This insight suggests that world disclosure also has a deep connection with how persons and subjects experience themselves and are able to change their circumstances.

# Notes

## Introduction

1 At the end of the 1980s I attended the last of three seminars that Jürgen Habermas and Axel Honneth offered on aesthetics at Frankfurt University (summer semester 1988; winter semester 1988/89, and summer semester 1989). They announced the first seminar as follows: 'The problem of aesthetics has once again become a central theme of philosophy. We would like to deal in the first seminar, of a series, with the pre-history of the contemporary discussion. In order to reach this goal we shall discuss six central positions in twentieth century philosophical aesthetics' (*Kommentiertes Vorlesungsverzeichnis*, University of Frankfurt, SS 1988, my translation). These six aesthetical 'positions' were Pragmatism (Dewey), Philosophical Anthropology (Gehlen), Marxism (Lukács), Phenomenology/Hermeneutics (Heidegger/Becker), Semiology (Bakhtin) and Critical Theory (Adorno). At the start of the last semester, Habermas and Honneth wrote: 'After we have discussed the theoretical arguments of Bakhtin, Lukács, Marcuse and Adorno in the previous semesters, we will use the central ideas of Benjamin in the upcoming semester as a bridge towards two positions in the contemporary aesthetical discussion: on the one hand the critical-theoretical contributions of A. Wellmer and M. Seel, and on the other hand the post-structural aesthetics of J. Derrida and J-F. Lyotard' (*Kommentiertes Vorlesungsverzeichnis*, University of Frankfurt, SS 1989, my translation).

2 Duvenage, *Die estetiese heling van die instrumentele rede* (unpublished D. Phil. diss.).

3 Weber, 'Aesthetic experience and self-reflection as emancipatory processes', p. 80.

4 Most prominently in his essays on Benjamin, Marcuse, Heine and Calvino. See Habermas, 'Bewussmachende oder rettende Kritik'; *idem*,

'Herbert Marcuse über Kunst und Revolution'; *idem*, 'Heinrich Heine und die Rolle des Intellektuellen in Deutschland'; and *idem*, *Nachmetaphysisches Denken*, pp. 242–63/205–28. (In this and subsequent citations, German pagination is given first, English pagination second.)

5   Habermas, 'Questions and counterquestions', p. 199.

6   The exceptions are Jay, 'Habermas and modernism'; Wellmer, *The Persistence of Modernity*; Keulartz, 'Over Kunst en Kultuur in het Werk van Habermas'; and Ingram, 'Habermas on aesthetics and rationality'. See Görtzen's bibliography in Rasmussen, *Reading Habermas*, pp. 114–40.

7   In the formulation of this paragraph I have benefited from Matuštík, 'Introduction', in *Jürgen Habermas: A Philosophical-Political Profile*; and J. Anderson, 'The "Third Generation" of the Frankfurt School'.

8   Wellmer, 'Reason, Utopia and the "Dialectic of Enlightenment"', pp. 48–9.

9   Although the distinction between the inner and outer circles of Critical Theorists plays an important role in this study, it should be qualified: Benjamin has some arguments in common with the inner circle, e.g. the many traces of instrumental reason in his own thinking. Adorno's position on autonomous art is also not so clear-cut. In 'Die Kunst und die Kunste' of his *Aesthetic Theory* he refers to transgression and even to the public use of art. In his 'Versuch Musik' he even prefers avant-garde art to Schönberg. I thank Hauke Brunkhorst for making me aware of this point.

10  Habermas, *Theorie des kommunikativen Handelns*, vol. 2, pp. 585–6/398–9.

11  Ibid., pp. 293/196–7.

12  Lyotard, *The Postmodern Condition*, p. xxiv. See also the work of Lacoue-Labarthe and Nancy, *The Literary Absolute*, and De Man, *The Rhetoric of Romanticism*.

13  Jay, 'Habermas and Modernism'.

14  Foucault, 'On the genealogy of ethics'; Whitebook, 'Reason and Happiness'.

15  Bürger, *Theory of the Avant-garde*; Keulartz, 'Over Kunst en Kultuur in het Werk van Habermas'.

16  J. M. Bernstein, 'Art against Enlightenment'; Wellmer, *Persistence of Modernity*.

17  See Kompridis, 'On world disclosure'.

## Chapter 1   Habermas and Aesthetics: The First Phase

1   Two of the best short introductions to Habermas's philosophical work remain R. J. Bernstein (ed.), *Habermas and Modernity*, pp. 1–32, and Dews, 'Introduction', pp. 1–34. For book-length studies on Habermas, see Sensat, *Habermas and Marxism*; Kortian, *Metacritique*; Gripp, *Jürgen*

*Habermas*; McCarthy, *The Critical Theory of Jürgen Habermas*; Roderick, *Habermas and the Foundations of Critical Theory*; Thompson, *Critical Hermeneutics*; Pusey, *Jürgen Habermas*; R. J. Bernstein, *Beyond Objectivism and Relativism*; Ingram, *Habermas and the Dialectic of Reason*; White, *The Recent Work of Jürgen Habermas*; Horster, *Habermas zur Einführung*; Rasmussen, *Reading Habermas*; Horster, *Jürgen Habermas*; Braaten, *Habermas's Critical Theory of Society*; Outhwaite, *Habermas*; Rehg, *Insight and Solidarity*; and Matuštík, *Jürgen Habermas*. For a discussion on some of these works (McCarthy, Kortian and Sensat), see Kellner and Roderick, 'Recent literature on Critical Theory', pp. 159–66.

There has also been a steady stream of compilations and readers on Habermas, see J. Thompson and Held (eds), *Habermas: Critical Debates*; R. J. Bernstein (ed.), *Habermas and Modernity*; Van Doorne and Korthals (eds), *Filosofie en Maatskapijkritiek*; *New German Critique* 35 (1985); Honneth et al., *Zwischenbetrachtungen*; Calhoun (ed.), *Habermas and the Public Sphere*; Outhwaite (ed.), *The Habermas Reader*; Deflem (ed.), *Habermas, Modernity and Law*; M. Passerin d'Entreves and Benhabib (eds), *Habermas and the Unfinished Project of Modernity*; White (ed.), *The Cambridge Companion to Habermas*; Rosenfeld and Arato (eds), *Habermas on Law and Democracy*; Dews (ed.), *Habermas: A Critical Reader*; Hahn (ed.), *Perspectives on Habermas*; Müller-Doohm (ed.), *Das Interesse der Vernunft*; and the comprehensive compilation by Rasmussen and Swindal (eds), *Jürgen Habermas* (4 vols).

For the reception of Habermas's work in the fields of theology, feminism and social health, see Arens (ed.), *Habermas und die Theologie*; Meehan (ed.), *Feminists Read Habermas*; and Fleming, *Emancipation and Illusion*; *Philosophy and Social Criticism* 26 (3) (2000); and Scambler (ed.), *Habermas, Critical Theory and Health*.

For extended bibliographies on Habermas's work till the mid-1990s, see Görtzen, *Jürgen Habermas*; Rasmussen, *Reading Habermas*, pp. 114–40; and White (ed.), *Cambridge Companion to Habermas*, pp. 325–39.

2   Habermas, *Autonomy and Solidarity*, p. 74.
3   See in this regard Wiggershaus, *The Frankfurt School*, p. 599: 'From 1949 to 1954 he [Habermas] studied philosophy, history, psychology, German literature, and economics, in Göttingen, Zurich, and Bonn. His most important teachers in philosophy were Eric Rothacker, a theorist of human sciences who followed Dilthey, and Oskar Becker, a student of Husserl's belonging to Heidegger's generation, who distinguished himself in the fields of mathematics and logic. Apart from one, Theodor Litt, all the professors who were of significance to him during the course of his studies had been either convinced Nazis or at least conformists, carrying on their work as usual during the Nazi regime.'
4   Habermas's doctorate, *Das Absolute und die Geschichte: Von der Zwiespältigkeit in Schellings Denken*, was completed in 1954 at the Uni-

versity of Bonn and never published. For a fine study of this aspect of Habermas's development, see Keulartz, *De verkeerde Wereld van Jürgen Habermas*, ch. 2.

5  See Habermas, 'Zur Veröffentlichung von Vorlesungen aus dem Jahre 1935'.

6  Habermas, 'Dialektik der Rationalisierung', p. 171/96: 'Already at that time, my problem was a theory of modernity, a theory of the pathology of modernity, from the viewpoint of the realization – the deformed realization – of reason in history.'

7  See Wittgenstein, *Philosophical Investigations*. For a recent appraisal of Wittgenstein, see Habermas, *Texte und Kontexte*, pp. 84–90. Later, Habermas was influenced by ethnomethodology (Circourel/Schütz), language action theory (Austin/Searle), and development psychology (Piaget and Kohlberg).

8  Habermas, 'Dialektik der Rationalisierung', p. 170/96.

9  Hohendahl, 'The dialectic of Enlightenment revisited', p. 6. The industrial-sociological research conducted by the Institute in Frankfurt after 1950 was strongly influenced by A. Sohn-Rethels. See in this regard Van Reijen, *Philosophie als Kritik*, p. 14.

10  Habermas's defence of a critical and rational public sphere is also discernible in the different debates and polemics in which he has participated in the last three decades. In the 1960s to 1970s he contributed to the positivism debate against Popper, the hermeneutics debate against Gadamer, and the systems-theory debate against Luhmann. (See Habermas and Luhmann, *Theorie der Gesellschaft oder Sozialtechnologie*; Greven, 'Power and communication in Habermas and Luhmann'; and Misgeld, 'Critical hermeneutics versus Neoparsonianism'.)

In the 1980s Habermas debated against postmodernists and conservative German historians. Regarding the former, see Fraser, 'Is Michel Foucault a young Conservative?'; Foster (ed.), *The Anti-aesthetic*; Benhabib, 'Epistemologies of postmodernism'; Wolin, 'Modernism vs postmodernism' Ingram, 'Foucault and the Frankfurt School'; Angern, 'Krise der Vernunft?'; Hoy, 'Two conflicting conceptions of how to naturalize philosophy'; Dews, *Logics of Disintegration*; Kamper and Van Reijen (eds), *Die unvollendete Vernunft*; Welsch, *Unsere postmoderne Moderne*; L. Dumm, 'The politics of post-modern aesthetics'; Müller, 'Hermeneutik als Modernitätskritik'; and Kirsten, 'Die postmoderne Projek'. On Habermas's critique of Derrida, see Kimmerle in Frank et al., *Die Frage nach dem Subjek*, pp. 267–82; Hoy, 'Splitting the difference'; and Norris, 'Deconstruction, postmodernism and philosophy'. With regard to the debate with the German historians, see Piper (ed.), *Historikerstreit*; Craig, 'The war of the German historians'; Betz, '"Deutschlandpolitik" on the margins'; Nolan, 'The "historikerstreit" and social history'; Torpey, 'Introduction: Habermas and the historians'; Wehler, *Entsorgung der deutschen Vergangenheit?*; and Duvenage, 'The politics of memory and forgetting'.

In the 1990s Habermas participated in debates on nationalism (see Habermas, *Die Normalität einer Berliner Republik*), on European identity (see Habermas, *Die postnationale Konstellation* and *Die Zeit der Übergänge*), and eugenics (Habermas, *Die Zukunft der menschlichen Natur*).

11  For a comprehensive study of Adorno's concept of mimesis, see Früchtl, *Mimesis: Konstellation des Zentralbegriffs bei Adorno*. On mimesis and the critique of conceptual rationality, see Honneth, *Critique of Power*, pp. 57–96. On Marcuse see, Honneth, 'Critical Theory', pp. 371–2; MacIntyre, *Herbert Marcuse*; Schoeman, *Waarheid en Werklikheid in die Kritiese Teorie van Herbert Marcuse*; Schoolman, *The Imaginary Witness*; Geoghegan, *Reason and Eros*; Kellner, *Herbert Marcuse and the Crisis of Marxism*; and Kearney, *Dialogues with Contemporary Continental Thinkers*. See also the biographical study of Katz, *Herbert Marcuse and the Art of Liberation*.

12  Bourdieu, 'Vive le Streit!'

13  Calhoun (ed.), *Habermas and the Public Sphere*, p. 1; Holub, *Jürgen Habermas*, p. 3.

14  Habermas, *Moralbewusstsein und kommunikatives Handeln*, p. 12/4; my emphasis.

15  For a clarification of 'representative publicness', see Habermas, *Strukturwandel der Öffentlichkeit*, pp. 17–25/5–13.

16  Ibid., p. 20/7–8.

17  Ibid., p. 31/18.

18  Ibid., p. 42/27: 'The bourgeois public sphere may be conceived above all as the sphere of private people come together as a public; they soon claimed the public sphere regulated from above against the public authorities themselves, to engage them in a debate over the general rules governing relations in the basically privatized but publicly relevant sphere of commodity exchange and social labor. The medium of this political confrontation was peculiar and without historical precedent; people's public use of their reason (i.e. *Räsonnement*). In our [German] usage this term (i.e. *Räsonnement*) unmistakably preserves the polemical nuances of both sides: simultaneously the invocation of reason and its disdainful disparagement as merely malcontent gripping.'

19  Ibid., pp. 71–2/53–4.

20  Calhoun (ed.), *Habermas and the Public Sphere*, pp. 10–11.

21  Habermas, *Strukturwandel der Öffentlichkeit*, pp. 67–8/49–50.

22  Ibid., p. 67/49–50.

23  Ibid., pp. 52–3/36–7. Although participation was supposedly open to 'all', Habermas's critics have pointed out that in practice it applied only to men.

24  Ibid., pp. 306–7/259: 'In principle anyone was called upon and had the right to make a free judgment as long as he participated in public discussion, bought a book, acquired a seat in a concert or theatre, or visited an art exhibition. But in the conflict of judgments he has not to shut

his ears to convincing arguments; instead, he had to rid himself of his "prejudices". With the removal of the barrier that representative publicity had erected between laymen and initiates, special qualifications . . . became in principle irrelevant . . . Hence, if the public acknowledged no one as privileged, it did recognize experts. They were permitted and supposed to educate the public, but only inasmuch as they convinced through arguments and could not themselves be corrected by better arguments.'

25   Ibid., p. 58/41.
26   Ibid., p. 46/31. See also Keulartz, 'Over Kunst en Kultuur in het Werk van Habermas', p. 15.
27   Calhoun (ed.), *Habermas and the Public Sphere*, p. 15; Habermas, *Strukturwandel der Öffentlichkeit*, p. 100/79.
28   Habermas, *Strukturwandel der Öffentlichkeit*, pp. 173–4/143–4, 244/205.
29   Ibid., p. 198/164.
30   Ibid., p. 173/142.
31   Ibid., p. 240/202.
32   Keulartz, 'Over Kunst en Kultuur in het Werk van Habermas', p. 17.
33   Hohendahl, 'Critical Theory, public sphere and culture', p. 90.
34   Habermas, *Strukturwandel der Öffentlichkeit*, p. 205/170–1.
35   Ibid., p. 200/166.
36   Calhoun (ed.), *Habermas and the Public Sphere*, pp. 25–6.
37   Habermas, *Strukturwandel der Öffentlichkeit*, p. 189/156.
38   It is no coincidence that Habermas refers to Adorno's famous essay 'Über den Fetischcharakter in der Musik und die Regression des Hörens' and the Adorno-influenced essays of Enzensberger, *Einzelheiten*, in his study.
39   Habermas, *Strukturwandel der Öffentlichkeit*, p. 294/250.
40   On the German reception see Luhmann, *Zweckbegriff und Systemrationalität*, and *idem, Soziologische Aufklärung*. See also Negt and Kluge, *Öffentlichkeit und Erfahrung*. The study was also an important impulse for the development of a critical literary science in post-war Germany. See in this regard Bürger and Schulte-Sasse (eds), *Aufklärung und Öffentlichkeit*, and Bürger et al., *Zur Dichotomisierung von hoher und niederer Literatur*. On the reception outside Germany, see Keulartz, 'Over Kunst en Kultuur in het Werk van Habermas', p. 13. For a contribution on the reception of Habermas's concept of the public sphere in recent debates, see the essays in Calhoun (ed.), *Habermas and the Public Sphere*.
41   On the liberal reception, see Hohendahl, 'Critical Theory, public sphere and culture', pp. 93, 95. He refers to the following studies in this regard: Glotz, *Buchkritik in deutschen Zeitungen*, and Jäger, *Öffentlichkeit und Parlementarismus. Eine Kritik an Jürgen Habermas* (Stuttgart, n.d.). On Luhmann's systems theory see Hohendahl, 'Critical Theory, public sphere and culture', pp. 99–100. See also Luhmann, *Soziologische Aufk-*

*lärung*, and *idem*, *Soziale Systeme*; Habermas and Luhmann, *Theorie der Gesellschaft oder Sozialtechnologie*; and Greven, 'Power and communication in Habermas and Luhmann'. For collected essays on Luhmann's work, see *New German Critique* 61 (1994); and *Theory, Culture and Society* 18 (1) (2001).

42  Hohendahl, 'Critical Theory, public sphere and culture', pp. 104–5. See Negt, *Soziologische Phantasie und exemplarisches Lernen*; Negt and Kluge, *Öffentlichkeit und Erfahrung*; and Prokop, *Massenkultur und Spontaneität*. For an overview of Kluge's films, see *New German Critique* 49, (1990), pp. 3–138. For a recent appreciation of Kluge, see Habermas, *Vom sinnlichen Eindruck zum symbolischen Ausdruck*, ch. 8.

43  Calhoun (ed.), *Habermas and the Public Sphere*, pp. 34–5.

44  Ibid., p. 32.

45  According to Jay, 'Habermas and Modernism', p. 126, an essay of Habermas in *Theorie und Praxis*, pp. 162–214/195–252, already contains some aesthetical elements.

46  On the positivism debate, see the contributions of Adorno, Albert, Dahrendorf, Habermas, Pilot and Popper in Adorno et al., *The Positivist Dispute in German Sociology*. See also Apel, 'Wissenschaft als Emanzipation?'; Alford, *Science and the Revenge of Nature*; Komesaroff, *Objectivity, Science and Society*, pp. 76–92; Hesse (in Thompson and Held, *Habermas: Critical Debates*, pp. 98–115); and Vogel, 'Habermas and Science'. On the debate between Habermas and Albert, see Ley and Müller, *Kritische Vernunft und Revolution*.

47  Habermas found the basis of this argument (and the distinction between *technē* and *praxis*) in the work of Aristotle, Arendt (*The Human Condition* and *On Revolution*) and Gadamer (*Wahrheit und Methode* and *Vernunft im Zeitalter der Wissenschaft*). For a clarification of *technē*, *phronēsis* and *praxis*, see Aristotle's *Nicomachēan Ethics* 1139b, Rackman trans., pp. 16–17.

48  Habermas, *Knowledge and Human Interests*, p. 4: '"Scientism" means science's belief in itself: that is the conviction that we can no longer understand science as one form of possible knowledge, but rather must identify knowledge with science.'

49  *Erkenntnis und Interesse*, pp. 395–400/368–71. On this work, see Dallmayr (ed.), *Materialen zu Erkenntnis und Interesse*; Bubner (in K. Apel et al., *Hermeneutik und Ideologiekritik*), pp. 160–209; Apel, 'Types of social science in the light of human interests of knowledge'; Overend, 'Enquiry and ideology'; Ottmann (in Thompson and Held, *Habermas: Critical Debates*, pp. 79–98), and more generally Keat, *The Politics of Social Theory*.

50  Habermas, *Technik und Wissenschaft als Ideologie*, p. 159 (*Knowledge and Human Interests*, p. 310).

51  Habermas, *Erkenntnis und Interesse*, pp. 378–81/358–60.

52  Dallmayr, *Between Freiburg and Frankfurt*, p. 19.

53  Habermas, *Erkenntnis und Interesse*, pp. 113–15/88–90, 223/177.

54  On Habermas's interpretation of psychoanalysis, see McIntosh, 'Habermas on Freud'; Flynn, 'Reading Habermas reading Freud'; Livesay, 'Habermas, narcissism, and status'; Whitebook, 'Reason and Happiness'; Alford, 'Habermas, post-Freudian psychoanalysis and the end of the individual'; Connolly, *Politics and Ambiguity*, pp. 56–60; and Whitebook, 'Intersubjectivity and the monadic core of the psyche'. More generally, see Jacoby, *Social Amnesia*, and Cahoone, *The Dilemma of Modernity*.

55  See Miller, 'Jürgen Habermas, *Legitimation Crisis*'; Held, 'Habermas' theory of crisis in late capitalism'; and Holton, 'The idea of crisis in modern society'.

56  Habermas, *Legitimationsprobleme im Spätkapitalismus*, pp. 68–9/46.

57  Hohendahl, 'Critical Theory, public sphere and culture', pp. 112–13.

58  Habermas, *Legitimationsprobleme im Spätkapitalismus*, p. 110/78.

59  Ibid., p. 120/85.

60  Habermas, 'Bewussmachende oder rettende Kritik', pp. 308–9/133–4.

61  Ibid., p. 306/132. See also Habermas's interpretation of Marcuse's aesthetics in 'Herbert Marcuse über Kunst und Revolution'. On Marcuse's example of the Paris students in 1968, see Prinz, *Der poetische Mensch im Schatten der Utopie*.

62  Habermas, 'Bewussmachende oder rettende Kritik', pp. 312–13/136.

63  On the difference between autonomous art (painting) and technically reproduced art (film), see Benjamin, *Illuminations*, p. 240: 'Let us compare the screen on which a film unfolds with the canvas of a painting. The painting invites the spectator to contemplation; before it the spectator can abandon himself to his associations. Before the movie frame he cannot do so. No sooner has his eye grasped a scene then it is already changed . . . The spectator's process of association in view of these images is indeed interrupted by their constant, sudden change. This constitutes the shock effect of the film, which, like all shocks, should be cushioned by heightened presence of mind. By means of its technical structure, the film has taken the physical shock effect out of the wrappers in which Dadaism had, as it were, kept it inside the moral shock effect.' On the concept of shock (*Chok*) and Baudelaire, see ibid., pp. 165–7.

64  See Benjamin, *Gesammelte Schriften*, vol. 1/2, pp. 203–408, on the baroque tragedy. On his interpretation of Goethe, see ibid., pp. 123–203. On his interpretation of Baudelaire's poetry, see ibid., vol. 4/1, pp. 65–83; and on his interpretation of Soviet films, ibid., vol. 2/2, pp. 747–51.

65  Habermas, 'Bewussmachende oder rettende Kritik', pp. 315–16/138–9. See the following quotation of Benjamin, ibid., p. 315/138: ' In every true work of art there is a place where a cool breeze like that of the approaching dawn breathes on whoever puts himself there. It follows from this that art, which was often enough regarded as refractory toward any relationship with progress, can serve as authentic distinc-

tiveness. Progress is at home not in the continuity of the flow of time, but in its interferences: wherever something genuinely new makes itself felt for the first time with the sobriety of dawn.'

66  On Habermas's ambivalent interpretation of the symbolic and the allegorical, see Jay, 'Habermas and modernism', p. 129.
67  Habermas, 'Bewussmachende oder rettende Kritik', p. 310/134.
68  Adorno, *Aesthetic Theory*, p. 25.
69  Habermas, 'Bewussmachende oder rettende Kritik', p. 310/134.
70  Ibid., pp. 320–1/142–3. For a defence of Adorno's aesthetics against Habermas, see J. M. Bernstein, 'Art against Enlightenment'.
71  Habermas, 'Bewussmachende oder rettende Kritik', pp. 310–11/134–5, 316–17/138–9. See also Benjamin, *Illuminations*, p. 223: 'One might generalize by saying: the technique of reproduction detaches the reproduced object from the domain of tradition [aura].'
72  Habermas, 'Bewussmachende oder rettende Kritik', pp. 322–4/143–5.
73  For a critique of Habermas's communicative interpretation of Benjamin, see Brewster and Buchner, 'Language and criticism'. They end their essay on the following note: 'Whether or not Habermas' conclusions will be borne out by further research is an open question. The usefulness of his conclusion as a basis for further research is questionable' (p. 29).
74  Habermas, 'Bewussmachende oder rettende Kritik', pp. 328–9/149.
75  Jay, 'Habermas and Modernism', p. 130.
76  Habermas, 'Bewussmachende oder rettende Kritik', pp. 335–6/153.
77  Ibid., pp. 338–9/155.
78  Ibid., pp. 340–1/156.
79  Ibid., p. 343/158.
80  Ibid., p. 343/159.
81  Horkheimer and Adorno were strong critics of Heidegger's thinking. Yet, despite this dislike, there is an interesting similarity in their analyses of the fate of Western rationality. There is a fine divide between Horkheimer and Adorno's analysis of instrumental reason, on the one hand, and Heidegger's analysis of determined thinking (*Gestell*) – the 'essence of technology' which he interpreted as the disclosed essence of Western metaphysics. See R. J. Bernstein (ed.), *Habermas and Modernity*, p. 6. On the relationship between Adorno and Habermas, see Honneth, 'Communication and reconciliation'; and the interesting recent work of Morris, *Rethinking the Communicative Turn*.
82  Hohendahl, 'Critical Theory, public sphere and culture', pp. 114–15.
83  Calhoun (ed.), *Habermas and the Public Sphere*, pp. 31–2.

## Chapter 2    Habermas and the Legacy of
## Aesthetics in Critical Theory

1  For an explanation of this interpretation, see Habermas, 'Die Frankfurter Schule in New York', and *idem, Theorie des kommunikativen*

*Handelns*, II, p. 558/380. The reading of Habermas's position in this chapter has been influenced by Honneth, 'Critical Theory', pp. 362–3. See also Honneth, 'Enlightenment and rationality', p. 692.

2   On the initial years of the Institute, see Jay, *The Dialectical Imagination*, pp. 3–40; Kilminster, *Praxis and Method*; Feenberg, *Lukács, Marx and the Sources of Critical Theory*; and Wiggershaus, *The Frankfurt School*, pp. 24–35.

3   Honneth, 'Critical Theory', p. 349; and Habermas, *Philosophisch-politische Profile*, p. 411.

4   See Horkheimer, 'The present situation of social philosophy and the tasks of an Institute for Social Research', in *Between Philosophy and Social Science*, p. 1.

5   Ibid., pp. 1–4.

6   Ibid., pp. 5–6.

7   On Horkheimer's path via Marx and Lukács, see Arato and Beines (eds), *The Young Lukács and the Origins of Western Marxism*; and Jay, *The Dialectical Imagination*, pp. 43–4. Marcuse's work, on the other hand, is to an extent influenced by Heidegger. See in this regard Schmidt, 'Existentialontologie und historischer Materialismus bei Marcuse'; Piccone and Delfini, 'Herbert Marcuse's Heideggerian Marxism'; Ahlers, 'Technologie und Wissenschaft bei Heidegger und Marcuse'; and Breuer, *Die Krise der Revolutionstheorie*.

8   There are extensive sources on Critical Theory. For a historical background, see Jay, *The Dialectical Imagination*; Dubiel, *Theory and Politics*; and Wiggershaus, *The Frankfurt School*.

   For more general studies on the first and second generations of Critical Theorists, see Therborn, 'The Frankfurt School'; P. Anderson, *Considerations on Western Marxism*; Klapwijk, *Dialektik der Verlichting*; Slater, *Origin and Significance of the Frankfurt School*; Tar (ed.), *The Frankfurt School*; Held, *Introduction to Critical Theory*; Connerton, *The Tragedy of Enlightenment*; Friedman, *The Political Philosophy of the Frankfurt School*; Geuss, *The Idea of a Critical Theory*; Bottomore, *The Frankfurt School*; Jay, *Marxism and Totality*; Warren, *The Emergence of Dialectical Theory*; Gmünder, *Kritische Theorie*; Jay, *Permanent Exiles*; Van Reijen, *Philosophie als Kritik*; Kearney, *Modern Movements in European Philosophy*; Jay, *Fin de siècle Socialism*; Kellner, *Critical Theory, Marxism and Modernity*; Ingram, *Critical Theory and Philosophy*; and J. M. Bernstein (ed.), *The Frankfurt School*. For an overview of literature on Critical Theory, up to the early eighties, see Kellner and Roderick, 'Recent literature on Critical Theory'.

   See also the following readers on Critical Theory: O'Neil (ed.), *On Critical Theory*; Arato (ed.), *The Essential Frankfurt School Reader*; Bonss and Honneth (eds), *Sozialforschung als Kritik*; Forester (ed.), *Critical Theory and Public Life*; Bronner and Kellner (eds), *Critical Theory and Society – A Reader*; Ingram and Simon-Ingram (eds), *Critical Theory*; Ray (ed.), *Critical Sociology*; Rasmussen (ed.), *Handbook of Critical Theory*; and Wilkerson and Paris (eds), *New Critical Theory*.

For the reinterpretation of Critical Theory by the second generation of Critical Theorists, see Habermas, *Theorie des kommunikativen Handelns*; Wellmer, *Critical Theory of Society*. There are interesting similarities, but also differences, between the second and third generations on Critical Theory. For the third generation's interpretation of Critical Theory, see. Benhabib, 'Modernity and the aporias of Critical Theory'; *idem, Critique, Norm and Utopia*; Honneth, *Critique of Power; idem,* 'Critical Theory'.

For feminist, postmodern and aesthetic perspectives on Critical Theory, see Mills, *Woman, Nature and Psyche*; Kellner, 'Postmodernism as social theory'; and Roblin (ed.), *The Aesthetics of the Critical Theorists*.

9   On Horkheimer's materialist social theory, see Korthals, 'Die kritische Gesselschaftstheorie des frühen Horkheimer', and Söllner, 'Erfahrungs- und Geschichtsabhängigkeit der Wahrheit'. See further Tar (ed.), *The Frankfurt School*; Geyer, *Kritische Theorie*; Held, *Introduction to Critical Theory*, pp. 175–99; Connerton, *The Tragedy of Enlightenment*, pp. 27–41; Küsters, *Der Kritikbegriff der Kritischen Theorie Max Horkheimers*; Habermas, *Philosophisch-politische Profile*, pp. 411–25; and Benhabib et al. (eds), *On Max Horkheimer*.

10  Honneth, 'Critical Theory', p. 350. Bonss and Honneth (eds), *Sozialforschung als Kritik*, p. 31, calls it 'interdisciplinary materialism'.

11  Honneth, 'Critical Theory', p. 352.

12  Horkheimer, 'The present situation of social philosophy and the tasks of an Institute for Social Research', pp. 9–10.

13  Wellmer, 'Reason, utopia and the "Dialectic of Enlightenment"', pp. 45–6.

14  Horkheimer, 'The present situation of social philosophy and the tasks of an Institute for Social Research', p. 11.

15  Kellner, *Critical Theory, Marxism and Modernity*, p. 18.

16  On Critical Theory and psychoanalysis, see Robinson, *The Freudian Left*. See further Jacoby, *Social Amnesia*; and Connolly, *Politics and Ambiguity*, pp. 56–60; Arato, *The Essential Frankfurt School Reader*, pp. 387–9.

17  Honneth, 'Critical Theory', pp. 354–5.

18  Habermas, *Theorie des kommunikativen Handelns*, vol. 2, pp. 559–61/381–2.

19  Habermas, 'Die Frankfurter Schule in New York', p. 424/64.

20  For studies of Adorno's philosophy, see Kaiser, *Benjamin, Adorno*; Buck-Morss, *The Origin of Negative Dialectics*; Tar (ed.), *The Frankfurt School*; G. Rose, *The Melancholy Science*; Held, *Introduction to Critical Theory*; Jay, *Adorno*; Snyman, *Theodor W. Adorno*; Jarvis, *Adorno*; Hohendahl, *Prismatic Thought*; and J. M. Bernstein, *Adorno*.

21  Korthals, 'Die kritische Gesellschaftstheorie des frühen Horkheimer', pp. 315–16, traces Horkheimer's pessimism back to the earlier phases of his intellectual development. Hence he argues that Horkheimer's work in the thirties is a theoretical exception in his broader pessimistic world-view.

22  Habermas, *Der philosophische Diskurs der Moderne*, p. 130/106.
23  Honneth, *Critique of Power*, p. xii.
24  Habermas, *Der philosophische Diskurs der Moderne*, p. 130/106.
25  Adorno and Horkheimer, *Dialectic of Enlightenment*, pp. 81–2.
26  Ibid., p. 25.
27  Ibid., p. 33.
28  Klapwijk, *Dialektik der Verlichting*, pp. 7–8.
29  R. J. Bernstein (ed.), *Habermas and Modernity*, pp. 6–7.
30  Klapwijk, *Dialektik der Verlichting*, p. 5.
31  Honneth, 'Critical Theory', p. 359. See also Baars, *Die Mythe van totale Beheersing*, on Horkheimer and Adorno's interpretation of totalitarianism and instrumentalism.
32  Adorno and Horkheimer, *Dialectic of Enlightenment*, pp. 120–1.
33  Ibid., p. 42.
34  Ibid., p. xvi.
35  Geyer, *Kritische Theorie*, pp. 67–8.
36  Van Reijen, *Philosophie als Kritik*, p. 48.
37  Adorno and Horkheimer, *Dialectic of Enlightenment*, p. xvi.
38  Wellmer, 'Reason, utopia and the "Dialectic of Enlightenment"', pp. 47–8.
39  Habermas, *Der philosophishe Diskurs der Moderne*, p. 138/114.
40  Ibid., p. 139/114.
41  Connerton, *The Tragedy of Enlightenment*, pp. 60ff.
42  Benhabib, *Critique, Norm and Utopia*, pp. 149–50.
43  Adorno and Horkheimer, *Dialectic of Enlightenment*, p. 120.
44  Adorno, *Dissonanzen*, pp. 24–6.
45  Ibid., p. 34.
46  Marcuse, 'The Affirmative Character of Culture', p. 88.
47  Adorno, *Aesthetic Theory*, p. 321. Adorno's defence of autonomous art has earned him the criticism of being 'elitist' and a 'left mandarin'. Zuidervaart, in *Adorno's Aesthetic Theory*, pp. 31, 321, though, has pointed to a remark of Adorno indicating an openness to both autonomous and mass art – both being part of a greater whole: 'Both bear the stigmata of capitalism, both contain elements of change . . . Both are torn halves of an integral freedom to which however they do not add up.'
48  On Adorno's aesthetics, see Lindner and Lüdke (eds), *Materialen zur ästhetischen Theorie Adornos Konstruktion der Moderne*; Sauerland, *Einführung in die Ästhetik Adornos*; Offermans and Prior, *Die estetiese Teorie van Adorno en Benjamin*; Slater, *Origin and Significance of the Frankfurt School*, pp. 119–48; Snyman, *Theodor W. Adorno*, pp. 258–357; Johnson, 'An aesthetic of negativity/an aesthetic of reception'; Liessmann, *Ohne Mitleid*; Osborne, 'Adorno and the metaphysics of modernism'; Zuidervaart, *Adorno's Aesthetic Theory*; Bürger in Habermas and von Friedeburg (eds), *Adorno Konferenz 1983*, pp. 133–97; Zuidervaart and Huhn (eds), *The Semblance of Subjectivity*; and the study by Weber-Nicholsen, *Exact Imagination, Late Work*. On the overlaps and dif-

ferences between Adorno and Derrida, see Wilke, *Zur Dialektik von Exposition und Darstellung*; and Menke, *Die Souveränität der Kunst.*

49  Keulartz, 'Over Kunst en Kultuur in het Werk van Habermas', p. 20.
50  Bürger, *Theory of the Avant-garde*, p. 46: 'To summarize: the autonomy of art is a category of bourgeois society. It permits the description of art's detachment from the context of practical life as a historical development – that among the members of those classes which, at least at times, are free from the pressures of the need for survival, a sensuousness could evolve that was not part of any means–ends relationships.'
51  Adorno, *Notes on Literature*, vol. 2, pp. 93–4.
52  Ibid., p. 90.
53  Zuidervaart, *Adorno's Aesthetic Theory*, p. 35. Benjamin, though, gave a greater role to the intellectual than Brecht.
54  Adorno, *Aesthetic Theory*, p. 342.
55  Zuidervaart, *Adorno's Aesthetic Theory*, pp. 40–1.
56  Adorno, *Aesthetic Theory*, p. 34.
57  Adorno, *Noten zur Literatur*, pp. 265, 273–4.
58  Ibid., pp. 259–62.
59  Adorno, *Aesthetic Theory*, pp. 353–4.
60  Ibid., pp. 200–1.
61  J. M. Bernstein, 'Art against Enlightenment', p. 55.
62  Adorno, *Aesthetic Theory*, pp. 141–2.
63  Ibid., p. 189.
64  Ibid., pp. 187, 86.
65  Ibid., pp. 79–80. See further Wellmer, *The Persistence of Modernity*, p. 9: 'Art can thus only be true in the sense of being faithful to reality to the extent that it makes reality appear *as* unreconciled, antagonistic, divided against itself. But it can only do this by showing reality in the light of reconciliation, i.e. by the non-violent aesthetic synthesis of disparate elements which produces the semblance of reconciliation. This means, however, that an antinomy is carried into the very *heart* of the aesthetic synthesis – which can only succeed by turning against itself and questioning its own underlying principle, for the sake of truth which nevertheless cannot be extracted except with recourse to this very principle.'
66  Wellmer, 'Reason, utopia, and the "Dialectic of the Enlightenment"', pp. 48–9.
67  Habermas, *Theorie des kommunikativen Handelns*, vol. 2, pp. 558–61/380–2; Honneth, 'Critical Theory', pp. 14–15.
68  See Kirchheimer and Neumann, *Social Democracy and the Rule of Law*, and the two studies of Söllner: 'Skizzen zu einer intellektuellen und politischen Biographie' and *Geschichte und Herrschaft.*
69  Neumann and Kirchheimer's analysis has remained influential. See Wilson, *Das Institut für Sozialforschung und seine Faschismusanalysen*, and Van Reijen, *Philosophie als Kritik*, pp. 38–9.
70  Honneth, 'Critical Theory', pp. 363–4.

71  See Söllner, *Geschichte und Herrschaft*, on the influence of Austro-Marxism on Neumann and Kirchheimer.

72  On Fromm, see Slater, *Origin and Significance of the Frankfurt School*, pp. 114–18; Schaar, *Escape from Authority*; Funk, *Eric Fromm*; Bonns and Honneth (eds), *Sozialforschung als Kritik*; and Rickert, 'The Fromm–Marcuse debate revisited'.

73  Honneth, 'Critical Theory', pp. 368–9.

74  See Bonss and Honneth (eds), *Sozialforschung als Kritik*, and Jay, *The Dialectical Imagination*, on Adorno's and Marcuse's critique of Fromm.

75  For appreciative essays on Benjamin, see G. Smith (ed.), *Benjamin*; Löwenthal, 'The integrity of the intellectual'; Unseld (ed.), *Zur Aktualität Walter Benjamins*; Tiedemann, *Studien zur Philosophie Walter Benjamins*; Roberts, *Walter Benjamin*; Wolin, *Walter Benjamin*; Kambas, *Walter Benjamin im Exil*; Witte, *Walter Benjamin*; Frisby, *Fragments of Modernity*. See also Bolz and Faber (eds), *Walter Benjamin*, and the biographical studies of Scholem, *Walter Benjamin*, and Fuld, *Walter Benjamin*. On the unity in Benjamin's work, see Habermas, 'Bewussmachende oder rettende Kritik'; and Tiedemann, *Studien zur Philosophie Walter Benjamins*. See further on Habermas's interpretation of Benjamin, Brewster and Buchner, 'Language and criticism'.

76  Arendt, 'Introduction', p. 11.

77  Benjamin, *Illuminations*, p. 226. On Benjamin's aesthetics, see the essays of Snyder, Radnoti, and Todd in G. Smith (ed.), *Benjamin*. See also Offermans and Prior, *Die estetiese Teorie van Adorno en Benjamin*; Radnoti, 'The effective power of art'; Steiner, *Die Geburt der Kritik aus dem Geiste der Kunst*; and Bürger, *Theory of the Avant-garde*, pp. 27–34. On the decline of the aura see Stoessel, *Aura*, pp. 23–42; Eagleton, *Walter Benjamin or Towards a Revolutionary Criticism*, pp. 25–42; and Witte, *Walter Benjamin*, pp. 101–16. See further Kaulen, *Rettung und Destruktion*, and Negrin, 'Two critiques of the autonomy of aesthetic consciousness', on the hermeneutical quality of Benjamin's thinking, and Allen, 'The aesthetic experience of modernity', on the different ideas of film theory in the work of Benjamin and Adorno.

78  Buck-Morss, *The Dialectic of Seeing*, p. 293, writes: 'The past haunts the present, but the latter denies it with good reason. For on the surface, nothing remains the same. World War I was a turning point in the fashions of everything from office buildings to women's clothing, from printing type to children's book illustrations . . . By the 1920's, in every one of the technical arts, and in the fine arts affected by technology, the change in style was total. In Germany Walter Gropius' Bauhaus heralded this transformation. In Paris Le Corbusier's work epitomized the functional side of the new style, while Surrealism signalled its reflection in the imagination.'

79  On the avant-garde, see Bürger, *Theory of the Avant-garde*, pp. 20–7, 117–30; Calinescu, *Five Faces of Modernity*, pp. 95–144; Bürger, 'The decline of the modern age'; Keulartz, 'Over Kunst en Kultuur in het

Werk van Habermas', pp. 29–31, and Snyman, 'Kan 'n Mens dit ooit Kuns noem?', pp. 22–5. Bürger, *Theory of the Avant-garde*, p. 49, writes on the avant-garde's critique of autonomous art: 'The avant-gardistes view its dissociation from the praxis of life as the dominant character-istics of art in bourgeois society. One of the reasons this dissociation was possible is that Aestheticism had made the element that defines art as an institution the essential content of works. Institution and work contents had to coincide to make it logically possible for the avant-garde to call art into question. The avant-gardistes proposed the subla-tion in the Hegelian sense of the term: art was not to be simply destroyed, but transferred to the praxis of life where it would be pre-served, albeit in a changed form.' On the avant-garde and postmod-ernism see Bürger and Bürger, *Postmoderne*.

80  Benjamin, *Illuminations*, p. 229.
81  Ibid., p. 236.
82  Ibid., pp. 223–5.
83  Honneth, *Critique of Power*, pp. 68–9.
84  Weber-Nicholsen, *Exact Imagination, Late Work*, pp. 183–4.
85  Honneth, 'Critical Theory', pp. 367–8.
86  Ibid., p. 368.

## Chapter 3   Habermas and Aesthetics: The Second Phase

1  Habermas, *Theorie des kommunikativen Handelns*, vol. 1, p. 523/390. Honneth and Joas (eds), *Communicative Action*, p. 1 writes: 'In 1981 Jürgen Habermas published his "Theory of Communicative Action" as a two-volume book . . . He thus brought to a provisional conclusion the intellectual efforts of twenty years of reflexion and research. The basic idea informing it, namely that an indestructible moment of commu-nicative rationality is anchored in the social form of human life, is defended in this book by means of a contemporary philosophy of lan-guage and science, and is used as the foundation for a comprehensive social theory.' For influences on Habermas in this regard, see Apel, *Transformation der Philosophie*, vol. 2, pp. 220–63; and Wellmer (in Honneth and Jaeggi (eds), *Theorien des historischen Materialismus*, p. 465).
2  Habermas, *Technik und Wissenschaft als Ideologie*, p. 163 (*Knowledge and Human Interests*, p. 314).
3  See Habermas, *Theorie des kommunikativen Handelns*. For interpreta-tions of this work, see R. J. Bernstein (ed.), *Habermas and Modernity*, pp. 15–25; Rasmussen, 'Communicative action and philosophy'; Giddens, 'Reason without revolution?'; Kuhlmann, 'Philosophie und Rekonstruktive Wissenschaft'; Honneth, 'Communication and recon-ciliation'; Giddens, 'Labour and interaction'. Habermas's position on language is influenced by Gadamer's philosophical hermeneutics,

Wittgenstein's philosophy of language, and analytic philosophy. The central text in the debate between Habermas and Gadamer is Apel et al., *Hermeneutik und Ideologiekritik*. See also D. Misgeld (in O'Neill (ed.), *On Critical Theory*); Ricoeur, *Hermeneutics and the Human Sciences*; Hekman's overview in *Hermeneutics and the Sociology of Knowledge* and *Cultural Hermeneutics*, 2 (February 1975).

4   Habermas, *Theorie des kommunikativen Handelns*, vol. 1, pp. 130–2/ 87–8.

5   Ibid., p. 28/10.

6   Habermas, *Theorie des kommunikativen Handelns*, vol. 1, pp. 370ff/ 273ff. Habermas's parting with the philosophy of the subject is criticized by Grondin, 'Hat Habermas die Subjektphilosophie verabschiedet?'. See also Nagl (in Frank et al., *Die Frage nach dem Subjek*, pp. 346–72), and Gerhardt, 'Metaphysik und Ihre Kritik'. Gerhardt links his position to that of Henrich. For his answer to Henrich, see Habermas, *Nachmetaphysisches Denken*, pp. 267–79/10–27.

7   Cooke, *Language and Reason*, pp. 9–10.

8   Habermas, 'Questions and counterquestions', p. 209.

9   Habermas, *Theorie des kommunikativen Handelns*, vol. 1, pp. 148ff/98ff.

10  Habermas used the debates between analytical philosophers and anthropologists in the 1970s as a starting point for reconstructing his theory of rationality. Against the argument that every culture/life-form/language game as a closed totality with its own incommensurable rational criteria and rules, Habermas opposes his theory of communicative reason by stressing the commensurable or shared rational criteria in cross-cultural (universal) human communication.

11  Dallmayr, *Between Freiburg and Frankfurt*, pp. 86–7.

12  There are various options open regarding agreement among speakers of different cultural backgrounds. Speakers can, in the first place, deny the meaning of an action, regarding it as brutal conduct. They can, secondly, attempt to mediate between a mythical and modern rationality with the help of depth hermeneutics, structural or development methodologies, and logical learning processes. Speakers can interpret actions, thirdly, as rationally unmotivated. According to Habermas, only the second option avoids the double danger of behaviourism and ethnocentrism (*Theorie des kommunikativen Handelns*, vol 1, pp. 171–2/ 117–18). When speakers agree on mutual terms, there is still the danger of self-deceit on the side of the social critic, who is both judge and critic (ibid., pp. 157–8/106–7). Gadamer, for example, argues that there is a relationship between structures of rationality and our 'everyday existence'. Understanding is possible from this perspective only if it aims for agreement. This process is led by an expectation of full understanding (*Vorgriff der Vollkommenheit*). This is the idea of a limitless community of discourse in which all opposing interpretations contribute to consensus (pp. 188–93/130–6). Habermas acknowledges Gadamer's idea of reflexive historical understanding, but he criticizes

the move whereby the critical-dialogical moment is connected to the conservative ideas of authority and tradition (pp. 193–6/134–6).

13  Ibid., vol. 1, pp. 427–8/319–20, 439/329.
14  Ibid., vol. 1, p. 30/11. Habermas argues that the matters and symbols uttered in sentences could be interpreted through a system of validity claims (pp. 35–6/15–16). Whereas the truth-conditional theories of Frege, Carnap, the early Wittgenstein, Davidson and Dummett con-centrate on the sentence as the primary unit of meaning, the later Wittgenstein links the meaning of a sentence with the common usage of language, or, more precisely, the rules which govern its social-accept-able usage. Habermas's universal pragmatics mediates Wittgenstein's intersubjective semantics with Bühler's functional semiotics, where every sign has a representative, performative and expressive function. Universal pragmatics exposes the universal aspects of dialogue in any discourse situation. Habermas also uses Austin's speech-act theory to emphasize this point (pp. 388–90/288–90).
15  Ibid., vol. 1, pp. 66ff/39ff.
16  For a more recent exposition of rationality as justification, see the studies in Habermas, *Wahrheit und Rechtfertigung*.
17  Habermas, *Theorie des kommunikativen Handelns*, vol. 1, p. 71/42.
18  Cooke, *Language and Reason*, p. 11.
19  Habermas, *Theorie des kommunikativen Handelns*, vol. 1, p. 28/10.
20  See Habermas, 'Dialektik der Rationalisierung', pp. 178–9/103–4, where he states that the central motives of the *Theory of Communica-tive Action* are a theory of communicative action and rationality, the dialectic of social rationalization, the concepts of system and life-world, and a critical diagnosis of modernity.
21  Habermas, *Theorie des kommunikativen Handelns*, vol. 1, pp. 234–5/164–5. On Habermas's interpretation of Weber, see T. Smith, 'The scope of the social science in Weber and Habermas', and A. A. Smith, 'Ethics and politics in the work of Jürgen Habermas'.
22  Piaget and Kohlberg relate the different levels of learning with the cognitive and moral development of children. In this process the objective reality is differentiated from normative-social relations and the individual inner self. Piaget describes this development as one of heightened decentredness. In this process of decentralization the child loses a strong experience of being ego-centred and discovers the important perspectives of others. Piaget's genetic-structural model distinguishes four phases of child development: the symbiotic, egocentric, sociocentric and universalist phases (Habermas, *Zur Rekon-struktion des historischen Materialismus*, p. 14/100). The key here is that the child moves through different phases to a higher level of critical reflection, thereby freeing him or her from the parochial power of tradition.
23  Whereas Hegel and some orthodox Marxists interpret history as an a priori development, Habermas connects history to a theory of social

evolution, developmental advances and regression (Habermas, *Zur Rekonstruktion des historischen Materialismus*, pp. 154–5/140–1). On the problematical concept of social evolution, Ingram remarks that Habermas advances the superiority of post-conventional morality. It is an open question whether there are not more appropriate ways of development in non-Western cultures. Are the problems of societies always cross-culturally universalizable? The difference between late capitalist and traditional societies remains a reality. Ingram also adds that it is problematic to link the ontogenetic model with the developmental phases of social evolution (Ingram, *Habermas and the Dialectic of Reason*, pp. 132–4).

24 Habermas, *Theorie des kommunikativen Handelns*, vol. 1, pp. 105–9/ 68–72.

25 On communicative ethics, see Habermas, *Moralbewußtsein und kommunikatives Handeln*; idem, *Vorstudien und Ergänzungen zur Theorie des kommunikativen Handelns*; and idem, *Erläuterungen zur Diskursethik*. For interpretations of this aspect of Habermas's work, see Weisshaupt, 'Überlegungen zur Diskursethik von Jürgen Habermas'; Ferrara, 'A critique of Habermas' *Diskursethik*'; White, *The Recent Work of Jürgen Habermas*; and the essays in *New German Critique* 62 (1994).

26 Habermas, *Theorie des kommunikativen Handelns*, vol. 2, pp. 171–293/ 113–98. For interpretations of this aspect of Habermas's work, see McCarthy, 'Introduction' to *The Theory of Communicative Action*; Baxter, 'System and life-world in Habermas' theory of communicative action'; Dallmayr, 'Life-world and communicative action'; and Ingram, *Habermas and the Dialectic of Reason*, pp. 115–35. For critical perspectives on life-world and system, see Honneth, *Critique of Power*, pp. 278–304, and the essays by Arnason, Berger, Joas and McCarthy in Honneth and Joas (eds), *Communicative Action*. For his reaction to this criticism, see Habermas 'Entgegnung', pp. 327–405/214–64, and *idem*, 'Questions and counterquestions', pp. 192–216.

27 Habermas, *Theorie des kommunikativen Handelns*, vol. 2, pp. 187–8/ 122–3. Habermas (pp. 74–5/46) writes: 'To the degree that the rationality potential ingrained in communicative action is released, the archaic core of the normative dissolves and gives way to the rationalization of worldviews, to the universalization of law and morality, and to an acceleration of the processes of individuation. It is upon this evolutionary trend that Mead bases in the end his idealistic projection of a communicatively rationalized society.'

28 Ibid., vol. 2, pp. 182–6/119–23, 219–23/146–8. According to McCarthy ('Introduction' to *The Theory of Communicative Action*, p. xxv), crises are issues such as a loss of meaning and motivation, legitimation problems, orientation uncertainty, anomie, destabilization of collective identity, alienation, psychopathologies and destruction of tradition.

29 Habermas, *Theorie des kommunikativen Handelns*, vol. 2, pp. 224–8/ 148–52.

30  On Habermas's relationship to Marxism, see Jay, *Marxism and Totality*, pp. 462–509, and Rockmore, 'Theory and practice again'.
31  Habermas, *Theorie des kommunikativen Handelns*, vol. 2, pp. 225–6/ 149–51. The separation of system and life-world has been criticized. Ingram argues (*Habermas and the Dialectic of Reason*, pp. 133–4) that the disconnection of the life-world leads to a reduction in practical rationality as against cognitive-instrumental rationality. Practical rationality aims at emancipating individuals in a universal sense. An emancipated society should mediate between particular and universal interests. This, for Ingram, is the basis of a cosmopolitical, egalitarian vision of democratic socialism. Important questions, such as the relationship between reason and tradition, individual autonomy, and the importance of economic growth and the life-world, should be asked in this context. McCarthy and Misgeld, for example, question Habermas's positive interpretation of systems theory in place of a historical-situated cultural critique (cf. McCarthy, 'Reflections on rationalization in *The Theory of Communicative Action*'; Misgeld, 'Critical hermeneutics versus Neoparsonianism'). For a feminist-inspired critique of the difference between life-world and system, see Fraser, 'What is critical about Critical Theory?'
32  R. J. Bernstein (ed.), *Habermas and Modernity*, p. 22, remarks: 'There have always been social scientists who have argued that the proper study of society is one that studies society as a complex system, where there are underlying interacting structures, and dynamic forms of systematic integration/or breakdown. In its extreme form a systems theory approach diminishes the significance of the role of social actors. They are seen as "place-holders" within a total system. But the other pole in sociological analyses gives primacy to the creative role of social actors, and the ways in which they construct, negotiate, and reconstruct the social meanings of their world. In its extreme form, advocates of this orientation claim that the very concepts of system and structure are reified fictions.'
33  Habermas, *Theorie des kommunikativen Handelns*, vol. 2, p. 250/167.
34  Ibid., vol. 2, pp. 275–6/185: 'the institutions that anchor steering mechanisms such as power and money in the lifeworld could serve as a channel either for the influence of the lifeworld on formally organized domains of action or, conversely, for the influence of the system on communicatively structured contexts of action. In the one case, they function as an institutional framework that subjects system maintenance to the normative restrictions of the lifeworld, in the other, as a base that subordinates the lifeworld to the systematic constraints of material reproduction and thereby "mediatizes" it.' See in this regard R. Pfeufer Kahn, 'The problem of power in Habermas'.
35  Habermas, *Theorie des kommunikativen Handelns*, vol. 2, p. 455/307.
36  For an early formulation on new social movements, see Habermas, *Zur Rekonstruktion des historischen Materialismus*, p. 116. On Habermas and

feminism, see Fraser, 'What is critical about Critical Theory?'; Simpson, 'On Habermas and particularity'; Benhabib (ed.), *Feminism as Critique*; and Mills, *Woman, Nature and Psyche*.

37  Habermas, *Theorie des kommunikativen Handelns*, vol. 2, p. 293/196–7. See also ibid., vol. 1, pp. 338–9/248–9. Habermas writes: 'The paradox, however, is that the rationalization of the lifeworld simultaneously gives rise to both the systematically induced reification of the lifeworld and the utopian perspective from which capitalist modernization has always appeared with the stain of dissolving traditional life-forms without salvaging their communicative substance. Capitalist modernization destroys these forms of life, but does not transform them in such a way that the intermeshing of cognitive-instrumental with moral-practical and expressive moments, which had obtained in everyday practice prior to its rationalization, could be retained at a higher level of differentiation' (ibid., vol. 2, pp. 486–7/329).

38  Ibid., vol. 2, p. 488/330–1: Habermas interprets Weber's vision of the 'steel cage' of modern society and Marx's concept of alienation as pathologies of the life-world.

39  On the rational dimension of Habermas's thinking, see White, 'Rationality and the foundations of political philosophy'; Giddens, 'Reason without revolution?'; Honneth, 'Enlightenment and rationality'; and Dallmayr, 'Habermas and rationality'.

40  See McCarthy, 'Introduction' to *The Theory of Communicative Action*, p. xxxvii.

41  Ibid., pp. v–vi.

42  R. J. Bernstein (ed.), *Habermas and Modernity*, p. 24.

43  See White, *The Recent Work of Jürgen Habermas*, p. 147.

44  Habermas, *Theorie des kommunikativen Handelns*, vol. 1, p. 41/20.

45  Ibid., vol. 1, p. 326/238. The three original formal-pragmatic relationships, i.e. cognitive and instrumental action (1.1), social responsibility (2.2) and emotion or self-expression (3.3) can be articulated linguistically in allegations, regulative and expressive utterances and can be rationalized in the context of theoretical, practical and aesthetic discourses. The mentioned relationships and their corresponding forms of discourse can *inter alia* be extended to strategic action (1.2), moral self-control and autonomy (2.3) and aesthetic taste (3.1). Habermas emphasized the cognitive-instrumental (1.1/2), moral-practical (2.2/3) and aesthetic-expressive (3.1/3) relationships as social spheres that are susceptible to rationalization. These forms of rationalization tolerate an argumentative-systematic accumulation of knowledge; only within these complexes is rationalization at all possible. This schematic representation, and more specifically the model of aesthetic rationality in it, have been criticized. McCarthy asks: in what way do the moments of rationality retain their unity in the midst of differentiation, and can this unity be adequately addressed through philosophical analysis? McCarthy (with Whitebook and Ottmann) also asks why the

subjective-objective relationship (1.3), objective-moral relationship (2.1) and moral-aesthetic relationship (3.2) are not rationalizable? (See McCarthy, 'Reflections on rationalization in *The Theory of Communicative Action*', pp. 176–91.) Secondly, it is not clear why a rationalizable aesthetic attitude towards the social reality is not possible. Habermas (p. 327/238–9) complicates this issue when he writes: 'that expressively determined forms of interaction (for example counter cultural forms of life) do not form structures that are rationalizable in and of themselves, but are parasitic in that they remain dependent on innovations in the other spheres of value'. Although Habermas acknowledges that subjects may assume a performative attitude towards external nature, may stand in a communicative relationship to it, and may experience it aesthetic-morally (2.1), he comes to the conclusion that there is only one productive approach in this regard: namely, the objective approach of the natural scientist, the experimental observer.

46   Ibid., vol. 1, p. 70/41.
47   Ibid., vol. 1, p. 36/16.
48   Habermas, 'Die Moderne – ein unvollendetes Projekt', p. 184/8.
49   Habermas (*Theorie des kommunikativen Handelns*, vol. 1, p. 329/240) writes that a selective model of rationality results when '(at least) one of the three constitutive components of the cultural tradition is not systematically worked up, or when (at least) one cultural value sphere is insufficiently institutionalized, that is, without any structure-forming effect on society as a whole, or when (at least) one sphere predominates to such an extent that it subjects life-orders to a form of rationality that is alien to them'.
50   Habermas, 'Questions and counterquestions', pp. 208–9.
51   Habermas, *Theorie des kommunikativen Handelns*, vol. 2, pp. 585–6/ 328–9.
52   Ibid., vol. 1, pp. 157ff/106ff; Habermas, 'Questions and counterquestions', pp. 199, 207.
53   Habermas, 'Questions and counterquestions', p. 201.
54   Habermas, 'Die Moderne – ein unvollendetes Projekt', p. 190/12.
55   Habermas, 'Questions and counterquestions', p. 200.
56   Habermas, 'Die Moderne – ein unvollendetes Projekt', p. 184/10.
57   Ibid.
58   Wellmer, *The Persistence of Modernity*, p. 33. Adorno's criticism of popular art – e.g. Jazz – could be interpreted as an answer to Benjamin's optimistic interpretation of modern mass culture. Adorno tends to interpret popular music as ideological (ibid., p. 32). Similarly, he criticizes sport as mass culture (see Morgan, 'Adorno on Sport'). For a more positive appreciation of popular and rock music as mass culture, see Buxton, 'Rock music, the star system and the rise of consumerism'; Olivier, 'Beyond music minus memory'; and Bloomfield, 'Is it sooner than you think, or where are we in the history of rock music?'

59  Habermas, 'Die Moderne – ein unvollendetes Projekt', p. 188/10–11.
60  Wellmer, *The Persistence of Modernity*, p. 34.
61  Zuidervaart, *Adorno's Aesthetic Theory*, p. 246.
62  Wellmer, *The Persistence of Modernity*, p. 3.
63  Zuidervaart, *Adorno's Aesthetics Theory*, p. 245.
64  Ibid., p. 242.
65  Habermas, 'Questions and counterquestions', p. 202.
66  Ibid., p. 211.
67  Ibid., p. 202.
68  Habermas explicitly tries to put forward a concept of communicative reason that escapes the grip of Western logocentrism. In place of Nietzsche's totalizing, self-referential critique of reason – followed by Heidegger/Derrida and Bataille/Foucault – Habermas argues that the potential for rationality can be apprehended in the everyday practice of communication. On this point the validity dimensions of propositional truth, normative correctness and subjective truthfulness mix with one another. Against this background, a major aporia of the philosophical tradition is addressed: from the network of embodied and interactively formed historically situated reason, only propositional reason is absolutized as a humanistic ideal. Von Humboldt's pragmatism, the later Wittgenstein's philosophy of language, and Austin's speech-act theory all problematize the semantic advantage of assertoric sentences and propositional truth, according to Habermas. Logocentrism means for Habermas the neglect of the complexity of rationality in the lifeworld and the restriction of reason to its cognitive-instrumental dimension – the selective privileged dimension of capitalist modernization. (ibid., pp. 196–7.)
69  Habermas, *Der philosophische Diskurs der Moderne*, pp. 63–4/49–50: 'Over against the dissolution of art into life . . . Schiller clings to the autonomy of the pure appearance . . . For Schiller an aestheticization of the lifeworld is legitimate only in the sense that art operates as a catalyst, as a form of communication, as a medium within which separated moments are rejoined into an uncoerced totality.'
70  Ibid., pp. 13–14/5–6.
71  Ibid., pp. 41–2/29–30.
72  Ibid., pp. 44–6/32–4.
73  Ibid., pp. 52–3/39–40.
74  Ibid., p. 53/40: 'If the absolute is then thought of as infinite subjectivity . . . then the moments of the universal and the individual can be thought of as unified only in the framework of monological self-knowledge: in the concrete universal, the subject as universal maintains a primacy over the subject as individual. For the sphere of the ethical, the outcome of this logic is the primacy of the *higher-level subjectivity of the state* over the subjective freedom of the individual.'
75  Ibid., p. 54/40.

76  Habermas, 'Questions and counterquestions', pp. 206, 210–12.
77  Ibid., p. 213.
78  Habermas, 'Die Moderne – ein unvollendetes Projekt', p. 190/12.
79  Habermas, 'Heinrich Heine und die Rolle des Intellektuellen in Deutschland', p. 29/73.
80  Ibid., p. 33/78–9.
81  On Weber's famous essay 'Politics as vocation', see ibid., p. 28/72: 'To the professional politician Weber ascribed realistic detachment, a sense of proportion, competence, and a willingness to accept responsibility – to the writer and philosopher engaged in politics as a dilettante, in contrast, a "romanticism" of the intellectually interesting . . . devoid of all feeling of objective responsibility.'
82  Ibid., p. 34/79. They argue that the intellectual has to burn '. . . the greater part of what he owes to his bourgeois descent before he can march in rank and file with the proletarian army'.
83  Ibid., p. 39/84–5.
84  Ibid., p. 31/75: 'this lifelong battle, fought with the weapons of the poet, as nourished by the same inspirations, the same partisan support of the universal and individualism of the Enlightenment'.
85  Ibid., pp. 38–9/82–4.
86  Ibid., p. 41/86.
87  Ibid., p. 43/88–9.

## Chapter 4    The Second Phase Continues: The Postmodern Challenge

1  On postmodernism and modern architecture, see Habermas, *Die neue Unübersichtlichkeit*, pp. 11–29; Kolb, *Postmodern Sophistications*, pp. 87–129; Wellmer, *The Persistence of Modernity*; and Duvenage, 'Filosofie en Argitektuur'.
2  For a critical interpretation of Habermas's *The Philosophical Discourse of Modernity*, see Dallmayr, 'The discourse of modernity'.
3  Dallmayr, 'The discourse of modernity', pp. 377–8.
4  Schelling argues in his *System of Transcendental Idealism* (1800) that aesthetic intuition and the development of a new collective mythology offer an answer to the derailment of modernity. 'Reason could no longer take possession of itself in its own medium of self-reflection; it could only rediscover itself in the prior medium of art' (Habermas, *Der philosphische Diskurs der Moderne*, p. 112/90). It is interesting that Habermas did his doctorate on Schelling.
5  Ibid., pp. 112–13/90–1. See also Kraus, *Naturpoesie und Kunstpoesie im Frühwerk Friedrich Schlegels*.
6  There is a difference between the Romantic and the Nietzschean interpretation of Dionysus. The dividing line is Nietzsche's anti-Christian

stance, which relate to his radical anti-Enlightenment and anti-rational thinking. The Romantics, on the other hand, identify 'the frenzied wine-god with the Christian saviour-god . . . only . . . because Romantic messianism aimed at a *rejuvenation* of, but not a departure from, the West' (Habermas, *Der philosophische Diskurs der Moderne*, p. 114/92). On Dionysus and Nietzschean aesthetics see Sallis, *Crossings*, and Young, *Nietzsche's Philosophy of Art*.

7  Habermas, *Der philosophische Diskurs der Moderne*, p. 116/93–4.
8  Ibid., pp. 118–20/95–7. See also Dallmayr, 'The discourse of modernity', p. 386.
9  Habermas, *Der philosophische Diskurs der Moderne*, p. 129/104–5.
10  Ibid., p. 121/97.
11  Heidegger, *Nietzsche*, vol. I, pp. 211–20. On Heidegger's aesthetics, see Megill, *Prophets of Extremity*; and Kockelmans, *Heidegger on Art and Art Works*.
12  Heidegger, 'What calls for thinking', p. 359.
13  Habermas, *Der philosophische Diskurs der Moderne*, pp. 163/136, 181/152–3. See also Dallmayr, 'The discourse of modernity', p. 390.
14  Heidegger, *Being and Time*, pp. 153–4.
15  McCarthy, 'Introduction', in Habermas, *The Philosophical Discourse of Modernity*, p. xii.
16  Habermas, *Der philosophische Diskurs der Moderne*, pp. 194–5/164–5. On Derrida's defence of writing (*grammatology*) and critique of Husserl's theory of meaning, see ibid., pp. 198–200/168–9.
17  Dews discusses the implications of Schelling's thinking for the post-Nietzschean discourse of Derrida. According to him, Schelling's critique of subjective idealism comes down to a critique of any form of privilege on behalf of the subject or object. Schelling seeks, rather, a more fundamental underlying identity – which can be proposed only in continuous absence. Dews (*Logics of Disintegration*, pp. 26–7) sees Schelling as a precursor of Adorno and Derrida: 'for in Derrida's work, *différance* cannot be defined through its oppositional relation to identity, since it is considered to be "nonoriginary origin" of presence and identity, and as such cannot be *dependent* upon them for its determination. But, if *différance* does not stand in opposition to presence and identity, then neither can it differ from them . . . Absolute difference, in other words, which is what Derrida must understand by a *différance* which is the "possibility of conceptuality," and thus of determination, necessarily collapses into absolute identity.' See also Baum, *Die Transzendierung des Mythos*.
18  Despite its replacement of transcendental subjectivity by writing, Habermas argues that Derrida's deconstructive project is still locked into a subject-based philosophy. Jay, 'Review of Habermas' *Philosophical Discourse of Modernity*', p. 101, writes: 'deconstruction ultimately remains in thrall to a philosophy of the subject, whose problematic it merely inverts. For in trying to get back "before" the subject, it can only

find a linguistically defined, absent infrastructural prime mover that functions in precisely the same way.' As in the case of the fate of Heidegger's Being, there is a movement away from public communication to an arbitrary play of signs where meaning is constantly deferred – an act of private relevation or a possible esoteric discourse of an absent god (Habermas, *Der philosophische Diskurs der Moderne*, pp. 212–13/180–1). Habermas argues that Derrida's project is a post-Nietzschean example of the aesthetic moment being privileged above the cognitive and ethical moments of modernity. The clearest example of this is the levelling of the genre distinction between philosophy and literature.

19   Habermas, *Der philosophische Diskurs der Moderne*, p. 221/187. For an appreciative account of Derrida's aesthetics, see Olivier, 'Derrida, art and truth'.

20   Habermas, *Der philosophische Diskurs der Moderne*, p. 224/190.

21   Ibid., p. 226/192. Habermas refers to the following statements by Norris and De Man: '[C]riticism is now crossing over into literature, rejecting its subservient . . . stance and taking on the freedom of interpretative style with a matchless gusto' (Norris, *On Deconstruction*, p. 98). De Man, *Blindness and Insight*, p. 110, writes: 'Since they are not scientific, critical texts have to be read with the same awareness of ambivalence that is brought to the study of non-critical literary texts.'

22   Habermas, *Der philosophische Diskurs der Moderne*, p. 233/198: 'As Gadamer has shown, the hermeneutic effort that would bridge over temporal and cultural distances remains oriented toward the idea of a possible consensus being brought about in the present.'

23   Ibid., p. 234/199: 'Everyday communicative practice, in which agents have to reach an understanding about something in the world, stands under the need to prove its worth, and it is the idealizing suppositions that make such testing possible in the first place. It is in relation to this need for standing the test within ordinary practice that one may distinguish, with Austin and Searle, between "usual" and "parasitic" uses of language.'

24   Ibid., p. 236/201.

25   Habermas, *Nachmetaphysisches Denken*, pp. 261–2/223–4.

26   Habermas, *Der philosophische Diskurs der Moderne*, pp. 240–1/204–5.

27   Ibid., pp. 222/188, 243/207.

28   Ibid., pp. 245–6/209–10.

29   Carroll calls his work on Foucault, Lyotard and Derrida, *paraesthetics*. He argues that postmodern thinkers do not prejudice philosophy against literature, and logic against rhetoric. These pairs are, rather, put in a playful and creative tension. Carroll, *Paraesthetics*, p. 11, writes: 'Today it seems to me just as urgent to say, and in a way that is anything but anti-Nietzschean, that there is just as great a danger of our perishing of art as of truth, and that it is this double danger that con-

fronts critical theory and art after Nietzsche.' In short, art for art's sake (the totalitarian autonomous artwork) is just as problematic as the aestheticization of life (the aesthetic state). In its place Carroll calls for a creative mediation between art and politics, art and theory, and art and ethics.

30 Habermas, *Der philosophische Diskurs der Moderne*, p. 246/210.
31 See Weiss, *The Aesthetics of Excess*.
32 Habermas, *Der philosophische Diskurs der Moderne*, p. 249/212.
33 Ibid., pp. 269–71/229–31.
34 Ibid., p. 281/240. On Habermas and Foucault, see Freundlieb, 'Rationalism versus irrationalism'.
35 Dreyfus and Rabinow, *Michel Foucault*, pp. 90ff.
36 Habermas, *Der philosophische Diskurs der Moderne*, p. 318/271.
37 Ingram, *Habermas and the Dialectic of Reason*, p. 99.
38 Jay, 'Review of Habermas' *Philosophical Discourse of Modernity*', p. 104.
39 Lyotard, *The Postmodern Condition*, p. xxiv. For a distinction between modern autonomous and postmodern art, see Foster, '(Post)modern polemics', p. 75. Foster writes that it is the ideal of autonomous art to maintain the high quality of past art 'and to ensure the aesthetic as a value in its own right; and to ground art – the medium, the discipline – ontologically and epistemologically'. Postmodern art 'is posed, at least, initially, against a modernism become monolithic in its self-referentiality and official in its autonomy'.
40 Lyotard, *The Postmodern Condition*, p. 15.
41 Ibid., p. 72.
42 Huyssen, 'The search for tradition', p. 38: 'Habermas ignores the fact that the very idea of wholistic (sic) modernity and of a totalizing view of history has become anathema in the 1970s, and precisely not on the conservative right.'
43 Lyotard, *The Postmodern Condition*, pp. 65–6. See also Wellmer, *The Persistence of Modernity*, p. 42: 'We might speak of a pluralistic and "punctualistic," a "post-Euclidian" concept of reason, in contrast to Habermas's consensual concept of reason, for example, which appears from Lyotard's point of view as a last supreme effort to cling to the "totalizing" categories of reconciliation characteristic of German Idealism (and the Marxist tradition), including the idea of the unity of truth, freedom and justice.' For another view on this issue, see Huyssen, 'The search for tradition', p. 36.
44 Lyotard, *The Postmodern Condition*, p. 72, writes: 'Jürgen Habermas . . . thinks that if modernity has failed, it is in allowing the totality of life to be splintered into independent specialities which are left to the narrow competence of experts, while the concrete individual experiences "desublimated meaning" and "destructed form," not as liberation but in the mode of that immense *ennui* which Baudelaire described over a century ago.'

45    Ibid., p. 72.

46    Ibid., p. 73.

47    Ibid., p. 75.

48    Ibid., p. 78.

49    Ibid.

50    Ingram, *Habermas and the Dialectic of Reason*, p. 76. Against this back-ground, Andreas Huyssen, *After the Great Divide*, p. 196, describes post-modern art as an 'ever wider dispersal and dissemination of artistic procedures all working out of the ruins of the modernist edifice, raiding it for ideas, plundering its vocabulary and supplementing it with ran-domly chosen images and motifs from pre-modern and non-modern cultures as well as from contemporary mass culture'.

51    Lyotard, *The Postmodern Condition*, p. 77.

52    Ibid., pp. 78, 81.

53    Ibid., pp. 81–2.

54    Derrida, *The Truth in Painting*, p. 117.

55    Jay, '"The aesthetic ideology" as ideology, or what does it mean to aestheticize politics?', p. 46.

56    Lacoue-Labarthe and Nancy, *The Literary Absolute*, p. 53.

57    De Man, *The Rhetoric of Romanticism*, p. 264.

58    Ibid., p. 289.

59    Jay, '"The aesthetic ideology" as ideology, or what does it mean to aestheticize politics?', p. 47.

60    Culler, *On Deconstruction*, writes: 'Deconstruction's demonstration that these hierarchies . . . [literal/metaphorical, truth/fiction] . . . are undone by the working of texts that propose them alters the standing of literary language . . . If serious language is a special case of non-serious, if truths are fictions whose fictionality has been forgotten, then literature is not a deviant, parasitical instance of language. On the con-trary, other discourses can be seen as cases of a generalized literature, or archi-literature.'

61    Jameson, 'The politics of theory', p. 62, points to four possible posi-tions on the relation between modernity and postmodernity: pro-postmodernism/anti-modernism (Wolfe, Jencks), pro-postmodernism/pro-modernism (Lyotard), anti-postmodernism/anti-modernism (Tafuri), anti-postmodernism/pro-modernism (Habermas).

62    Ingram, *Habermas and the Dialectic of Reason*, pp. 75–7. Ingram argues that Habermas's recent work has enlarged the rhetorical aspects of lan-guage and communication. This 'moment of deconstruction,' moves away from the strict differentiation of the validity spheres in *The Theory of Communicative Action*. Despite Habermas's critique of postmoder-nity, Ingram (ibid., p. 103) argues that it plays a role in his concept of communicative rationality. Postmodernism mediates between the mate-rial impulse of pre-discursive life and the form impulse of reflective dis-course without elevating one above the other.

63    Megill, *Prophets of Extremity*.

## Chapter 5 Critical Perspectives on Habermas's Aesthetics

1 Ingram, *Habermas and the Dialectic of Reason*, pp. 131–2.
2 Ibid., p. 73. Ingram refers to Habermas's usage of the concepts of aesthetic rationality and mimesis.
3 Ibid., pp.131–2.
4 Habermas, 'Questions and counterquestions', p. 209. Critics such as McCarthy, Whitebook and Ottmann also ask how the moments of rationality retain their unity in the midst of differentiation.
5 Some of Habermas's critics argue that he underestimates mimesis as a 'technical act of human production'. Similarly, Habermas is criticized for not using the expressive moments of semantic potential in Benjamin's theory of language. Rabinbach argues that although Benjamin did not thematize language explicitly in communicative terms, he strongly criticized a technical or instrumental concept of language use. Wolin, *Walter Benjamin*, p. 246, writes: '[the] rejection of an instrumentalist view of language and [the] emphasis on language as a privileged medium through which a "flashing image" of reconciliation between man and nature can be glimpsed'. Benjamin found, according to Jay, a mimetic and communicative (semiotic) dimension in language.
6 Jay, 'Habermas and modernism', p. 222. Habermas is sceptical as to whether Piaget's genetic psychology is applicable on the level of aesthetic learning processes ('Questions and counterquestions', p. 201).
7 Jay, 'Habermas and modernism', p. 139.
8 Ingram, 'Habermas on aesthetics and rationality', p. 75, argues that Habermas 'is torn between two types of modernist aesthetic: the formalism of the one establishing a critical distance from the antiformalism of the other . . . everyday life'. As a possible solution, Ingram suggests that Habermas should mediate between these two elements.
9 Thompson, 'Universal pragmatics', pp. 125–8; Norris, 'Deconstruction, postmodernism and philosophy', p. 426; White, *The Recent Work of Jürgen Habermas*, p. 31.
10 Cooke, *Language and Reason*, pp. 21–2, 25. For a recent position in this regard, see Habermas, *Vom sinnlichen Eindruck zum symbolischen Ausdruck*.
11 Cooke, *Language and Reason*, pp. 75–7, 80–2, 83–4.
12 Habermas, 'A reply to my critics', pp. 270–1.
13 Foucault, *The History of Sexuality*, vol. i, pp. 140, 155–9. For critical studies of the relationship between Foucault and Habermas, see Honneth, *Critique of Power*; Ashenden and Owen, *Foucault contra Habermas*; and Kelly (ed.), *Critique and Power*.
14 Foucault, 'On the genealogy of ethics', pp. 230–1, 235.
15 Foucault, *The Foucault Reader*, pp. 41–2.
16 Taylor, 'Overcoming epistemology', p. 472, writes: 'the subject withdraws even from his own body, which he is able to look on as an object

... the ... demand for a neutral, objectifying science of human life and action'.

17    Foucault, 'On the genealogy of ethics', p. 230. For a defence of Foucault, see Visker, *Michel Foucault*.

18    White, *The Recent Work of Jürgen Habermas*, p. 177, counters that Foucault was aware of the limitations of his thinking in this regard. He refers, for example, to an interview in which Foucault (*The Foucault Reader*, p. 379) made the following statement on political consensus: 'The furthest I would go is to say that perhaps one must not be for con-sensuality, but one must be against nonconsensuality.'

19    On the concept of the 'aesthetics of existence', Foucault ('On the genealogy of ethics', p. 231) writes: 'Recent liberation movements suffer from the fact that they cannot find any principle on which to base the elaboration of a new ethics.' Against the background of Habermas's nor-mative concept of the subject it is relevant to ask in what sense does Foucault allow the aesthetic subject to take up political and ethical positions. Although Foucault resisted a judicial or norm-oriented con-ception of subjectivity, he also, like Habermas, supported new social movements. There was apparently no real tension between the aesthetic subject and his or her political involvement in new social movements. See also the article of Huijer, 'The aesthetics of existence in the work of Michel Foucault'.

20    Whitebook, 'Reason and happiness', pp. 140–1.

21    Ibid., pp. 150–1.

22    Ibid., pp. 155–7.

23    The disconcerting conclusion, as indicated in chapter 1, is that an eman-cipated, just society can simultaneously be an unhappy society. 'Is it possible that one day an emancipated human race could encounter itself within an expanded space of discursive formation of will and yet be robbed of the light in which it is capable of interpreting its life as something *good*?' (Habermas, 'Bewussmachende oder rettende Kritik', p. 343/158).

24    Whitebook, 'Reason and happiness', p. 157.

25    Habermas, 'Questions and Counterquestions', pp. 213–15.

26    Habermas criticizes the argument of many Protestants that the balance of happiness does not change in the long run; consequently, it is not necessary for every generation to have utopian dreams. Such a stand-point is for Habermas – against the background of the overwhelming experiences of individual unhappiness, collective suffering and social catastrophes – not true to reality. These experiences are so tragic because, despite their quasi-naturalness, they do not stem from natural grounds. Thus the necessary conditions for a good life are violated. It is this experience which gave both Marx and Freud their inspiration. Habermas agrees with Whitebook that this kind of materialism should not be discarded. He writes: 'I do not want to pass over in silence the fact that McCarthy and Whitebook touch upon a basic philosophical

problem, which, if I am correct, still awaits an adequate resolution this side of the Hegelian logic: How is it possible to weaken the claims of statements about totalities so that they might be joined together with the stronger statements about general structure?' (ibid., p. 216).

27 Whitebook, 'Reason and Happiness', pp. 159–60.
28 Kunneman and Keulartz, *Rondom Habermas*, p. 246.
29 Habermas, *Theorie des kommunikativen Handelns*, vol. 2, p. 482/326.
30 Ibid., vol. 1, pp. 41/20, 69/41, 137/91.
31 Keulartz, 'Over Kunst en Kultuur in het Werk van Habermas', p. 12.
32 Kunneman and Keulartz, *Rondom Habermas*, pp. 183–5.
33 Keulartz argues that the metaphor of the court, with its clashing validity claims, makes room for the metaphor of birth (Keulartz, 'Over Kunst en Kultuur in het Werk van Habermas', pp. 24–5). The metaphor of birth, according to him, plays an important role in the philosophy of consciousness. He also points to the intimate link between production aesthetics and a philosophy of consciousness. The contemplative attitude of production aesthetics forms the basis of a dialectical philosophy of consciousness.
34 Habermas, 'Die Moderne – ein unvollendetes Projekt', p. 186/9.
35 Keulartz, 'Over Kunst en Kultuur in het Werk van Habermas', p. 33.
36 Ibid., pp. 25–6.
37 Habermas, *Theorie des kommunikativen Handelns*, vol. 2, p. 585/398.
38 Kunneman and Keulartz, *Rondom Habermas*, pp. 163–83.
39 Keulartz, 'Over Kunst en Kultuur in het Werk van Habermas', p. 36.
40 Bürger, 'The institution of "art" as a category in the sociology of literature'.
41 Bürger, *Theory of the Avant-garde*, p. 22. See also pp. 8, 13–14.
42 Ibid., p. 19.
43 Ibid., pp. 36, 46.
44 Ibid., p. 49.
45 Ibid., p. 87.
46 Ibid., pp. 6–14, 20–7, 83–8.
47 Ibid, p. 87.
48 Ibid., pp. 50–4, 57–8.
49 Zuidervaart, *Adorno's Aesthetic Theory*, p. 218.
50 Bürger, 'Avant-garde and contemporary aesthetics'.
51 Ibid., p. 20.
52 Ibid., pp. 21–2.
53 Bürger, *Theory of the Avant-garde*, p. 94.
54 See Zuidervaart, *Adorno's Aesthetic Theory*, pp. 240–2, 246. See also Bürger, *Theory of the Avant-garde*, p. 99.
55 Jay, 'Habermas and modernism', pp. 133, 137.
56 Habermas, 'A reply to my critics', p. 235.
57 J. M. Bernstein, 'Art against Enlightenment', p. 49.
58 Ibid., p. 50.

59 Adorno, *Aesthetic Theory*, pp. 180, 182.
60 Ibid., p. 199.
61 Ibid., p. 173: 'Aesthetics cannot hope to grasp works of art if it treats them as hermeneutical objects.'
62 Ibid., p. 185.
63 Wellmer, *The Persistence of Modernity*, p. 9, writes: 'Art can thus only be true in the sense of being faithful to reality to the extent that it makes reality appear *as* unreconciled, antagonistic, divided against itself. But it can only do this by showing reality in the light of reconciliation, i.e. by the non-violent aesthetic synthesis of disparate elements which produces the semblance of reconciliation. This means, however, that an antinomy is carried into the very *heart* of the aesthetic synthesis – which can only succeed by turning against itself and questioning its own underlying principle, for the sake of truth which nevertheless cannot be extracted except with recourse to this very principle.'
64 J. M. Bernstein, 'Art against Enlightenment', p. 58.
65 Adorno, *Aesthetic Theory*, p. 86.
66 J. M. Bernstein, 'Art against Enlightenment', p. 59.
67 Habermas, *Theorie des kommunikativen Handelns*, Vol. 1, p. 524/391.
68 J. M. Bernstein, 'Art against Enlightenment', p. 61, quoting Adorno, *Aesthetic Theory*, pp. 343, 338.
69 J. M. Bernstein, 'Art against Enlightenment', p. 62.
70 Ibid., p. 65. For a more extended version of Bernstein's argument, see his *Recovering Ethical Life*, chs 4, 6–7.
71 Wellmer, *The Persistence of Modernity*, p. 12.
72 Adorno, *Aesthetic Theory*, p. 186.
73 Wellmer, *The Persistence of Modernity*, pp. 7, 23.
74 Ibid., pp. 8–9.
75 Zuidervaart, *Adorno's Aesthetics*, pp. 285–6.
76 Wellmer, *The Persistence of Modernity*, p. 34.
77 According to Habermas, Weber defended the differentiation of the value spheres in modern Europe – which was introduced by the neo-Kantians Emil Lask and Heinrich Rickert – on two levels: first, on the level of ideas being the product of tradition (scientific theories, moral and judicial views, and artistic production); and second, on the level of cultural action systems, with their corresponding discourses, activities and professional institutions. The differentiation of value spheres corresponds to a decentred understanding of the world which is an important prerequisite for the professional treatment of cultural traditions which leads to questions of truth, justice and taste. This modern understanding of the world involves a hypothetical approach to phenomena and experiences, which can be isolated from the complexity of life-world perspectives and submitted to experimental, changeable conditions. This is applicable to objective natural conditions, normative forms of action, and boundless subjectivity (Habermas, 'Questions and Counterquestions', pp. 206-7).

78  Habermas, *Theorie des kommunikativen Handelns*, vol. 2, p. 584/397: 'And an art that has become autonomous pushes toward an ever purer expression of the basic aesthetic experiences of a subjectivity that is decentred and removed from the spatiotemporal structures of everyday life. Subjectivity frees itself here from the conventions of daily perception and of purposive activity, from the imperatives of work and of what is merely useful.'

79  Wellmer, *The Persistence of Modernity*, p. 13.

80  Wellmer, 'Reason, utopia and the *Dialectic of Enlightenment*', p. 49.

81  Wellmer's interpretation of aesthetic reconciliation also influences his understanding of subjectivity, where the diffuse, unintegrated, and 'meaningless' elements can be gathered 'in an arena for non-violent communication which would encompass the opened forms of art as well as the open structures of a no longer rigid type of individuation and socialization' (Wellmer, *The Persistence of Modernity*, p. 20).

82  Ibid., p. 22. The fact that there may be a dispute about the evaluation of an artwork in aesthetic discourse indicates for Habermas the inherent presentness of validity claims in art. The aesthetic validity or 'unity' of a work of art points to its illuminating power to open one's eyes to the 'known' – to reveal 'reality' anew. Such a validity claim stands open for the 'truth potential' which is freed from the full complexity of life's experience. Such a 'truth potential' belongs, though, not to one of the three validity claims of communicative action. The one to one relation between the prescriptive validity of normative validity claims in regulative speech-acts is, according to Habermas, not a proper model for the relationship between the truth potential of the art work and the transformed relationship between the subject and the world which is accomplished by aesthetic experience. Habermas repeats this position in 'Questions and Counterquestions', p. 203.

83  Wellmer, *The Persistence of Modernity*, pp. 23–4.

84  See Habermas, *Theorie des kommunikativen Handelns*, vol. 1, pp. 40–2/19–20, where he distinguishes between theoretical argumentation, moral-practical discourses and aesthetic critique.

85  Wellmer, *The Persistence of Modernity*, p. 27.

86  My interpretation of Wellmer on this point has been influenced by Lara, 'Albrecht Wellmer'.

87  Ibid., pp. 15–16.

88  Ibid, pp. 5–6, 9.

89  Ibid., pp. 11–13.

90  Zuidervaart, *Adorno's Aesthetics*, p. 289.

91  Ibid., p. 241.

92  Zuidervaart (ibid., p. 290), argues that further reflection is needed in the following areas: 'artistic truth, the status of philosophical claims about artistic truth, the historiographic patterns surrounding such claims, and the language in which Adorno couches his conception of truth.'

93  Habermas, 'Questions and Counterquestions', p. 202.
94  Ibid., p. 209.
95  Wellmer, 'Reason, utopia and the *Dialectic of Enlightenment*', pp. 42–3.

## Chapter 6   The Reciprocity of World Disclosure and Discursive Language

1  Apart from its aesthetic implications, the concept of world disclosure has wandered into the fields of linguistics, epistemology and even cultural anthropology. See Bohman, 'World disclosure and radical criticism', p. 82. According to Bohman, quite different phenomena could be included under the term 'world disclosure': from ordinary classification schemes to novel artistic and poetic language and epochal-historical experiences of radical innovation in whole cultures. The issue of making and finding, construction and discovery, are mutual.
2  Bohman's reference to *Disclosure A* and *Disclosure B* follows very much the same logic (ibid, pp. 82–3). *Disclosure A* is a language or culture disclosing a 'world', in that it already shapes how we see and question reality through its habitual categories and presupposed categories. *Disclosure B* indicates that innovators and poets disclose the 'world' in the opposite sense. See also Kompridis, 'On world disclosure', p. 29. My interpretation of world disclosure in this chapter has been influenced by Kompridis. For more detailed positions by Kompridis, see his forthcoming books *In Times of Need: Habermas, Heidegger and the Future of Critical Theory* (Evanston, Ill.: Northwestern University Press) and *Crises and Transformation: The Aesthetic Critique of Modernity from Hegel to Habermas* (Berkeley: University of California Press).
3  Bohman, 'World disclosure and radical criticism', p. 83.
4  Kompridis, 'On world disclosure', pp. 30, 37.
5  Kompridis (ibid., p. 37) argues that Habermas pursues a middle course between the unifiers (Taylor, Dreyfus, Gadamer), and those thinkers who move beyond the common space (Rorty, Castoriades, Derrida). In the process he steers a middle course between a too tight holism which disallows criticism, on the one hand, and an incoherent pluralism, which decentres one meaning horizon after another, on the other hand. He agrees with Taylor that social practices, capacities for intersubjectivity, and the forming of individual and collective identities are made possible by the world-disclosing function of language. There is, though, a danger of totalizing this function – its exclusive power to create or re-create a common space. There is something here of Heidegger's emphatic holism in its prioritizing of the shared ontological pre-understanding disclosed by language and the 'We perspective' articulating common space. Rorty is partly right that the bonds that bind can limit the scope of individually initiated action.

6   For a later formulation of this famous expression, see Heidegger, 'Letter on humanism', p. 217.
7   Lafont, 'World disclosure and reference', pp. 51–2.
8   See Heidegger, *Being and Time*, pp. 256–73, on the relationship between *Dasein*, disclosedness and truth.
9   Heidegger, 'The origin of the work of art', p. 200.
10  Heidegger, 'The essence of truth', p. 119: 'The impression arises that this definition of the essence of truth is independent of the interpretation of the essence of the Being of all beings, which always includes a corresponding interpretation of the essence of man as the bearer and executor of intellectus.'
11  Ibid., p. 122.
12  Ibid., p. 121.
13  Ibid., p. 125. Heidegger emphasizes the ambiguity of the concept of *aletheia*, because every uncovering leaves things covered in other respects. Therefore the proposition that '*Dasein* is in the truth' also means that '*Dasein* is in untruth'.
14  Ibid., pp. 123, 126–7. Freedom, or letting be (*Gelassenheit*), is also intrinsically a concealment/disclosure. In so far as *Da-sein ek-sists*, it conserves the first and broadest undisclosedness, untruth proper. Heidegger describes the proper non-essence of truth as mystery (p. 130). In the simultaneity of disclosure and closure, errancy holds sway (p. 134).
15  See Heidegger's essays 'On the essence of truth', 'On the essence of reason', and his writings on Nietzsche and Hölderlin in this regard.
16  Bohman, 'World disclosure and radical criticism', p. 83. Responsive gestures include those of praise (*ruhmen*) and dedication (*weihen*). In less fortunate cases they entail resignation. See in this regard Heidegger's 'The origin of the work of art', p. 169, and 'The question concerning technology', p. 341: 'The closer we come to danger, the more brightly do the ways into the saving power begin to shine and the more questioning we become.'
17  Heidegger, 'The origin of the work of art', p. 143.
18  Ibid., pp. 165, 169.
19  Ibid., pp. 197–8. The quintessential art for Heidegger is poetry – the setting-itself-into-work of truth on which both the artwork and the artist depend. Poetry is the saying of the disclosure of beings. Actual language at any given moment is the happening of the saying, in which a people's world historically arises for it and the earth is preserved as that which remains closed. The essence of poetry is the founding of truth. Heidegger understands founding as (a) bestowing (*Schenken*), (b) grounding (*Grunden*), and (c) beginning (*Anfangen*). A genuine beginning is a leap, is always a head start, in which everything to come is already leaped over, even if as something still veiled (p. 199). The beginning already contains the end latent within itself. Such a founding, according to Heidegger, happened historically among the Greeks as a forerunner for a possible way of Western thinking.

20  Ibid., pp. 170–2, 173–4. One of the characteristics of earth is that it shatters any attempt to penetrate it.
21  Ibid., p. 187. Preserving the artwork, as the domain of strife, does not reduce people to their private experiences, but brings them into contact with the truth happening in the work.
22  Ibid., pp. 186, 193. Only when science passes beyond correctness and proceeds to a truth, which means that it arrives at the essential disclosure of being-as-such, is it philosophy.
23  White, 'Heidegger and the difficulties of a postmodern ethics and politics', p. 85.
24  Lafont, 'World disclosure and reference', p. 54.
25  Seel, 'On rightness and truth', pp. 64–5, refers to Habermas and Tugendhat. He also finds Goodman's explanation of a certain kind of rightness in *Ways of Worldmaking*, despite terminological differences, similar to Heidegger's argument. See Tugendhat, 'Heidegger's idea of truth'.
26  Bohman, 'World disclosure and radical criticism', p. 86. According to Seel, 'On rightness and truth', p. 67, this argument puts Heidegger (and thinkers such as Taylor, Foucault and Derrida) at odds with the whole philosophical tradition.
27  Bohman, puts his case too strongly though, when in 'World disclosure and radical criticism', p. 87, he writes that the 'truth of an assertion is independent of disclosure'. See sections 6.3 and 6.4 in this regard.
28  Kompridis, 'On world disclosure', p. 35.
29  Heidegger, 'The origin of the work of art', pp. 204–5.
30  For a clear discussion of Heidegger's link with Hegel's aesthetics, see Kompridis, 'On world disclosure', p. 36. See also J. M. Bernstein, *The Fate of Art*, ch. 2; and Taminiaux, *Poetics, Speculation, and Judgment*.
31  Lafont, 'World disclosure and reference', pp. 46–7. For a more comprehensive position, see Lafont, *The Linguistic Turn in Hermeneutic Philosophy*, and *idem*, *Heidegger, Language and World-Disclosure*.
32  Lafont, 'World disclosure and reference', pp. 50–1, 55.
33  Ibid., pp. 48–9.
34  Ibid., pp. 55–6. Lafonte uses the theories of Kripke, Putnam and Donnellan to develop her alternative. Donnellan introduces the distinction between an 'attributive' and 'referential' use of characterization. The description of the referent contained in the indicator is correctable, and is in competition with other descriptions.
35  Ibid., pp. 58–60.
36  Kompridis, 'On world disclosure', p. 33.
37  Ibid., p. 34.
38  White, 'Heidegger and the difficulties of a postmodern ethics and politics', pp. 81–2.
39  For a defence of Heidegger's non-authoritarian politics, see Schürmann, *Heidegger on Being and Acting*. Schürmann uses the concept of 'anarchic praxis', which refers to a broader, more radical suggestion about

how action in general must be understood, once we accept Heidegger's arguments that our prevailing thinking about action condemns us to a compulsive reiteration of a technologizing, grasping attitude. Such an orientation would celebrate the utterly plural, unstable, mobile and unhierarchical character of being as presencing.

40    White, 'Heidegger and the difficulties of a postmodern ethics and politics', pp. 89–90.

41    See Habermas, *Das Absolute und die Geschichte*. This aspect of Habermas's intellectual development has not received the kind of attention it deserves. The only notable exception is the fine study of Keulartz, *De verkeerde Wereld van Jürgen Habermas*.

42    See Habermas, 'Mit Heidegger gegen Heidegger denken'.

43    Cf. Habermas, 'Dialektik der Rationalisierung', p. 96/171.

44    Habermas, *Theorie des kommunikativen Handelns*, vol. 1 pp. 10/28, 87–8/130–2, 273ff/370ff.

45    Ibid., vol. 1, pp. 11/30, 15–16/35–6, 98ff/148ff, 288–90/388–90.

46    Ibid., vol. 1, p. 10/28: 'This concept of communicative rationality carries with it connotations based ultimately on the central experience of the unconstrained, unifying, consensus bringing force of argumentative speech, in which different participants overcome their merely subjective views and, owing to the mutuality of rationally motivated convictions, assure themselves of both the unity of the objective world and the intersubjectivity of their lifeworld.'

47    See Habermas, *Nachmetaphysisches Denken*, pp. 50–1/42–3: 'Language's power to create meaning is promoted by the later Heidegger to the rank of the absolute. But from this there results another problem: the prejudicing force of linguistic world-disclosure devalues all innerworldly learning-processes. The ontological preunderstanding that dominates in any given period forms a fixed framework for the practices of the socialized individuals who are in the world. The encounter with what is innerworldly moves fatalistically along the path of antecedently regulated contexts of meaning, such that these contexts themselves cannot be affected by successful problem solutions, by accumulated knowledge, by the transformed state of productive forces, or by moral insights. It thus becomes impossible to account for the dialectical interplay between the shifting horizons of meaning, on the one hand, and the dimensions in which these horizons must in fact prove their viability, on the other.'

48    It has been pointed out (in chapter 4) that Habermas criticizes Heidegger for taking his critique of metaphysics beyond the framework of discursive thinking or reason. He contends that Heidegger's subject–object scheme of conceptual language performance and his interpretation of the disclosure of truth underestimate ontologically and epistemologically the communicative praxis of the life-world and intersubjectivity.

49    Kompridis, 'On world disclosure', pp. 38–9.

50   Habermas, *Der philosophische Diskurs der Moderne*, pp. 204–5/240–1, 207/243.
51   Ibid., pp. 209–10/245–6.
52   According to White, 'Heidegger and the difficulties of a postmodern ethics and politics', p. 91, Habermas conceptualizes human projects in such a way as to essentialize human beings under the sway of the responsibility to act, and he forgets thereby the problem of finitude.
53   Habermas, *Theorie des kommunikativen Handelns*, vol. 1, p. 41/70.
54   Kompridis, 'On world disclosure', p. 39.
55   Lara, 'Albrecht Wellmer', pp. 15–16. For a recent position of Wellmer, see his essays in *Endgames*.
56   White, 'Introduction', p. 10, argues that Habermas's ethical perspective and critique of Western rationalization seemed to distance him in the 1970s from the existing institutions of liberal democracy as a political system. At that time Habermas continued to think in terms of a fundamental transition from a liberal, constitutional state to some sort of socialist system with more radicalized democratic institutions. In *The Theory of Communicative Action* this perspective underwent modification in the form of certain modes of resistance in advanced industrial societies. Healthy democratic impulses seem largely confined to the periphery of organized politics. The force of communicative reason, as manifest in new social movements, can, in effect, only hurl themselves against an administrative Leviathan.
57   Ibid., pp. 11–12.
58   Ibid., p. 13.
59   See Rasmussen, *Reading Habermas*, p. 12.
60   Kompridis, 'On world disclosure', p. 40.
61   Kompridis (ibid., p. 41) refers to the following statement of Dewey in *Philosophy and Civilization*: 'meaning is wider in scope as well as more precious in value than truth . . . truth is but one class of meaning'.
62   Habermas, *Nachmetaphysisches Denken*, p. 185/145.
63   Kompridis, 'On world disclosure', p. 41, refers to the following statement of Dewey: 'Not just doing and undergoing in alternation, but . . . in relationship.' See Dewey, *Art as Experience*, pp. 50–1.
64   See Dewey, *Art as Experience*, p. 349: 'disclosure . . . of possibilities that contrast with actual conditions . . . are . . . the most penetrating 'criticism' of the latter that can be made. It is by a sense of possibilities opening up before us that we become aware of the constrictions that hem us and of burdens that oppress.'
65   Wellmer, *The Persistence of Modernity*, pp. 4–5.
66   Adorno, *Aesthetic Theory*, p. 178: 'If we try to grasp the ineffable by seeking to penetrate its aesthetic appearance it eludes us like the end of the proverbial rainbow.'
67   Wellmer, *The Persistence of Modernity*, p. 12.
68   Ibid., p. 20.

69 Ibid., p. 22. This distinction of Koppe broadly corresponds to Habermas's pragmatic differentiation between cognitive-instrumental, moral-practical and aesthetic-expressive rationality types.

70 Lara, 'Albrecht Wellmer', pp. 4–5, argues that Wellmer's concept of a plurality of rationalities is more radical than Habermas's model, but lacks the relativistic overtones of Heidegger's proposal. Communication and intersubjectivity are conditions for a re-dimensioning of the role of aesthetics as a form of rationality. Wellmer conceives of a model of rationalities in which there remain no traces of the aporetical view of the other of reason (Adorno) or the scientist conceptualization of communicative rationality (Habermas).

71 Seel, 'On rightness and truth', p. 76. Seel describes Wellmer's position, in confrontation with metaphysical realism, epistemic idealism (early Putnam, Habermas and Apel), and epistemic relativism (Rorty), as a position of a pragmatic realism or corrective pragmatism working with a fallibilist and differentiated concept of truth. Seel differs from Habermas by giving a more prominent place to aesthetics in the model of rational differentiation. He describes the main features of a corrective pragmatism in the following way: a theory of truth must account for the existence of relativity and irrelativity. True propositions can only be formulated in relative languages; that is to say, truth exists only relative to a language. The claim to truth is nevertheless often a non-relative one, in the sense that it is meant to be valid at any point in time and in any language. Truth claims also do not involve the belief that one's own ideas are not revisable, only the expectation that they will not be revised. The ideal of truth possession, even as a regulative idea, should be rejected. If truth claims are essentially fallible, the idea of an ultimate possession of knowledge, a final grasp of truth, is empty. The idea of truth is no longer that of a complete hold of truth, nor that of an infinite quest for truth; it implies the rectifiable justification of belief.

72 Lara, 'Albrecht Wellmer', pp. 10–11.

73 Ibid., pp. 12–13.

74 Ibid., pp. 15–16.

75 Ibid., p. 6.

76 It should be clear by now that world disclosure 1 should not be placed prior to world disclosure 2 as Habermas and Bohman suggest.

77 Kompridis, 'On world disclosure', p. 43.

78 Bohman, 'World disclosure and radical criticism', p. 84.

79 Bohman argues, though, that it is not the artist, but the critic who provides, in the first place, the best paradigm for the analysis of what it means to disclose new possibilities of action and thought. He goes on to argue that one should not make a distinction between innovative and everyday discourses, but rather a contrast between a disclosive and rigid relation to the world – a contrast found by analogy in pathologies of reasoning, perception and speech that are often marked by a special rigidity and lack of multi-dimensionality (ibid., pp. 84–5).

80   Ibid., pp. 94–5.
81   Seel, 'On rightness and truth', pp. 76, 78.
82   Wellmer, *The Persistence of Modernity*, p. 92. Alessandro Ferrara has for-
     mulated a fascinating position in this regard; see his *Reflective Authen-
     ticity* and *Justice and Judgment*.
83   Wellmer, *The Persistence of Modernity*, p. 93.
84   Benhabib, 'The utopian dimension of communicative ethics', p. 389.
85   Ibid., pp. 393–94.
86   Ibid., p. 395. See also Habermas, *Die Einbeziehung des Anderen*.
87   Benhabib, 'The utopian dimension of communicative ethics', pp. 396–7.

# Bibliography

## Primary sources

### Books

Habermas, J., *Das Absolute und die Geschichte: Von der Zwiespältigkeit in Schellings Denken.* Unpublished D. Phil. diss., University of Bonn, 1954.

Habermas, J., *Strukturwandel der Öffentlichkeit: Untersuchungen zu einer Kategorie der bürgerlichen Gesellschaft.* Darmstadt: Luchterhand, 1962. / *The Structural Transformation of the Public Sphere*, trans. T. Burger and F. Lawrence. Cambridge: Polity, 1989.

Habermas, J., *Theorie und Praxis: Sozialphilosophische Studien.* Frankfurt: Suhrkamp, 1963. / *Theory and Practice*, trans. J. Viertel. London: Heinemann, 1974 (abridged translation).

Habermas, J., *Technik und Wissenschaft als Ideologie.* Frankfurt: Suhrkamp, 1968. / *Toward a Rational Society*, trans. J. J. Shapiro. London: Heinemann, 1971 (only the last three essays are translated).

Habermas, J. and Luhmann, N., *Theorie der Gesellschaft oder Sozialtechnologie.* Frankfurt: Suhrkamp, 1971.

Habermas, J., *Legitimationsprobleme im Spätkapitalismus.* Frankfurt: Suhrkamp, 1973. / *Legitimation Crisis*, trans. T. McCarthy. London: Heinemann, 1979.

Habermas, J., *Zur Rekonstruktion des historischen Materialismus.* Frankfurt: Suhrkamp, 1976. / *Communication and the Evolution of Society*, trans. T. McCarthy. London: Heinemann, 1979 (partial translation).

Habermas, J., *Theorie des kommunikativen Handelns*, Band I–II. Frankfurt: Suhrkamp, 1981. / *The Theory of Communicative Action*, vols. 1–2, trans. T. McCarthy. New York: Beacon Press, 1984, 1987.

Habermas, J., *Philosophisch-politische Profile.* Frankfurt: Suhrkamp, 1981. / *Philosophical-Political Profiles*, trans. F. G. Lawrence. Cambridge, Mass.: MIT Press, 1983 (partial translation).

Habermas, J., *Moralbewußsein und kommunikatives Handeln*. Frankfurt: Suhrkamp, 1983. / *Moral Consciousness and Communicative Action*, trans. C. Lenhardt and S. W. Nicholsen. Cambridge: Polity, 1990.

Habermas, J. and Von Friedeburg, L. (eds), *Adorno Konferenz*. Frankfurt: Suhrkamp, 1983.

Habermas, J., *Vorstudien und Ergänzungen zur Theorie des kommunikativen Handelns*. Frankfurt: Suhrkamp, 1984.

Habermas, J., *Der philosophische Diskurs der Moderne*. Frankfurt: Suhrkamp, 1985. / *The Philosophical Discourse of Modernity*, trans. F. Lawrence. Cambridge, Mass.: MIT Press, 1987.

Habermas, J., *Die neue Unübersichtlichkeit: Kleine Politische Schriften, V*. Frankfurt: Suhrkamp, 1985.

Habermas, J., *Autonomy and Solidarity: Interviews*, ed. P. Dews. Norfolk: Thetford Press, 1986. (Contains some translations *Die neue Unübersichtlichkeit*.)

Habermas, J., *Eine Art Schadensabwicklung: Kleine politischen Schriften VI*. Frankfurt: Suhrkamp. / *The New Conservatism: Cultural Criticism and the Historians' Debate*, trans. S. W. Nicholsen. Cambridge: Polity, 1990 (partial translation).

Habermas, J., *Nachmetaphysisches Denken*. Frankfurt: Suhrkamp, 1988. / *Postmetaphysical Thinking*, trans. W. M. Hohengarten. Cambridge: Polity, 1992 (partial translation).

Habermas, J., *Erläuterungen zur Diskursethik*. Frankfurt: Suhrkamp, 1991. / *Justification and Application: Remarks on Discourse Ethics*, trans. C. Cronin. Cambridge: Polity, 1993 (partial translation).

Habermas, J., *Texte und Kontexte*. Frankfurt: Suhrkamp, 1991.

Habermas, J., *Die Normalität einer Berliner Republik. Kleine politischen Schriften, VIII*. Frankfurt: Suhrkamp, 1995 / *A Berliner Republic*, trans. P. Hohendahl. Cambridge: Polity, 1997.

Habermas, J., *Die Einbeziehung des Anderen: Studien zur politischen Theorie*. Frankfurt: Suhrkamp, 1996. / *The Inclusion of the Other*, trans. and ed. C. Cronin and P. de Greiff. Cambridge: Polity, 1998.

Habermas, J., *Vom sinnlichen Eindruck zum symbolischen Ausdruck: Philosophische Essays*. Frankfurt: Suhrkamp, 1996. / *The Liberating Power of Symbols: Philosophical Essays*, trans. P. Dews. Cambridge: Polity, 2001.

Habermas, J., *Die postnationale Konstellation*. Frankfurt: Suhrkamp, 1998. / *The Postnational Constellation*, trans. M. Pensky. Cambridge: Polity, 2000.

Habermas, J., *Wahrheit und Rechtfertigung: Philosophische Aufsätze*. Frankfurt: Suhrkamp, 1999.

Habermas, J., *Die Zeit der Übergänge: Kleine politischen Schriften, IX*. Frankfurt: Suhrkamp, 2001.

Habermas, J., *Die Zukunft der menschlichen Natur: Auf dem Weg zu einer liberale Eugenik*. Frankfurt: Suhrkamp, 2001.

## Articles

Habermas, J., 'Bewussmachende oder rettende Kritik – Die Aktualität Walter Benjamins'. In *Kultur und Kritik* (1973). pp. 302–44. / 'Walter Benjamin: consciousness-raising or rescuing critique'. In *Philosophical-Political Profiles*, pp. 129–64.

Habermas, J., 'Herbert Marcuse über Kunst und Revolution'. In *Kultur und Kritik* (1973), pp. 345–54. / 'Herbert Marcuse: on art and revolution'. In *Philosophical-Political Profiles*, pp. 165–70.

Habermas, J., 'Zur Veröffentlichung von Vorlesungen aus dem Jahre 1935'. In *Philosophisch-politische Profile* (1981), pp. 65–72.

Habermas, J., 'Die Frankfurter Schule in New York'. In *Philosophisch-politische Profile* (1981), pp. 411–25. / 'Foundations of the Frankfurt School of Social Research'. In J. Marcus and Z. Tar (eds), *Foundations of the Frankfurt School of Social Research*, New Brunswick, NJ: Transaction Books, 1984, pp. 55–65.

Habermas, J., 'A reply to my critics'. In J. B. Thompson and D. Held (eds), *Habermas: Critical Debates*, Basingstoke: Macmillan, 1982.

Habermas, J., 'Dialektik der Rationalisierung'. In *Die neue Unübersichtlichkeit* (1985), pp. 167–208. / 'The dialectics of rationalization'. In *Autonomy and Solidarity*, pp. 93–130.

Habermas, J., 'Questions and counterquestions'. In R. J. Bernstein (ed.), *Habermas and Modernity*, Cambridge: Polity, 1985.

Habermas, J., 'Entgegnung'. In A. Honneth and H. Joas (eds), *Kommunikativen Handelns*. Frankfurt: Suhrkamp, 1986. / 'A reply'. In *Communicative Action*, trans. J. Gaines and D. Jones, Cambridge, Mass.: MIT Press, 1991.

Habermas, J., 'Heinrich Heine und die Rolle des Intellektuellen in Deutschland'. In *Eine Art Schadensabwicklung* (1987), pp. 25–54. / 'Heinrich Heine and the role of the intellectual in Germany'. In *The New Conservatism*, pp. 71–99.

Habermas, J., 'Die Moderne – ein unvollendetes Projekt'. In W. Welsch (ed.), *Wege aus der Moderne*, Weinheim: VCH, 1988. / 'Modernity versus postmodernity'. trans. S. Benhabib. *New German Critique* 22 (1981): 3–14.

## Secondary sources

Adorno, T. W., *Dissonanzen: Einleitung in die Musiksoziologie*. Schriften 14. Frankfurt: Suhrkamp, 1973.

Adorno, T. W., *Noten zur Literatur*. Schriften 11. Frankfurt: Suhrkamp, 1974.

Adorno, T. W., *Aesthetic Theory*. London: Routledge and Kegan Paul, 1984.

Adorno, T. W., *Notes to Literature*, vol. 2, trans. S. W. Nicholsen. New York: Columbia University Press, 1992.

Adorno, T. W. and Horkheimer, M., *Dialectic of Enlightenment*, trans. J. Cumming. London: Verso, 1979.

Adorno, T. W., et al., *The Positivist Dispute in German Sociology*. London: Heinemann, 1976.

Ahlers, R., 'Technologie und Wissenschaft bei Heidegger und Marcuse'. *Zeitschrift für Philosophische Forschung* 25: (1971): 575–90.

Alford, C. F., *Science and the Revenge of Nature: Marcuse and Habermas*. Gainesville: University of Florida Press, 1985.

Alford, C. F., 'Habermas, post-Freudian psychoanalysis and the end of the individual'. *Theory, Culture and Society* 4 (1987): 3–29.

Allen, R., 'The aesthetic experience of modernity: Adorno, Benjamin and contemporary film theory'. *New German Critique* 40 (1987): 225–40.

Anderson, J., 'The "third generation" of the Frankfurt School'. *Intellectual History Newsletter* 22 (2000): 49–61.

Anderson, P., *Considerations on Western Marxism*. Atlantic Highlands, N.J.: Humanities Press, 1976.

Angern, E., 'Krise der Vernunft? Neuere Beiträge zur Diagnose und Kritik der Moderne'. *Philosophische Rundschau* 33 (1986): 161–209.

Apel, K-O., 'Wissenschaft als Emanzipation? Eine kritische Würdigung der Wissenschaftskonzeption der Kritischen Theorie'. *Zeitschrift für allgemeine Wissenschaftsteorie* 1 (1970): 173–95.

Apel, K-O., *Transformation der Philosophie*, 2 vols. Frankfurt: Suhrkamp, 1973.

Apel, K-O., 'Types of social science in the light of human interests of knowledge'. *Social Research* 44 (1977): 425–70.

Apel, K-O. et al., *Hermeneutik und Ideologiekritik*. Frankfurt: Suhrkamp, 1971.

Arato, A., (ed.), *The Essential Frankfurt School Reader*. Oxford: Basil Blackwell, 1978.

Arato, A. and Beines, P. (eds), *The Young Lukács and the Origins of Western Marxism*. New York: Seabury Press, 1979.

Arendt, H., *The Human Condition*. Chicago: University of Chicago Press, 1958.

Arendt, H., *On Revolution*. New York: Viking Press, 1963.

Arendt, H., 'Introduction'. In W. Benjamin, *Illuminations*, trans. H. Zohn, New York: Harcourt, Brace and World, 1968.

Arens, E. (ed.), *Habermas und die Theologie*. Düsseldorf: Patmos, 1989.

Aristotle, *The Nicomachean Ethics*, trans. H. Rackman. London: Williams and Heineman, 1926.

Ashenden, S. and Owen, D., *Foucault contra Habermas*. London: Sage, 1999.

Baars, J., *Die Mythe van totale Beheersing*. Amsterdam: SUA, 1987.

Baum, K., *Die Transzendierung des Mythos: Zur Philosophie und Ästhetik Schellings und Adornos*. Würzburg: Königshausen und Neumann, 1988.

Baxter, H., 'System and life-world in Habermas' theory of communicative action'. *Theory and Society* 16 (1987): 39–86.

Benhabib, S., 'Modernity and the aporias of Critical Theory'. *Telos* 49 (1981): 39–59.

Benhabib, S., 'Epistemologies of postmodernism'. *New German Critique* 33 (1984): 103–26.

Benhabib, S., *Critique, Norm and Utopia: A Study of the Foundations of Critical Theory*. New York: Columbia University Press, 1986.

Benhabib, S., 'The utopian dimension in communicative ethics'. In D. Ingram and J. Simon-Ingram, (eds), *Critical Theory: The Essential Readings*, New York: Paragon House, 1990.

Benhabib, S. (ed.), *Feminism as Critique: Essays on the Politics of Gender in Late-Capitalist Societies*. Cambridge: Polity, 1987.

Benhabib, S.; Bonss, W.; and McCole, J. (eds), *On Max Horkheimer: New Perspectives*. Cambridge, Mass.: MIT Press, 1993.

Benjamin, W., *Illuminations*, trans. H. Zohn. London: Jonathan Cape, 1970.

Benjamin, W., *Gesammelte Schriften*, Band I–IV. Frankfurt: Suhrkamp, 1974.

Bernstein, J. M., 'Art against Enlightenment: Adorno's critique of Habermas'. In A. Benjamin (ed.), *The Problems of Modernity*, London: Routledge, 1989.

Bernstein, J. M., *The Fate of Art: Aesthetic Alienation from Kant to Derrida to Adorno*. Cambridge: Polity, 1992.

Bernstein, J. M., *Recovering Ethical Life: Jürgen Habermas and the Future of Critical Theory*. London: Routledge, 1995.

Bernstein, J. M., *Adorno: Disenchantment and Ethics*. Cambridge: Cambridge University Press, 2001.

Bernstein, J. M., (ed.), *The Frankfurt School: Critical Assessments*, 6 vols. London: Routledge, 1994.

Bernstein, R. J., *Beyond Objectivism and Relativism*. Oxford: Basil Blackwell, 1983.

Bernstein, R. J., (ed.), *Habermas and Modernity*. Cambridge: Polity, 1985.

Betz, H-G., '"Deutschlandpolitik" on the margins: on the evolution of contemporary new right nationalism in the Federal Republic'. *New German Critique* 44 (1988): 127–57.

Bloomfield, T., 'Is it sooner than you think, or where are we in the history of rock music?' *New Left Review* 190 (1991): 59–81.

Bohman, J., 'World disclosure and radical criticism'. *Thesis Eleven* 37 (1994): 82–97.

Bolz, N. W. and Faber, R. (eds), *Walter Benjamin*. Würzburg: Königshausen und Neumann, 1982.

Bonss, W. and Honneth, A. (eds), *Sozialforschung als Kritik*. Frankfurt: Suhrkamp, 1982.

Bottomore, T., *The Frankfurt School*. London: Tavistock Publications, 1984.

Bourdieu, P., 'Vive le Streit! Jürgen Habermas zum Geburtstag'. *Suddeutsche Zeitung*, 18 June. 1999.

Braaten, J., *Habermas's Critical Theory of Society*. New York: SUNY Press, 1991.

Breuer, S., *Die Krise der Revolutionstheorie*. Frankfurt: Suhrkamp, 1977.

Brewster, P. and Buchner, C. H., 'Language and criticism: Habermas on Benjamin'. *New German Critique* 17 (1979): 15–29.

Bronner, B. E. and Kellner, D. M. (eds), *Critical Theory and Society – A Reader*. New York: Routledge, 1989.

Buck-Morss, S., *The Origin of Negative Dialectics: Adorno, Benjamin and the Frankfurt Institute*. New York: Free Press, 1977.

Buck-Morss, S., *The Dialectic of Seeing: Walter Benjamin and the Arcades Project*. Cambridge, Mass.: MIT Press, 1989.

Bürger, C. and Bürger, P., *Postmoderne: Alltag, Allegorie und Avantgarde*. Frankfurt: Suhrkamp, 1987.

Bürger, C. and Schulte-Sasse, J. (eds), *Aufklärung und Öffentlichkeit*. Frankfurt: Suhrkamp, 1980.

Bürger, C. et al., *Zur Dichotomisierung von hoher und niederer Literatur*. Frankfurt: Suhrkamp, 1982.

Bürger, P., 'Avant-garde and contemporary aesthetics: a reply to Jürgen Habermas'. *New German Critique* 22 (1981): 19–22.

Bürger, P., *Theory of the Avant-garde*, trans. M. Shaw. Minneapolis: University of Minnesota Press, 1984.

Bürger, P., 'The decline of the modern age'. *Telos* 62 (1984): 117–30.

Bürger, P., 'The institution of "art" as a category in the sociology of literature'. *Cultural Critique* 2 (1986): 5–33.

Buxton, D., 'Rock music, the star system and the rise of consumerism'. *Telos* 57 (1983): 93–101.

Cahoone, L. E., *The Dilemma of Modernity: Philosophy, Culture and Anti-culture*. New York: SUNY Press, 1988.

Calhoun, C., (ed.), *Habermas and the Public Sphere*. Cambridge, Mass.: MIT Press, 1992.

Calinescu, M., *Five Faces of Modernity: Modernism, Avant-garde, Decadence, Kitsch, Postmodernism*, Durham, N. C.: Duke University Press, 1987.

Carroll, D., *Paraesthetics: Foucault, Lyotard, Derrida*. New York: Methuen, 1987.

Connerton, P., *The Tragedy of Enlightenment: An Essay on the Frankfurt School*. Cambridge: Cambridge University Press, 1980.

Connolly, W. E., *Politics and Ambiguity*. Madison: University of Wisconsin Press, 1987.

Cooke, M., *Language and Reason: A Study of Habermas's Pragmatics*. Cambridge, Mass.: MIT Press, 1994.

Craig, G. A., 'The war of the German historians'. *New York Review*, 15 January 1987: 16–19.

Culler, J., *On Deconstruction*. Ithaca, N. Y.: Cornell University Press, 1983.

Dallmayr, F., 'Life-world and communicative action'. In B. Parekh (ed.), *Political Discourse*, New Delhi: Sage, 1987.

Dallmayr, F., 'Habermas and rationality'. *Political Theory* 16 (1988): 553–79.

Dallmayr, F., 'The discourse of modernity: Hegel, Nietzsche, Heidegger (and Habermas)'. *Praxis International* 8 (1989): 377–406.

Dallmayr, F., *Between Freiburg and Frankfurt: Toward a Critical Ontology*. Amherst: University of Massachusetts Press, 1991.

Dallmayr, F., (ed.) *Materialen zu Erkenntnis und Interesse*. Frankfurt: Suhrkamp, 1974.

Deflem, M. (ed.), *Habermas, Modernity and Law*. London: Sage, 1996.

d'Entreves, M. P. and Benhabib, S. (eds), *Habermas and the Unfinished Project of Modernity*. Cambridge: Polity, 1996.

De Man, P., *Blindness and Insight*. Oxford: Oxford University Press, 1983.

De Man, P., *The Rhetoric of Romanticism*. New York: Columbia University Press, 1984.

Derrida, J., *The Truth in Painting*, trans. G. Bennington and I. McLeod. Chicago: University of Chicago Press, 1987.

Dewey, J., *Art as Experience*. New York: Capricorn Books, 1959.

Dews, P., 'Introduction'. In J. Habermas, *Autonomy and Solidarity: Interviews*, ed. P. Dews, Norfolk: Thetford Press, 1986.

Dews, P., *Logics of Disintegration: Post-structuralist Thought and the Claims of Critical Theory*. London: Verso, 1987.

Dews, P. (ed.), *Habermas: A Critical Reader*. Oxford: Blackwell, 1999.

Dreyfus, R. and Rabinow, P., *Michel Foucault: Beyond Structuralism and Hermeneutics*. Chicago: University of Chicago Press, 1983.

Dubiel, H., *Theory and Politics: Studies in the Development of Critical Theory*, trans. B. Gregg. Cambridge, Mass.: MIT Press, 1985.

Dumm, T. L., 'The politics of post-modern aesthetics: Habermas contra Foucault'. *Political Theory* 16 (1988): 209–28.

Duvenage, P., 'Filosofie en Argitektuur: Moderniteit en Post-moderniteit'. *South African Journal of Art and Architectural History* 2 (1991): 69–77.

Duvenage, P., *Die estetiese Heling van die Instrumentele Rede. 'n Kritiese interpretasie van Jürgen Habermas se Sosiale Filosofie*. Unpublished D. Phil. diss., University of Port Elizabeth, 1994.

Duvenage, P., 'The politics of memory and forgetting after Auschwitz and apartheid'. *Philosophy and Social Criticism* 28/3 (1999): 1–28.

Eagleton, T., *Walter Benjamin or Towards a Revolutionary Criticism*. London: Verso, 1981.

Enzensberger, H. M., *Einzelheiten*. Frankfurt: Suhrkamp, 1962.

Feenberg, A., *Lukács, Marx and the Sources of Critical Theory*. Totowa, N.J.: Rowman and Littlefield, 1981.

Ferrara, A., 'A critique of Habermas' Diskursethik'. *Telos* 64 (1985): 45–74.

Ferrara, A., *Reflective Authenticity: Rethinking the Project of Modernity*. London: Routledge, 1998.

Ferrara, A., *Justice and Judgment: The Rise and Prospect of the Judgment Model in Contemporary Political Philosophy*. London: Sage, 1999.

Fleming, M., *Emancipation and Illusion: Rationality and Gender in Habermas's Theory of Modernity*. Philadelphia: Penn State University, 1997.

Flynn, B. C., 'Reading Habermas reading Freud'. *Human Studies* 8 (1985): 57–76.

Forester, J. (ed.), *Critical Theory and Public Life*. Cambridge, Mass.: MIT Press, 1985.

Foster, H., '(Post)modern polemics'. *New German Critique* 33 (1984): 68–78.

Foster, H. (ed.), *The Anti-aesthetic: Essays on Postmodern Culture*. Seattle: Bay Press, 1983.

Foucault, M., *The History of Sexuality*, vol. I. New York: Random House, 1980.

Foucault, M., 'On the genealogy of ethics'. In R. Dreyfus and, P. Rabinow, *Michel Foucault: Beyond Structuralism and Hermeneutics,* Chicago: University of Chicago Press, 1983.

Foucault, M., *The Foucault Reader,* ed. P. Rabinow. Harmondsworth: Penguin, 1984.

Frank, M., Raulet, G. and Van Reijen, W. (eds), *Die Frage nach dem Subjek.* Frankfurt: Suhrkamp, 1987.

Fraser, N., 'Is Michel Foucault a young Conservative'? *Ethics* 96 (1985): 165–84.

Fraser, N., 'What is critical about Critical Theory? The case of Habermas and gender'. *New German Critique* 35 (1985): 97–131.

Freundlieb, D., 'Rationalism versus irrationalism: Habermas' response to Foucault'. *Inquiry* 31 (1988): 171–92.

Friedman, G., *The Political Philosophy of the Frankfurt School.* Ithaca, N.Y.: Cornell University Press, 1981.

Frisby, D., *Fragments of Modernity: Theories of Modernity in the Work of Simmel, Kracauer and Benjamin.* Cambridge, Mass.: MIT Press, 1986.

Früchtl, J., *Mimesis: Konstellation des Zentralbegriffs bei Adorno.* Wurzburg: Königshauser und Neumann, 1986.

Fuld, W., *Walter Benjamin: Zwischen den Stühlen.* Munich: Hauser, 1979.

Funk, R., *Eric Fromm: The Courage to be Human.* New York: Continuum, 1982.

Gadamer, H-G., *Wahrheit und Methode,* 4th edn. Tübingen: Mohr, 1975.

Gadamer, H-G., *Vernunft im Zeitalter der Wissenschaft.* Frankfurt: Suhrkamp, 1976.

Geoghegan, V., *Reason and Eros: The Social Theory of Herbert Marcuse.* London: Pluto Press, 1981.

Gerhardt, V., 'Metaphysik und Ihre Kritik: Aus Anlaß der Jüngsten Debatte über die Metaphysik'. *Zeitschrift für Philosophische Forschung* 42 (1988): 45–70.

Geuss, R., *The Idea of a Critical Theory.* Cambridge: Cambridge University Press, 1981.

Geyer, C-F., *Kritische Theorie: Max Horkheimer und Theodor W. Adorno.* Munich: Alber, 1982.

Giddens, A., 'Labour and interaction'. In J. B. Thompson and D. Held (eds), *Habermas: Critical Debates,* London: Macmillan, 1982.

Giddens, A., 'Reason without revolution? Habermas's *Theorie des kommunikativen Handelns*'. In R. J. Bernstein (ed.), *Habermas and Modernity,* Cambridge: Polity, 1985.

Glotz, P., *Buchkritik in deutschen Zeitungen.* Hamburg: Verlag für Buchmarkt-Forschung, 1968.

Gmünder, U., *Kritische Theorie: Horkheimer, Adorno, Marcuse, Habermas.* Stuttgart: Metzler Verlag, 1985.

Görtzen, R., *Jürgen Habermas: Eine Bibliographie seiner Schriften und der Sekundärliteratur.* Frankfurt: Suhrkamp, 1982.

Greven, M. T., 'Power and communication in Habermas and Luhmann'. In B. Parekh (ed.), *Political Discourse*, New Delhi: Sage, 1987.

Gripp, H., *Jürgen Habermas*. Paderborn: Schöningh, 1984.

Grondin, J., 'Hat Habermas die Subjektphilosophie verabschiedet?' *Allgemeine Zeitschrift für Philosophie* 12 (1987): 25–37.

Hahn, L. E. (ed.), *Perspectives on Habermas*. Chicago: Open Court Publishers, 2000.

Heidegger, M., *Being and Time*, trans. J. Macquarrie and E. Robinson. Oxford: Blackwell, 1962.

Heidegger, M., *Nietzsche*, vol. I. trans. D. F. Krell. New York: Harper Collins, 1991.

Heidegger, M., 'What calls for thinking'. In *Basic Writings*, ed. David Ferrell Krell, London: Routledge, 1993.

Heidegger, M., 'Letter on humanism'. In *Basic Writings*, ed. David Ferrell Krell, London: Routledge, 1993.

Heidegger, M., 'The essence of truth'. In *Basic Writings*, ed. David Ferrell Krell, London: Routledge, 1993.

Heidegger, M., 'The question concerning technology'. In *Basic Writings*, ed. David Ferrell Krell, London: Routledge, 1993.

Heidegger, M., 'The origin of the work of art'. In *Basic Writings*, ed. David Ferrell Krell, London: Routledge, 1993.

Hekman, S. K., *Hermeneutics and the Sociology of Knowledge*. Cambridge: Polity, 1986.

Held, D., 'Habermas' theory of crisis in late capitalism'. *Radical Philosophers Journal* 6 (1976): 1–19.

Held, D., *Introduction to Critical Theory*. London: Hutchinson, 1980.

Hohendahl, P., 'Critical Theory, public sphere and culture: Jürgen Habermas and his critics'. *New German Critique* 16 (1979): 89–118.

Hohendahl, P., 'The dialectic of Enlightenment revisited: Habermas' critique of the Frankfurt School'. *New German Critique* 35 (1985): 3–26.

Hohendahl, P., *Prismatic Thought: Theodor W. Adorno*. Lincoln, Nebr.: Nebraska University Press, 1995.

Holton, R. J., 'The idea of crisis in modern society'. *British Journal of Sociology* 38 (1987): 502–20.

Holub, R. C., *Jürgen Habermas: Critic in the Public Sphere*. London: Routledge, 1991.

Honneth, A., 'Communication and reconciliation: Habermas' critique of Adorno'. *Telos* 39 (1979): 45–61.

Honneth, A., 'Enlightenment and rationality'. *Journal of Philosophy* 84 (1987): 692–9.

Honneth, A., 'Critical Theory'. In A. Giddens and J. Turner (eds), *Social Theory Today*, Cambridge: Polity, 1987.

Honneth, A., *Critique of Power: Reflective Stages in a Critical Social Theory*. Cambridge, Mass.: MIT Press, 1991.

Honneth, A. and Jaeggi, U. (eds), *Theorien des historischen Materialismus*. Frankfurt: Suhrkamp, 1977.

Honneth, A. et al., *Zwischenbetrachtungen: Im Prozess der Aufklärung*. Frankfurt: Suhrkamp, 1989.

Honneth, A. and Joas, H. (eds), *Communicative Action.* Cambridge, Mass.: MIT Press, 1991.

Horkheimer, M., *Between Philosophy and Social Science. Selected Early Writings,* trans. G. F. Hunter et al. Cambridge, Mass.: MIT Press, 1993.

Horster, D., *Habermas zur Einführung.* Hamburg: SOAK, 1988.

Hoy, D. C., 'Two conflicting conceptions of how to naturalize philosophy: Foucault versus Habermas'. In D. Henrich and R. Horstmann (eds), *Metaphysik nach Kant,* Stuttgart: Klett-Cotta, 1987.

Hoy, D. C., 'Splitting the difference: Habermas' critique of Derrida'. *Praxis International* 8 (1989): 447–64.

Huijer, M., 'The aesthetics of existence in the work of Michel Foucault'. *Philosophy and Social Criticism* 25/2 (1999): 61–86.

Huyssen, A., 'The search for tradition: avant-garde and postmodernism in the 1970's'. *New German Critique* 22 (1981): 23–40.

Huyssen, A., *After the Great Divide: Modernism, Mass Culture, Postmodernism.* Bloomington: Indiana University Press, 1986.

Ingram, D., 'Foucault and the Frankfurt School: a discourse on Nietzsche, power and knowledge'. *Praxis International* 6 (1986): 311–27.

Ingram, D., *Habermas and the Dialectic of Reason.* New Haven: Yale University Press, 1987.

Ingram, D., *Critical Theory and Philosophy.* New York: Paragon House, 1990.

Ingram, D., 'Habermas on aesthetics and rationality: completing the project of Enlightenment'. *New German Crritique* 53 (1991): 67–103.

Ingram, D. and Simon-Ingram, J., *Critical Theory: The Essential Readings.* New York: Paragon House, 1990.

Jacoby, R., *Social Amnesia.* Boston: Beacon Press, 1976.

Jameson, F., 'The politics of theory: ideological positions in the postmodernism debate'. *New German Critique* 33 (1984): 53–65.

Jarvis, S., *Adorno: A Critical Introduction.* Cambridge: Polity, 1998.

Jay, M., *The Dialectical Imagination: A History of the Frankfurt School and the Institute of Social Research.* London: Heinemann, 1973.

Jay, M., *Marxism and Totality: The Adventures of a Concept from Lukács to Habermas.* Cambridge: Polity, 1984.

Jay, M., *Adorno.* Cambridge, Mass.: Harvard University Press, 1984

Jay, M., 'Habermas and modernism'. In R. J. Bernstein (ed.), *Habermas and Modernity,* Cambridge: Polity, 1985.

Jay, M., *Permanent Exiles: Essays on the Intellectual Migration from Germany to America.* New York: Columbia University Press, 1986.

Jay, M., *Fin de siècle Socialism.* New York: Routledge, 1988.

Jay, M., 'Review of Habermas' *Philosophical Discourse of Modernity*'. *History and Theory* 28 (1989): 94–112.

Jay, M., '"The aesthetic ideology" as ideology, or what does it mean to aestheticize politics?' *Cultural Critique* 21 (1992): 41–61.

Johnson, P., 'An aesthetic of negativity/an aesthetic of reception: Jauss's dispute with Adorno'. *New German Critique* 42 (1987): 51–70.

Kaiser, G., *Benjamin, Adorno: Zwei Studien.* Frankfurt: Suhrkamp, 1974.

Kambas, C., *Walter Benjamin im Exil: Zum Verhältnis von Literaturpolitik und Ästhetik*. Tübingen: Niemeyer, 1983.

Kamper, D. and van Reijen, W. (eds), *Die unvollendete Vernunft: Moderne versus Postmoderne*. Frankfurt: Suhrkamp, 1987.

Katz, B., *Herbert Marcuse and the Art of Liberation: An Intellectual Biography*. London: Verso, 1982.

Kaulen, H., *Rettung und Destruktion: Untersuchungen zur Hermeneutik Walter Benjamins*. Tübingen: Niemeyer, 1987.

Kearney, R., *Dialogues with Contemporary Continental Thinkers*. Manchester: Manchester University Press, 1984.

Kearney, R., *Modern Movements in European Philosophy*. Manchester: Manchester University Press, 1986.

Keat, R., *The Politics of Social Theory: Habermas, Freud and the Critique of Positivism*. Oxford: Basil Blackwell, 1981.

Kellner, D., *Herbert Marcuse and the Crisis of Marxism*. Berkeley: University of California Press, 1984.

Kellner, D., 'Postmodernism as social theory: some problems and challenges'. *Theory, Culture and Society* 5 (1988): 239–70.

Kellner, D., *Critical Theory, Marxism and Modernity*. Cambridge: Polity, 1989.

Kellner, D. and Roderick, R., 'Recent literature on Critical Theory'. *New German Critique* 23 (1981): 141–71.

Kelly, M. (ed.), *Critique and Power*. Cambridge, Mass.: MIT Press, 1994.

Keulartz, J., 'Over Kunst en Kultuur in het Werk van Habermas'. In F. van Doorne and M. Korthals (eds), *Filosofie en Maatskappijkritiek*, Amsterdam: Boom, 1986.

Keulartz, J., *De verkeerde Wereld van Jürgen Habermas*. Amsterdam: Boom, 1992.

Kilminster, R., *Praxis and Method* and Kegan Paul, *A Sociological Dialogue with Lukács, Gramsci and the Early Frankfurt School*. London: Routledge, 1979.

Kirchheimer, O. and Neumann, F., *Social Democracy and the Rule of Law*, trans. L. Tanner and K. Tribe. London: Allen and Unwin, 1987.

Kirsten, J. M., 'Die postmoderne Projek: Aspekte van die hedendaagse afskeid van die Moderne'. *South African Journal of Philosophy* 7 (1988): 18–36.

Klapwijk, J., *Dialektik der Verlichting*. Amsterdam: Van Gorcum, 1976.

Kockelmans, J. J., *Heidegger on Art and Art Works*. Dordrecht: Nijhoff, 1986.

Kolb, D., *Postmodern Sophistications: Philosophy, Architecture and Tradition*. Chicago: University of Chicago Press, 1990.

Komesaroff, P. A., *Objectivity, Science and Society*. London: Routledge and Kegan Paul, 1976.

Kompridis, N., 'On world disclosure: Heidegger, Habermas, and Dewey'. *Thesis Eleven* 37 (1994): 29–45.

Korthals, M., 'Die kritische Gesellschaftstheorie des frühen Horkheimer'. *Zeitschrift für Soziologie* 14 (1985): 315–29.

Kortian, G., *Metacritique: The Philosophical Arguments of Jürgen Habermas*. Cambridge: Cambridge University Press, 1980.

Kraus, G., *Naturpoesie und Kunstpoesie im Frühwerk Friedrich Schlegels*. Erlangen: Verlag Palm und Enke, 1985.

Kuhlmann, W., 'Philosophie und Rekonstruktive Wissenschaft'. *Zeitschrift für Philosophische Forschung* 40 (1986): 224–34.

Kunneman, H. and Keulartz, J., *Rondom Habermas: Analyses en kritieken*. Amsterdam: Boom Meppel, 1985.

Küsters, G., *Der Kritikbegriff der Kritischen Theorie Max Horkheimers*. Frankfurt: Campus, 1980.

Lacoue-Labarthe, P. and Nancy, J-L., *The Literary Absolute: The Theory of Literature in German Romanticism*, trans. P. Barnard and C. Lester. Albany: SUNY Press, 1988.

Lafont, C., 'World disclosure and reference'. *Thesis Eleven* 37 (1994): 46–63.

Lafont, C., *The Linguistic Turn in Hermeneutic Philosophy*, trans. J. Medina. Cambridge, Mass.: MIT Press, 1999.

Lafont, C., *Heidegger, Language, and World-Disclosure*. Cambridge: Cambridge University Press, 2000.

Lara, M. P., 'Albrecht Wellmer: between spheres of validity'. *Philosophy and Social Criticism* 21/2 (1995): 1–22.

Ley, H. and Müller, T., *Kritische Vernunft und Revolution: Zur Kontroverse zwischen Hans Albert und Jürgen Habermas*. Köln: Paul Rugenstein, 1971.

Liessmann, K., *Ohne Mitleid: Zum Begriff der Distanz als ästhetische Kategorie mit ständiger Rücksicht auf Theodor W. Adorno*. Vienna: Passagen Verlag, 1991.

Lindner, B. and Lüdke, W. M. (eds), *Materialen zur ästhetischen Theorie Adornos Konstruktion der Moderne*. Frankfurt: Suhrkamp, 1979.

Livesay, J., 'Habermas, narcissism, and status'. *Telos* 64 (1985): 75–90.

Löwenthal, L., 'The integrity of the intellectual: in memory of Walter Benjamin'. In G. Smith (ed.), *Benjamin*, Chicago: University of Chicago Press, 1989.

Luhmann, N., *Zweckbegriff und Systemrationalität*. Tübingen: Mohr, 1968.

Luhmann, N., *Soziologische Aufklärung*, vols I-3. Opladen: Westdeutscher Verlag, 1972.

Luhmann, N., *Soziale Systeme: Grundriß einer allgemeinen Theorie*. Frankfurt: Suhrkamp, 1984.

Lyotard, J-F., *The Postmodern Condition*, trans. G. Bennington and B. Marsuni. Manchester: Manchester University Press, 1984.

MacIntyre, A., *Herbert Marcuse*. London: Fontana, 1970.

Marcuse, H., 'The affirmative character of culture'. In *Negations*, trans. J. J. Shapiro, Harmondsworth: Penguin, 1968.

Matuštík, M., *Jürgen Habermas: A Philosophical-Political Profile*. Lanham, Md.: Rowman and Littlefield, 2001.

McCarthy, T., 'Introduction'. In J. Habermas, *Communication and the Evolution of Society*, trans. T. McCarthy, London: Heinemann, 1979.

McCarthy, T., *The Critical Theory of Jürgen Habermas*. Cambridge, Mass.: MIT Press, 1984.

McCarthy, T., 'Introduction'. In J. Habermas, *The Theory of Communicative Action*, vol. I., Boston: Beacon Press, 1984.

McCarthy, T., Reflections on rationalization in *The Theory of Communicative Action'*. In R. J. Bernstein (ed.), *Habermas and Modernity*, Cambridge: Polity, 1985.

McCarthy, T., 'Introduction'. In J. Habermas, *The Philosophical Discourse of Modernity*, trans. F. Lawrence, Cambridge, Mass.: MIT Press, 1987.

McIntosh, D., 'Habermas on Freud'. *Social Research* 44 (1977): 562–98.

Meehan, J. (ed.), *Feminists Read Habermas: Gendering the Subject of Discourse*. London: Routledge, 1995.

Megill, A., *Prophets of Extremity: Nietzsche, Heidegger, Foucault and Derrida*. Berkeley: University of California Press, 1985.

Menke, C., *Die Souveränität der Kunst: Ästhetische Erfahrung nach Adorno und Derrida*. Frankfurt: Suhrkamp, 1991.

Miller, J., 'Jürgen Habermas, *Legitimation Crisis'*. *Telos* 25 (1975): 210–20.

Mills, P., *Woman, Nature and Psyche*. New Haven: Yale University Press, 1987.

Misgeld, D., 'Critical hermeneutics versus Neoparsonianism'. *New German Critique* 35 (1985): 55–87.

Morgan, W. J., 'Adorno on sport: the case of the fractured dialectic'. *Theory and Society* 17 (1988): 813–38.

Morris, M., *Rethinking the Communicative Turn: Adorno, Habermas and the Problem of Communicative Freedom*. New York: SUNY Press, 2001.

Müller, U., 'Hermeneutik als Modernitätskritik'. *Philosophisches Jahrbuch* 94 (1987): 209–21.

Müller-Doohm, S. (ed.), *Das Interesse der Vernunft: Rückblicke auf das Werk von Jürgen Habermas seit 'Erkenntnis und Interesse'*. Frankfurt: Suhrkamp, 2000.

Negrin, L., 'Two critiques of the autonomy of aesthetic consciousness: a comparison of Benjamin and Gadamer'. *Philosophy and Social Criticism* 13 (1988): 343–66.

Negt, O., *Soziologische Phantasie und exemplarisches Lernen*. Frankfurt: Europäische Verlag, 1968.

Negt, O. and Kluge, A., *Öffentlichkeit und Erfahrung: Zur Organisationsanalyse von bürgerlicher und politischer Öffentlichkeit*. Frankfurt: Suhrkamp, 1972.

Nolan, M., 'The "Historikerstreit" and social history'. *New German Critique* 44 (1988): 51–80.

Norris, C., *On Deconstruction: Theory and Practice*. London: Methuen, 1982.

Norris, C., 'Deconstruction, postmodernism and philosophy: Habermas and Derrida'. *Praxis International* 8 (1989): 426–46.

Offermans, C. and Prior, F., *Die estetiese Teorie van Adorno en Benjamin*. Nijmegen: Socialistiese Uitgeverij, 1973.

Olivier, B., 'Contemporary art and Hegel's thesis of the death of art'. *South African Journal of Philosophy* 2 (1983): 1–7.

Olivier, B., 'Derrida, art and truth'. *Journal of Literary Studies* 1 (1985): 27–48.

Olivier, B., 'Beyond music minus memory'. *South African Journal of Philosophy* 9 (1990): 9–17.

O'Neill, J. (ed.), *On Critical Theory*. London: Heinemann, 1976.

Osborne, P., 'Adorno and the metaphysics of modernism: the problem of a "postmodern art"'. In A. Benjamin (ed.), *The Problems of Modernity*, London: Routledge, 1989.

Outhwaite, W., *Habermas: A Critical Introduction*. Cambridge: Polity, 1994.

Outhwaite, W. (ed.), *The Habermas Reader*. Cambridge: Polity, 1996.

Overend, T., 'Enquiry and ideology: Habermas' trichotomous conception of science'. *Philosophy and the Social Sciences* 8 (1978): 1–13.

Pfeufer Kahn, R., 'The problem of power in Habermas'. *Human Studies* 11 (1988): 361–87.

Piccone, P. and Delfini, A., 'Herbert Marcuse's Heideggerian Marxism'. *Telos* 9 (1970): 36–47.

Pries, C. (ed.), *Das Erhabene. Zwischen Grenzerfahrung und Grossenwahn*. Weinheim: VCH, 1989.

Prinz, A., *Der poetische Mensch im Schatten der Utopie*. Würzburg: Königshausen und Neumann, 1990.

Prokop, D., *Massenkultur und Spontaneität: Zur veränderten Warenform der Massenkommunikation im Spätkapitalismus*. Frankfurt: Suhrkamp, 1974.

Pusey, M., *Jürgen Habermas*. Chichester: Ellis Horwood, 1978.

Radnoti, S., 'The effective power of art: on Benjamin's aesthetics'. *Telos* 49 (1981): 61–82.

Rasmussen, D., 'Communicative action and philosophy: reflections on Habermas's "Theorie des kommunikativen Handelns"'. *Philosophy and Social Criticism* 9 (1982): 3–28.

Rasmussen, D., *Reading Habermas*. Oxford: Basil Blackwell, 1990.

Rasmussen, D., (ed.), *The Handbook of Critical Theory*. Oxford: Basil Blackwell, 1996.

Rasmussen, D. and Swindal, J. (eds), *Jürgen Habermas*. 4 vols. London: Sage, 2002.

Ray, L. (ed.), *Critical Sociology*. Aldershot: Edward Elgar, 1990.

Rehg, W., *Insight and Solidarity: A Study in the Discourse Ethics of Jürgen Habermas*. Berkeley: University of California Press, 1997.

Rickert, J., 'The Fromm–Marcuse debate revisited'. *Theory and Society* 15 (1986): 351–400.

Ricoeur, P., *Hermeneutics and the Human Sciences*, trans. and ed. J. B. Thompson. Cambridge: Cambridge University Press, 1981.

Roberts, J., *Walter Benjamin*. London: Macmillan, 1982.

Robinson, P. A., *The Freudian Left: Wilhelm Reich, Geza Roheim, Herbert Marcuse*. New York: Harper, 1969.

Roblin, R. (ed.), *The Aesthetics of the Critical Theorists*. New York: Edwin Mellen Press, 1990.

Rockmore, T., 'Theory and practice again: Habermas and historical materialism'. *Philosophy and Social Criticism* 13 (1987): 211–25.

Roderick, R., *Habermas and the Foundations of Critical Theory*. London: Macmillan, 1986.

Rose, G., *The Melancholy Science: An Introduction to the Thought of Adorno*. New York: Columbia University Press, 1978.

Rose, M., *Marx's Lost Aesthetic: Karl Marx and the Visual Arts*. Cambridge: Cambridge University Press, 1984.

Rosenfeld, M. and Arato, A. (eds), *Habermas on Law and Democracy*. Berkeley: University of California Press, 1998.

Sallis, J., *Crossings: Nietzsche and the Space of Tragedy*. Chicago: University of Chicago Press, 1991.

Sauerland, K., *Einführung in die Ästhetik Adornos*. Berlin: Walter de Gruyter, 1979.

Scambler, G. (ed.), *Habermas, Critical Theory and Health*. London: Routledge, 2001.

Schaar, J. H., *Escape from Authority: The Perspectives of Eric Fromm*. New York: Harper, 1961.

Schmidt, A., 'Existentialontologie und historischer Materialismus bei Marcuse'. In J. Habermas (ed.), *Antworten auf Herbert Marcuse*, Frankfurt: Suhrkamp, 1969.

Schoeman, M. J., *Waarheid en Werklikheid in die Kritiese Teorie van Herbert Marcuse*. Pretoria: Van Schaik, 1979.

Scholem, G., *Walter Benjamin: Die Geschichte einer Freundschaft*. Frankfurt: Suhrkamp, 1975.

Schoolman, M., *The Imaginary Witness: The Critical Theory of Herbert Marcuse*. New York: Free Press, 1980.

Schor, N., *Reading in Detail: Aesthetics and the Feminine*. London: Methuen, 1987.

Schürmann, R., *Heidegger on Being and Acting: From Principles to Anarchy*. Bloomington, Id.: Indiana University Press, 1987.

Seel, M., 'On rightness and truth: reflections on the concept of world disclosure'. *Thesis Eleven* 37 (1994): 64–81.

Sensat, J., *Habermas and Marxism: An Appraisal*. Beverly Hills, Calif.: Sage, 1978.

Simpson, L., 'On Habermas and particularity: is there room for race and gender on the glassy plains of ideal discourse'. *Praxis International* 6 (1986): 328–40.

Slater, P., *Origin and Significance of the Frankfurt School*. London: Routledge and Kegan Paul, 1977.

Smith, A. A., 'Ethics and politics in the work of Jürgen Habermas'. *Interpretation* 11 (1983): 333–51.

Smith, G. (ed.), *Benjamin: Philosophy, History, Aesthetics*. Chicago: University of Chicago Press, 1989.

Smith, T., 'The scope of the social science in Weber and Habermas'. *Philosophy and Social Criticism* 1 (1981): 69–83.

Snyman, J. J., *Theodor W. Adorno: Kritiek en Utopie*. Unpublished D. Litt. et Phil. diss., Rand Afrikaans University. Johannesburg, 1985.

Snyman, J. J., 'Kan 'n Mens dit ooit Kuns noem? Oor die probleem van 'n definisie van Kuns'. *Acta Academica* 23 (1991): 1–28.

Söllner, A., 'Skizzen zu einer intellektuellen und politischen Biographie'. In F. Neumann, *Wirtschaft, Staat und Demokratie 1930–1954*, Frankfurt: Suhrkamp, 1978.

Söllner, A., *Geschichte und Herrschaft*. Frankfurt: Suhrkamp, 1979.

Söllner, A., 'Erfahrungs- und Geschichtsabhängigkeit der Wahrheit'. *Philosophisches Jahrbuch* 86 (1979): 113–47.

Steiner, U., *Die Geburt der Kritik aus dem Geiste der Kunst*. Würzburg: Königshausen, Neumann, 1989.

Stoessel, M., *Aura: Das vergessene Menschliche zu Sprache und Erfahrung bei Walter Benjamin*. Munich: Carl Hanser Verlag, 1983.

Taminiaux, J., *Poetics, Speculation, and Judgment: The Shadow of the Work of Art from Kant to Phenomenology*. Albany: SUNY Press, 1993.

Tar, Z. (ed.), *The Frankfurt School*. New York: John Wiley and Sons, 1977.

Taylor, C., 'Overcoming epistemology'. In K. Baynes et al. (eds),: *After Philosophy: End or Transformation?*, Cambridge, Mass.: MIT Press, 1987.

Therborn, G., 'The Frankfurt school'. *New Left Review* 63 (1970): 65–96.

Thompson, J. B., *Critical Hermeneutics: A Study of the Thought of Paul Ricoeur and Jürgen Habermas*. Cambridge: Cambridge University Press, 1981.

Thompson, J. B., 'Universal pragmatics'. In J. B. Thompson and D. Held (eds), *Habermas: Critical Debates*, Basingstoke: Macmillan, 1982.

Thompson, J. B. and Held, D., *Habermas: Critical Debates*. Basingstoke: Macmillan, 1982.

Tiedemann, R., *Studien zur Philosophie Walter Benjamins*. Frankfurt: Suhrkamp, 1973.

Torpey, J., 'Introduction: Habermas and the historians'. *New German Critique* 44 (1988): 5–24.

Tugendhat, E., 'Heidegger's idea of truth'. In C. Macann (ed.), *Martin Heidegger: Critical Assessments*, London: Routledge, 1992.

Unseld, S. (ed.), *Zur Aktualität Walter Benjamins*. Frankfurt: Suhrkamp, 1972.

Van Doorne, F. and Korthals, M. (eds), *Filosofie en Maatskapijkritiek: In Debat met Habermas*. Amsterdam: Boom Meppel, 1986.

Van Reijen, W., *Philosophie als Kritik: Einführung in die Kritische Theorie*. Königstein: Athenäum, 1986.

Van Reijen, W., 'Die Aushöhlung der abendländischen Kultur'. In D. Horster: *Habermas zur Einführung*. Hamburg: SOAK, 1988.

Visker, R., *Michel Foucault. Genealogy as Critique*. London: Verso, 1995.

Vogel, S., 'Habermas and science'. *Praxis International* 8 (1988): 329–49.

Weber, S., 'Aesthetic experience and self-reflection as emancipatory processes'. In J. O'Neil (ed.), *On Critical Theory*, London: Heinemann, 1976.

Weber-Nicholsen, S., *Exact Imagination, Late Work: On Adorno's Aesthetics*. Cambridge, Mass.: MIT Press, 1997.

Wehler, H-U., *Entsorgung der deutschen Vergangenheit? Ein polemischer Essay zum 'Historikerstreit'*. Munich: C. H. Beck, 1988.

Weiss, A. S., *The Aesthetics of Excess*. Albany: SUNY Press, 1989.

Weisshaupt, B., 'Überlegungen zur Diskursethik von Jürgen Habermas'. *Studia Philosophica* 44 (1985): 78–88.

Wellmer, A., *Critical Theory of Society*. New York: Seabury Press, 1971.

Wellmer, A., 'Reason, utopia and the *Dialectic of Enlightenment*'. In R. J. Bernstein (ed.), *Habermas and Modernity*, Cambridge: Polity, 1985.

Wellmer, A., *The Persistence of Modernity: Essays on Aesthetics, Ethics and Post-modernism*. Cambridge: Polity, 1991.

Wellmer, A., *Endgames: The Irreconcilable Nature of Modernity*. Essays and Lectures. Cambridge, Mass.: MIT Press, 2000.

Welsch, W., *Unsere postmoderne Moderne*. Weinheim: VHC, 1987.

Wilkerson, W. S. and Paris, J. (eds), *New Critical Theory: Essays on Liberation*. Lanham, Md.: Rowman and Littlefield, 2001.

White, S. K., 'Rationality and the foundations of political philosophy: an introduction to the recent work of Jürgen Habermas'. *Journal of Politics* 41 (1979): 1156–71.

White, S. K., 'Reason and authority in Habermas'. *American Political Science Review* 74 (1980): 1006–17.

White, S. K., *The Recent Work of Jürgen Habermas: Reason, Justice and Modernity*. Cambridge: Cambridge University Press, 1988.

White, S. K., 'Heidegger and the difficulties of a postmodern ethics and politics'. *Political Theory* 18 (1990): 80–103.

White, S. K., 'Introduction'. In S. K. White (ed.), *The Cambridge Companion to Habermas*, Cambridge: Cambrige University Press, 1995.

White, S. K. (ed.), *The Cambridge Companion to Habermas*. Cambridge: Cambridge University Press, 1995.

Whitebook, J., 'Reason and happiness: some psychoanalytic themes in Critical Theory'. In R. J. Bernstein (ed.), *Habermas and Modernity*, Cambridge: Polity, 1985.

Whitebook, J., 'Intersubjectivity and the monadic core of the psyche: Habermas and Castoriadis on the unconscious. *Praxis International* 9 (1990): 347–64.

Wiggershaus, R., *The Frankfurt School*. Cambridge, Mass.: MIT Press, 1994.

Wilke, S., *Zur Dialektik von Exposition und Darstellung*. Frankfurt: Peter Lang, 1988.

Wilson, M., *Das Institut für Sozialforschung und seine Faschismusanalysen*. New York: Campus, 1982.

Witte, B., *Walter Benjamin*. Hamburg: Reinbek bei Rowohlt, 1985.

Wittgenstein, L., *Philosophical Investigations*, trans. G. E. M. Anscombe. Oxford: Basil Blackwell, 1953.

Wolin, R., *Walter Benjamin: An Aesthetic of Redemption*. New York: Columbia University Press, 1982.

Wolin, R., 'Modernism vs postmodernism'. *Telos* 62 (1984): 9–29.

Wolin, R., 'Introduction'. In J. Habermas, *The New Conservatism: Cultural Criticism and the Historians' Debate*, trans. S. W. Nicholsen, Cambridge, Mass.: MIT Press, 1989.

Young, J., *Nietzsche's Philosophy of Art*. Cambridge: Cambridge University Press, 1992.

Zammitto, J., *The Genesis of Kant's Critique of Judgment*. Chicago: University of Chicago Press, 1992.

Zuidervaart, L., *Adorno's Aesthetic Theory*. Cambridge, Mass.: MIT Press, 1991.

Zuidervaart, L. and Huhn, T. (eds), *The Semblance of Subjectivity: Essays in Adorno's Aesthetic Theory*. Cambridge, Mass.: MIT Press, 1997.

# Index

Whitebook, Joel, 6, 20, 47, 96,
101–4, 117, 119
will to power, 78, 79, 80, 86, 87,
89
Wittgenstein, Ludwig, 11, 54, 90
world disclosure, 7, 44, 60, 77, 80,
81, 82, 83, 84, 85, 98, 115, 118,
120, 121, 122, 123, 124, 126,
127, 128, 129, 130, 131, 132,
133, 134, 135, 136, 137, 138,
139, 140, 141
world images, 55

world perspectives: inner world, 54,
105, 106; objective world, 52,
53, 54, 55, 84, 105, 129; one-
world ontology, 52; social world,
52, 54, 84, 105, 129; subjective
world, 52, 53, 84, 105, 129;
three-world ontology, 51, 52, 53,
73, 128
writing, 82

Zuidervaart, Lambert, 64, 110,
117